THE CONSTITUTION OF ITALY

This book introduces the reader to the Italian Constitution, which entered into force on 1 January 1948. It examines whether it has successfully managed the political and legal challenges that have occurred since its inception, and fulfilled the three main functions of a Constitution: maintaining a community, protecting the fundamental rights of citizens and ensuring the separation of powers.

Pictorial Narrative

The pictorial composition features elements of Italian constitutionalism in allegorical form. Top right, the figure dressed emblematically in black symbolises the pivotal requirement of 'never returning to fascism' that underpins the entire 1948 constitutional project. Echoing Casper David Friedrich, former President Sandro Pertini (identifiable by his pipe)* who championed wartime resistance to Fascism is in motion, striding confidently forward towards a future horizon with hand waving while turning his back on an inglorious phase in national history. The Escher-style multi-directional and multi-dimensional floating stairways frame the composition from the bottom right in order to represent the vertical and horizontal division of powers under the constitution incorporated to avoid the concentration of authority in a single state organ or individual.

Framed within a central red and orange rectangle is a distinctive female figure at the head of a procession of 21 women representing the constitutional recognition of equal voting rights, while the megaphone announces metaphorically that women acquire a political voice. Beneath her the central grouping of statesmen illustrate the vital co-operation of opposing political parties in the promulgation of the 1948 Constitution. Each figure bears the insignia of their political party: seated with hammer and sickle (Italian Communist Party), in the centre with DC (Christian Democrat Party) and the figure on the right, with LIB (Liberals). As trustee of Italian culture the towering red robed figure of Dante Alighieri (1265–1321) oversees the process. The signed document between them refers to the Constitution promulgated on 27th December 1947.

Bordering the left hand side, the Pantheon as a reminder of ancient Rome is juxtaposed with the home of the Chamber of Deputies, displaying its bell tower with the clock face sited on top of the Palazzo Montecitorio. Finally, an umbrella carrying the tricolours of the Italian flag signifies the nation and the confirmation of its unification.

Putachad
Artist

* Big thank you to Professor Martina Conticelli for proposing Pertini.

Constitutional Systems of the World

General Editors: Benjamin L Berger, Rosalind Dixon, Andrew Harding, Heinz Klug, and Peter Leyland

In the era of globalisation, issues of constitutional law and good governance are being seen increasingly as vital issues in all types of society. Since the end of the Cold War, there have been dramatic developments in democratic and legal reform, and post-conflict societies are also in the throes of reconstructing their governance systems. Even societies already firmly based on constitutional governance and the rule of law have undergone constitutional change and experimentation with new forms of governance; and their constitutional systems are increasingly subjected to comparative analysis and transplantation. Constitutional texts for practically every country in the world are now easily available on the internet. However, texts which enable one to understand the true context, purposes, interpretation and incidents of a constitutional system are much harder to locate, and are often extremely detailed and descriptive. This series seeks to provide scholars and students with accessible introductions to the constitutional systems of the world, supplying both a road map for the novice and, at the same time, a deeper understanding of the key historical, political and legal events which have shaped the constitutional landscape of each country. Each book in this series deals with a single country, or a group of countries with a common constitutional history, and each author is an expert in their field.

Published volumes

The Constitution of the United Kingdom; The Constitution of the United States; The Constitution of Vietnam; The Constitution of South Africa; The Constitution of Japan; The Constitution of Germany; The Constitution of Finland; The Constitution of Australia; The Constitution of the Republic of Austria; The Constitution of the Russian Federation; The Constitutional System of Thailand; The Constitution of Malaysia; The Constitution of China; The Constitution of Indonesia; The Constitution of France; The Constitution of Spain; The Constitution of Mexico; The Constitution of Israel; The Constitutional Systems of the Commonwealth Caribbean; The Constitution of Canada; The Constitution of Singapore; The Constitution of Belgium; The Constitution of Taiwan; The Constitution of Romania; The Constitutional Systems of the Independent Central Asian States; The Constitution of India; The Constitution of Pakistan; The Constitution of Ireland; The Constitution of Brazil; The Constitution of Myanmar; The Constitution of Czechia; The Constitution of New Zealand; The Constitution of Italy

Link to series website

www.bloomsbury.com/uk/series/constitutional-systems-of-the-world

The Constitution of Italy

A Contextual Analysis

Marta Cartabia
and
Nicola Lupo

•HART•
OXFORD • LONDON • NEW YORK • NEW DELHI • SYDNEY

HART PUBLISHING

Bloomsbury Publishing Plc

Kemp House, Chawley Park, Cumnor Hill, Oxford, OX2 9PH, UK

1385 Broadway, New York, NY 10018, USA

29 Earlsfort Terrace, Dublin 2, Ireland

HART PUBLISHING, the Hart/Stag logo, BLOOMSBURY and the Diana logo are trademarks of Bloomsbury Publishing Plc

First published in Great Britain 2022

A catalogue record for this book is available from the British Library.

A catalogue record for this book is available from the Library of Congress.

Library of Congress Control Number: 2021950757

ISBN: HB: 978-1-50990-572-0
ePDF: 978-1-50990-574-4
ePub: 978-1-50990-573-7

Typeset by Compuscript Ltd, Shannon
Printed and bound in Great Britain

Acknowledgements

Every book is the result of a collective work. For a number of reasons, this is particularly true of this book on the Italian Constitution.

First, the two co-authors have worked closely together from the book's initial broad conception and first plan, through the (numerous) drafts of each chapter, until the final revisions of page after page. The book is unquestionably the result of a strong collaboration. We can only identify the author of the first draft of each chapter: Marta Cartabia wrote chapters 2, 7, 8, 9 and 10 and Nicola Lupo wrote chapters 1, 3, 4, 5 and 6. However, each one is the result of intense dialogue and close cooperation between the two authors.

Second, we would like to thank a number of colleagues who provided us with assistance across many different stages of this work. Thanks are due in relation to the bibliographical research, comments and suggestions provided, and editing of the text. Special thanks to Pietro Faraguna, Cristina Fasone, Micol Ferrario, Elisabetta Lamarque, Davide Paris, Giovanni Piccirilli and Diletta Tega. The usual disclaimers apply: the two co-authors are solely responsible for any and all ideas, mistakes, lacunae, misinterpretations, etc. This book was written directly in English, but professional language editing was provided by Francesca M Genova, Miranda Harding and especially by Breony Allen, whose work was invaluable. Thanks also to Putachad Leyland for her artistic contribution in imagining and designing the cover, brilliantly synthetising several elements of the Italian constitutional history and culture, and for her warm friendship and support.

Third, a special mention must be given to the editors of the series, and especially to Peter Leyland and Andrew Harding. A big thank you to them for trusting us, for sharing their expertise and for their patience: this book was planned a few years ago and was delayed a number of times due to unexpected obligations arising that required prioritisation over all other commitments. In the meantime, the two authors have acquired some experience as public servants, so this book now reflects both a theoretical approach – the two co-authors being university professors of Constitutional law, who both also teach the subject in English at their respective universities – and a practical one. Ultimately, we hope that this dual perspective can offer the reader some added value, despite being delayed, with respect to understanding and encouraging the analysis, within the international community of public law scholars, of such an important, rich and dynamic constitutional experience as the Italian one.

Last, but not least, thanks to our spouses and children for patiently accepting that, over the last few years, our breaks – whether in winter or summer – were busy times, always largely devoted to the finalisation of this book.

Marta Cartabia
Professor of Constitutional Law, Bocconi University, Milan

Nicola Lupo
Professor of Public Law, LUISS Guido Carli University, Rome

Contents

Table of Cases

Italy

Other Jurisdictions

European Court of Human Rights

European Court of Justice

Germany

BVerfG

United States

Table of Legislation

Italy

Other Jurisdictions

National

France

Germany

Japan

Spain

United Kingdom

United States

International

Council of Europe

European Union

United Nations

1

The Making of the Italian Constitution and its Evolution

History – Albertine Statute – Fascist Regime – Political Parties – Flexible Constitution – Rigid Constitution – Constitutional Amendments – Supreme Principles – 'Bribesville' – Majoritarian Democracy

I. INTRODUCTION

THIS CHAPTER EXAMINES the origins of the Italian Constitution of 1947. Starting at the dawn of the Italian unification process (*Risorgimento*) with the pre-Republican period, which was ushered in by the conceding in 1848 of the Albertine Statute (*Statuto Albertino*) in the Kingdom of Sardinia and Piedmont, it continues through the events of the Fascist regime (1922–1943) and the Second World War. It then turns to the founding period and the subsequent constitutional history of the Italian Republic, which has been deeply marked by the fracture that took place in the political system in 1993, involving the fall of all the anti-fascist political parties – the 'fathers of the Constitution'.

In particular, it addresses Italy's transition from a modern liberal state to a contemporary constitutional democracy, and accounts for the problems that have arisen during this process. A brief discussion of the Italian Republic's constitutional history is provided, including a comparison between the Albertine Statute and the Republican Constitution. In order to fully understand the Italian Constitution, the effects of the Fascist regime must be taken into account: after two world wars and 20 years of fascism, Italian leaders were faced with the reconstruction and reunification of a devastated country. Due to its relationship with the past, the Italian Constitution is undeniably a 'never-again' constitution: renouncing the previous regime, it is based on principles that provide a safeguard against a totalitarian state. Nevertheless, in consideration for the future of the polity, the features of the new Republic were open and, in a sense, 'undecided'. The Constitution is imbued with anti-fascist principles; yet, the construction of the new polity was successful because of its inclusive, dialogical and incremental approach to constitutional change. The Italian Republic was not founded upon a single political idea, but was the result of a coming together of Catholic, Marxist and liberal ideologies. In a joint reaction to the past, these were united by an anti-fascist commitment, but had no shared vision of the future. The Constitution, firmly grounded on this commitment, was intended to prevent a relapse into the abuses of the totalitarian regime. Yet, the common will to adopt an anti-fascist constitution was not enough when it came to determining the features of the new forms of the State and the Government.[1]

This origin had consequences for the implementation of the new regime. First, the *mise en oeuvre* of the new constitutional architecture was neither immediate nor swift, and was certainly not complete. Moreover, this delayed implementation affected some institutions that were supposed to play a crucial role in the constitutional system, including the Constitutional Court and the Regions, and the instrument of the popular referendum. Second, the new constitutional order soon began to experience recurrent periods of crisis due to increasing political fragmentation and governmental instability: in the 1980s, calls for constitutional reform began to be widely heard.

Italy has undergone a number of political crises, reaching an acute phase in the early 1990s with a massive anticorruption investigation that implicated the vast majority of political leaders – coming to the point where the period is commonly, and yet inaccurately, referred to as the beginning of the 'Second Republic'. It was an inordinately difficult time: for a number of historical reasons, all the political forces that had led the constituent process – notably the Christian Democratic Party, the Socialist Party and the Communist Party – either disappeared or were transformed into something different, and a challenging new transition began.

Prompted by this political instability, the perennially incomplete debate on constitutional reform has over the past 40 years produced a number of drafts, many of which were ultimately not approved by Parliament or were subsequently rejected by the people in referendums.

[1] L Paladin, *Per una storia costituzionale dell'Italia repubblicana* (Bologna, Il Mulino, 2004) 35. See also M Luciani, 'Antifascismo e nascita della Costituzione' (1991) 21(2) *Politica del diritto* 183ff.

Nonetheless, in 1993 a new political phase began, bringing a series of electoral reforms and some major transformations of the political system.

An overview of the constitutional amendments that have been approved since 1948 is provided here, along with a discussion of the four constitutional referendums: two with a positive outcome (2001 and 2020), and two with a negative result (2006, Berlusconi government, and 2016, Renzi government). Specific attention is given to the rigid character of the Italian Constitution and its amendment procedure, which mirror the main features of the process that led to its approval, as well as the explicit limits to constitutional amendments.

II. THE ALBERTINE STATUTE

The first Constitution of Italy was not intended to apply to the entire Italian peninsula, which at that time was divided into as many as 10 States. It was enacted in 1848, well before the unification of Italy in 1861. The unification was a long process that brought together a people who, in spite of having shared a common classical culture since the end of the Roman Empire, used a variety of dissimilar languages and dialects (among which Italian as a spoken language was used by less than 10 per cent of the population)[2] and had been ruled by different royal families and governments (including the Catholic Church, in the central part of the peninsula) for many centuries.

The Albertine Statute was *conceded* on 4 March 1848 by King Charles Albert of Savoy, referring exclusively to the Kingdom of Sardinia and Piedmont. This concession was precipitated by the revolutionary riots that were taking place that year all over Europe, and clearly correlated with the events occurring at the same time in Paris. Of all the charters enacted in the Italian peninsula in 1848–49, the Albertine Statute was the only one to escape the repression that came to pass in all the other States after 1849. This made it possible for the Kingdom of Sardinia and Piedmont to lead the *Risorgimento*. In 1861 the *unification process*, led by the then King of Savoy (Victor Emmanuel II, first son of Charles Albert) and his Prime Minister (Camillo Benso, Count of Cavour), was solidified and the Albertine Statute became the fundamental charter of the Kingdom of Italy. Another decade had to pass, however, before Rome became part of the Kingdom and its new capital.

[2] See T De Mauro, *Storia linguistica dell'Italia unita* (Rome-Bari, Laterza, 1970) 43.

This document was not given the title of 'constitution', as the term evoked the traumatic events of the French Revolution and those taking place contemporaneously in Paris. 'Statute' was a more neutral term that recalled the Italian municipal tradition.[3]

In all respects except in name, the Albertine Statute was a classic example of the constitution of a liberal modern state. It was formally conceded by the King 'with regal loyalty and fatherly love', and substantively drafted by a Royal Council (*Consiglio di Conferenza*), whose proceedings were held in French. Thus, the literature refers to the Statute as a *charte octroyée* – a 'conceded charter'.[4]

The Albertine Statute declared itself 'perpetual and irrevocable'. However, as it did not provide any special procedure for its own revision, it was soon deemed a '*flexible*' constitution (ie not hierarchically superior to ordinary legislation).[5] It was also a *short* constitution: it included a very limited bill of rights, and no social rights were declared. The protection of these constitutional rights was only assured by the Parliament, whose legislation was called upon to implement them and to define their scope.

The Albertine Statute remained in force for almost a century until 1944, when, at the end of the Fascist regime, the first provisional constitution, issued during the Second World War, launched a new constituent process. When Benito Mussolini took power in 1922, the Albertine Statute was still formally in force. It was gradually suspended, and it was ultimately recalled in 1943, by King Victor Emmanuel III (grandson of Victor Emmanuel II), who had for two decades accepted its suspension.[6]

In order to demonstrate the flexible nature of the Albertine Statute, it suffices here to refer to a couple of provisions that were later overridden by legislation and constitutional practice.

First, the Albertine Statute stated that the Executive power was vested in the King alone (Article 5), thereby creating, similarly to many

[3] S Cassese, 'The Italian Constitutional Architecture: from Unification to the Present Day' in (2012) 17(1) *Journal of Modern Italian Studies* 2.

[4] See P Colombo, *Con lealtà di Re e con affetto di padre. Torino, 4 marzo 1848: la concessione dello Statuto albertino* (Bologna, Il Mulino, 2003) 49f.

[5] The distinction between rigid and flexible constitutions that we refer to is elaborated on in J Bryce, *Constitutions* (New York, Oxford University Press, 1901) 3–94 and then further developed by AV Dicey, *Introduction to the Study of the Law of the Constitution* (London, Macmillan, 1965) ch II. These theories had a clear influence on Italian literature: see A Pace, *La causa della rigidità costituzionale: una rilettura di Bryce, dello Statuto Albertino e di qualche altra costituzione* (Padua, Cedam, 1996).

[6] Cf G Rebuffa, *Lo Statuto albertino* (Bologna, Il Mulino, 2003) 145f.

constitutions conceded in continental Europe at the beginning of the nineteenth century, a so-called pure constitutional system. This means that the form of government was a 'division of power system'. Nevertheless, soon after the Albertine Statute came into force, the Prime Minister's autonomy and the influence of the elective Chamber of Deputies changed the form of government, which gradually evolved towards *a quasi-parliamentary system*.[7] Similarly to what had happened a couple of centuries earlier in the evolution of the British form of government, the King stopped presiding over the Executive's meetings, thereby granting a special role to the emerging figure of the Prime Minister and at the same time permitting the Executive to derive its legitimacy, first additionally, and then exclusively, from the (elected) Parliament.

Second, while the Albertine Statute forbade (Article 50) senators and deputies from receiving any monetary compensation, a lump sum, in the guise of a reimbursement, was in fact provided to them, by law no 655/1912.

Furthermore, neither the bearers of the right to vote nor the features of the electoral system were directly defined by the Albertine Statute, which assigned these fundamental choices to legislation (Articles 29 and 30). Indeed, both these matters changed significantly during the Statute's rather long life. The right to vote was progressively extended, especially before the elections held in 1882, 1913 and 1919 (when universal male suffrage was experimented with for the first time). The electoral system was, for the most part, a two-round plurality system, with generally single-member constituencies. It was transformed into a proportional system after the First World War in order to acknowledge the role of the new mass political parties. In fact, the elections of 1919 ended up being victories for the Socialist Party (32 per cent of the votes) and the Popular Party (21 per cent of the votes), while a relative defeat was suffered by the Liberals, who up to that point had almost exclusively covered the representative spectrum, but subsequently remained fragmented in many local lists and never restructured as a mass political party.

In the years following the First World War, Italy's young and fragile liberal State could not resist the impact of the popular masses and universal suffrage. The clash between the People's, Fascist, Socialist and Communist Parties gave rise to the authoritarian, one-party regime led by Mussolini.

[7] The reference is to G Maranini, *Storia del Potere in Italia (1848–1967)* (Florence, Vallecchi, 1967) 25ff (seeing it as a synonym for assemblearism).

III. THE FASCIST REGIME, THE SECOND WORLD WAR AND THE TRANSITION TO THE REPUBLIC (1922–1945)

Mussolini originally came to power in October 1922 without overtly breaching any constitutional rules. He was appointed President of the Council of Ministers through procedures that, at least on the face of it, were not inconsistent with those required by the Albertine Statute, which had been followed for the purposes of establishing previous Italian Governments.

Once he had been appointed to that role, Mussolini gradually but steadily expanded his powers, systematically violating the fundamental rights, freedoms and procedural guarantees provided for by the Albertine Statute. Some have therefore called his reign a '*dictatorship by stealth*'.[8]

To summarise the main institutional steps on Mussolini's path towards dictatorship – leaving aside the use of censorship, violence and, later on, the enactment of racial legislation – we can recall the creation of the Fascist 'militia' (in 1923); the adoption of electoral systems initially assigning (in 1923) two-thirds of the seats to the list that received the most votes and subsequently (in 1928) allowing a single list of candidates; the so-called *leggi fascistissime* (in 1925–26, shortly after the kidnapping and assassination of Giacomo Matteotti, a socialist member of Parliament), transforming the President of the Council into a Head of Government, allowing the Government to issue legislative acts and limiting the freedom of the press; the limitations on rights to meet and associate; the insertion into the State of the structures of the Fascist party, starting with the *Gran Consiglio del Fascismo* (created in 1922 and 'constitutionalised' in 1928); and, finally, the transformation of the Chamber of Deputies into the non-elective Chamber of Fasci and Corporations (in 1939).

The Fascist regime created new structures and bodies which, especially at the beginning, were conceived of as additions to the institutions of the liberal state. Indeed, the latter continued to exist, albeit substantially deprived of any political role. The Senate and the Monarchy, for instance, were never entirely suppressed, although their political influence was dramatically reduced. This formal persistence of some institutions of the liberal state, along with the pact made with the Catholic Church (via the signing of the Conciliation between the Vatican and the Fascist government in 1929), explains why the debate is unsettled as to whether

[8] Cf P Morgan, *Italian Fascism: 1915–1945* (Basingstoke, Palgrave, 2004) 80f.

the Fascist regime effectively achieved its goal of establishing a 'totalitarian state', or whether, despite its aspirations, it 'only' managed to set up an 'authoritarian state'.[9]

However, the Albertine Statute had not been explicitly repealed, so formally speaking it was still in place after a 20 year long dictatorship. Therefore in 1943, it was possible for the King to dismiss the Mussolini Government when, in the midst of the Second World War, favourable political conditions provided him with the opportunity to do so.

In fact, the dismissal of the Mussolini Government might be characterised, from a constitutional viewpoint, as a late application of the old Albertine rules, which, after 20 years of almost complete obsolescence, were somewhat reanimated by the Monarchy.[10] On 25 July 1943, when Anglo-American military forces had already arrived in Sicily, it was King Victor Emmanuel III (the same man who had appointed Mussolini as Prime Minister in 1922) who, after the collegial body of the Government (*Gran Consiglio del Fascismo*) voted against Mussolini, appointed a new transitional government (headed by a member of the Army, Marshal Pietro Badoglio) and ordered the imprisonment of Mussolini, thereby ending the Fascist regime.

The three years that followed the fall of the Mussolini Government were confusing, tragic and bloody, but at the same time extremely fertile from a constitutional point of view. On the one hand, Italian territory became the stage for some of the most violent battles of the Second World War and of the resistance to the allied military forces of Fascists and German Nazis. On the other hand, it was at this moment that the foundations of the new republican democratic regime were laid. The country was split into two parts, with the Monarchy and its government ruling the South of Italy and the remaining components of the Fascist regime entrenched in a small portion of the Northern territory – the Republic of Salò, led by Mussolini, who had been released by the Germans.

The new bases for the emerging Italian democracy were not established by the Monarchy – the Savoy family had been too close to the Fascist government, and was suspected of complicity – but by the *political parties*, which, especially in the Northern areas of the country, were fighting Mussolini and his puppet government, still allied with the Nazis.

[9] On the debate see DD Roberts, 'Myth, Style, Substance and the Totalitarian Dynamic in Fascist Italy' (2007) 16(1) *Contemporary European History* 1.

[10] Cf C Ghisalberti, *Storia costituzionale d'Italia: 1848–1948* (Rome-Bari, Laterza, 1981) 381ff and B Ackerman, *Revolutionary Constitutions: Charismatic Leadership and the Rule of Law* (Cambridge, Harvard University Press, 2019) 133.

Thus, it is correct to affirm that political parties came first (from 1943), while the Republic came later, chosen by the people through a rather divisive referendum in 1946.

Indeed, it was during these years that the anti-fascist political parties, reunited in the National Liberation Committee (later on coupled with an Advisory Assembly, called the *Consulta Nazionale*), made the most important decisions regarding the future institutional structure of the democratic regime, which would replace the previous arrangements once the war ended.

These decisions are enshrined in two documents, unsurprisingly referred to unofficially as '*provisional constitutions*' (and both signed by Umberto III, appointed lieutenant of the King, by his father Victor Emmanuel III).[11]

The first document was legislative decree no 151/1944, enacted in the aftermath of the Salerno unity pact between the anti-fascist parties and the liberation of Rome on 25 June 1944. This envisaged the election of a Constituent Assembly, thereby ensuring beyond further doubt the end of the long life of the Albertine Statute.

The second document was legislative decree no 98/1946, enacted on 16 March 1946, soon after the liberation of the entire country. This removed the choice between Monarchy and Republic from the competence of the Constituent Assembly, and entrusted it instead to the people through an *institutional referendum*. Essentially, political parties and allied forces preferred to avoid making such a potentially divisive choice themselves, as they were themselves internally divided on the issue, and the Constituent Assembly needed to try to unify the country and to work towards a constitutional agreement.

IV. THE CONSTITUENT ASSEMBLY (1946–1948)

On 2 June 1946, all Italian citizens were called to the polls to serve two different goals: deciding, through a referendum, whether Italy would remain a Monarchy or become a Republic; and electing, according to a proportional system, the Constituent Assembly, tasked with drafting and approving a new democratic Constitution. This was the first time ever in Italian history that women were given the franchise in a general political election.

[11] See U De Siervo, 'La transizione costituzionale (1943–1946)' (1996) 2(3) *Diritto pubblico* 543; Paladin (n 1) 19ff.

As just described, the political parties ultimately preferred to leave the first decision to the citizens, fearing that it would cause profound divisions within the parties. Indeed, the referendum's close result (around 12 and a half million in favour of the Republic; around 10 and a half million in favour of the Monarchy; and around one and a half million blank or invalid votes) sharply divided the country more or less along the military lines of 1945: with the North in favour of the Republic and the South in favour of keeping the Monarchy.

In the following days, the last King of Savoy, Umberto II, who succeeded his father, left the country and was soon replaced by a *Provisional Head of State*, Enrico De Nicola. De Nicola, who was elected by the Constituent Assembly with a large majority on 28 June 1946, was a Liberal politician from the pre-fascist period. He had been the President of the Chamber of Deputies while the Mussolini Government was ascending to power, and was monarchic and southern, being born and based in Naples. To a certain extent, therefore, he was a figure called upon – in an attempt to maintain the political unity of the country – to compensate for the people's choice of the Republic and the disconnection from the liberal regime.

By contrast, responsibility for the second goal, the framing of the new Constitution, had been handed over in its entirety to the negotiations and agreement between the political parties. The citizens were merely called upon to elect their own representatives, determining the relative numbers of each of the parties. However, the final outcome needed to be decided exclusively by those representatives in the Constituent Assembly, without any further involvement of the people. The concern, in this case, was that the country could not bear to suffer (another) divisive vote, carrying with it the risk of the new Constitution being rejected altogether, as happened in France in May 1946.[12]

The *elections of 2 June 1946* were a success for the Christian Democrats, the party of the then President of the Council, Alcide De Gasperi (207 seats); the Socialist and Communist parties also obtained good results (115 and 104 seats respectively). Percentages around 5 per cent or below were obtained by parties that were neither connected with the Catholic Church nor carried a Marxist ideology, such as the Liberal Party (heir to pre-fascist Italy), the Republican Party, also connected to *Risorgimento* traditions, and the Actionist (who were among the leaders

[12] Cf M Morabito, *Histoire Constitutionnelle de la France de 1789 à nos jours* (Paris, LGDJ, 2016) 400ff.

of the resistance but only obtained seven seats). In total, there were 556 members of the Constituent Assembly, of whom 21 were women. The political components of the Constituent Assembly were very polarised in many respects. They favoured opposing understandings of the very role of the state and its relationship with civil society. Their economic, social and religious views were mismatched. Their domestic cleavages echoed the more dramatic divide that was taking place during those same years on the international stage, with the Communist and Socialist parties aligning themselves with the USSR and the Christian Democrats leaning towards the USA.

According to the second provisional Constitution, the Constituent Assembly needed to concentrate its attention on the framing of the new fundamental charter, while the Government – with the advice of four standing committees of the Constituent Assembly – took care of ordinary legislation. The only exceptions related to legislation concerning constitutional and electoral issues and international treaties (as the peace treaty was to be signed and ratified), all of which, given their strategic significance, were reserved for the Constituent Assembly.

This division of labour revealed itself to be very wise and forward-looking, as it contributed to ensuring a clear-cut distinction between the governmental and legislative dynamics, on the one hand, and the constitution-framing activity, on the other, in relation to which a broad consensus among the anti-fascist political parties was systematically sought and often achieved. The most important compromises between the main political parties and the three cultural areas that were represented within the Constituent Assembly – *the Catholic, the Marxist and the Liberal* – took place particularly within the *Committee for the Constitution*. This internal body, composed of 75 deputies, presided over by Meuccio Ruini, and divided into three sub-committees, eventually issued a first draft Constitution on 31 January 1947. The text issued by the Committee for the Constitution was also based on preparatory work completed by the Government the previous year, since from June 1945 onward the Government had maintained the position of *Minister for the Constituent Assembly*, to which the leader of the socialists, Pietro Nenni, was appointed.

So, a large part of the work had already been accomplished, with the active participation of all the anti-fascist political parties, when political divisions increased due to the establishment, during those same months, of the new international alliances. Indeed, the crucial moment occurred in May 1947, when De Gasperi, returning from an official visit to the United States, and consistently with the international alliances which would divide the world into two blocs, formed a new Government supported by a different majority. Up until that point, all the anti-fascist political parties had been members of the Government. At that time, however, the Socialist and the Communist parties moved to the opposition, where they stayed for a long while – until the 1960s and the 1970s, respectively.

Notwithstanding these events, the activity of the Constituent Assembly went on without any great discontinuity and ultimately led to the approval – via a secret ballot – of the *new Constitution*, on 22 December 1947, with 453 votes in favour and 62 against (no abstentions). The new Constitution was then published in the Official Journal (*Gazzetta Ufficiale*) on 27 December 1947 and entered into force on 1 January 1948.

The *three signatures* that sealed the Italian Republican Constitution are the greatest symbol of the convergence of political positions that had been reached within the Constituent Assembly: the document was signed by Enrico De Nicola, a liberal, as the Head of State; Umberto Terracini, a communist, as the President of the Constituent Assembly; and Alcide De Gasperi, a Christian Democrat, as the Head of the Government.

The first elections for the new Chamber of Deputies and for two-thirds of the members of the new Senate of the Republic took place, following a very tough electoral campaign, on 18 April 1948.

From a substantive point of view, the Republican Constitution fundamentally overhauled the constitutional values of the Italian State. In a nutshell, the transition from the liberal modern state to the democratic contemporary state is clearly represented through a comparison between the basic principles of the Albertine Statute and those on which the Republican Constitution is based: (a) the former conceded (by the King), the latter approved (by a Constituent Assembly); (b) the former short, the latter long (as a result of the inclusion of social rights); (c) the former founded on the principle of formal equality, the latter also including the principle of substantive equality; (d) the former providing for a unitary and centralised state, the latter fostering regional and local autonomies; (e) the former elitist, the latter democratic, including granting the right to vote to all citizens, both men and women; and (e) most significantly, with respect to the procedure for constitutional amendments, the former flexible, the latter rigid.

V. THE RIGIDITY OF THE REPUBLICAN CONSTITUTION

One of the main features of the Republican Constitution is its *rigidity*. This means that, by contrast with the Albertine Statute, the Republican Constitution established both a special procedure (more onerous than the ordinary legislative process) for its amendment and a system of judicial review of legislation. After the failure of liberal constitutions to impede the success of authoritarian and totalitarian regimes in Europe, the constitutions of the second half of the twentieth century were built on more solid foundations, with more robust and powerful fortifications. Unsurprisingly, a rigid character and the presence of judicial review of legislation are among the main traits that distinguish the constitutions of the twentieth century from their predecessors.[13]

The dramatic events of the first half of the twentieth century – wars and totalitarianism – obliged 'all the players to embark on a fundamental rethinking of the foundations of the European constitutional model of the liberal age'. In the new democratic contemporary State, constitutionalism and democracy are asked to coexist: 'democracy is regulated by the constitution, while the constitution acknowledges its political origin, stemming from the will of the sovereign people'.[14] The aim is to ensure a stronger protection of the supreme value of the human person and of the principles affirmed by the Constitution, defending them from the abuses of the public powers and the political parties.[15]

That is why the definition that best captures the nature of the new State is 'constitutional democracy'. From a legal perspective, this means that all the provisions embedded in the new Constitution are hierarchically superior to ordinary legislation and bolstered by an 'ad hoc' judicial body – the Constitutional Court – entrusted with ensuring that ordinary legislation is fully compliant with the Constitution.

Of course, the fact that the Constitution is hierarchically superior to the other sources of law was not sufficient by itself to ensure the immediate effectiveness of the new institutions created by it, and the fundamental rights and principles enshrined in it. Indeed, the *implementation process* for the new Constitution was far from easy.

On the institutional side, it took almost a decade to establish the Constitutional Court (1956) and a few more years to set up the High Council of the Judiciary (1958). It took more than 20 years to put the ordinary Regions and the referendum into place (1970). As for fundamental

[13] Ackerman (n 10) 142ff.

[14] M Fioravanti, 'Constitutionalism' in E Pattaro (ed), *A Treatise of Legal Philosophy and General Jurisprudence. Vol 9: A History of the Philosophy of Law in the Civil Law World, 1600–1900* (Dordrecht, Springer, 2009) 263.

[15] See V Barsotti and others, *Italian Constitutional Justice in Global Context* (New York, Oxford University Press, 2016) 12ff (also quoting De Gasperi).

rights and principles, the story of the implementation of the Republican Constitution is always a work in progress. However, to a certain extent, this is understandable, given the dynamic nature of all rights and the very ambitious programs and objectives of the Constitution.

Moreover, an attempt was made to downplay the legal value of the Constitutional provisions, (dis)qualifying them as political declarations to be implemented by the political bodies, rather than legal ones, and not susceptible to enforcement by the Constitutional Court. Along these lines, in particular, a very dangerous attack on the authority of the Constitution was launched by a landmark decision of the Supreme Court of Cassation on 7 February 1948 (a few weeks after the entry into force of the Constitution).[16] This decision drew a distinction between *preceptive rules* on the one hand, which were to be treated as justiciable, and *merely programmatic principles* on the other hand, the binding force of which was conditional upon legislative implementation. In doing so, the Court of Cassation was giving a voice to a very conservative position that was circulating among some legal scholars[17] and in the judiciary, where the vast majority of the judges had served in the previous regime.

Had this doctrine taken root, the innovative driving force of the Constitution would have been neutralised, in particular its more innovative principles on social rights, healthcare, working conditions, and pensions and social assistance. Had the implementation process been left to Parliament, the translation of the constitutional framework into practice would have been distorted or, at least, slow and incomplete.

However, once established, the Constitutional Court immediately rejected that distinction and relied on the preceptive character and the rigidity of the new Constitution as a whole and in each of its provisions, in order to support its principles and values and to progressively shape the legal order accordingly. Starting with Judgment no 1/1956,[18] the Constitutional Court, instead of taking sides in existing political disputes, emerged as a defender of the anti-fascist constitution that

[16] Court of Cassation, Criminal United Sessions, 7 February 1948, II, *Foro italiano*, 57ff (1948).

[17] VE Orlando, 'Studio intorno alla forma di governo vigente in Italia secondo la Costituzione del 1948' (1951) 1(1) *Rivista trimestrale di diritto pubblico* 5ff. See also F Gentile and PG Grasso (eds), *La Costituzione criticata* (Naples, Edizioni scientifiche, 1999) 137ff.

[18] See Barsotti and others (n 15) 30–34 (who qualify Judgment no 1/1956 as the 'Italian Marbury v. Madison'). See also ch 9.

was hammered out on the basis of an agreement between all the political parties. Despite the personal and professional records of some of its members,[19] the Constitutional Court was able to do its job and to disseminate the new constitutional principles within a legal system that was very much in need of renovation.

In fact, it is worth noting that, at the outset, Italian legislation maintained a high degree of continuity with the previous regime. For example, all four codes enacted during the fascist regime – although mainly written by high-level legal scholars, some of them not particularly fervent supporters of Fascism – remained in force throughout the first 40 years of the Republic, albeit with the repeal of those provisions which were clearly incompatible with the new Constitution. It was only in 1988 that one of them (the code of criminal procedure) was completely replaced by a new code, while the civil code (1942), the code of civil procedure (1942) and even the criminal code (1931) are still in force, although they have undergone many modifications via the legislature and the interventions of the Constitutional Court.[20] The sub-constitutional legal framework of the new Republic was imbued with Fascist culture. The responsibility for getting rid of all the legal dross of the fascist epoch would later be taken on by the Constitutional Court. Instead of resetting the legal system from scratch, the Republic was reconstructed within the legal framework of the Fascist state, which was itself broadly based on the model of the liberal state. Step by step, norm by norm, the legislation in place was gradually brought into line with constitutional principles by the judiciary: that is, the Constitutional Court and the ordinary courts together. This incremental renovation took decades, and the business is still unfinished.

The alignment of the old legislation with the new constitutional principles was slow and difficult because the civil servants working in the public administration and the judiciary had been educated within the Fascist culture and were still in office. The administrative personnel of the State were mostly still those from the Fascist state, and the continuity was not only in the people themselves, but also in their mindset.[21]

[19] The most astonishing example is probably Gaetano Azzariti, President of the Constitutional Court from 1957 to 1961, who had held the post of President of the 'Race Tribunal' under the Fascist regime.

[20] Cf S Cassese, *Lo Stato fascista* (Bologna, Il Mulino, 2010) 47ff and M Cartabia, 'The Italian Constitution as a Revolutionary Agreement' in R Albert (ed), *Revolutionary Constitutionalism: Law, Legitimacy, Power* (London, Hart, 2020) 313ff.

[21] Cf A Lepre, *Storia della prima Repubblica: L'Italia dal 1942 al 1992* (Bologna, Il Mulino, 1993) 56.

The bureaucratic bodies had not been overhauled, and the employees were still the same 'conservative, authoritarian, and bureaucratic' people.[22]

VI. PROCEDURES FOR AND LIMITS ON CONSTITUTIONAL AMENDMENTS

The origins of the Italian Republic described above and the need to avoid repeating the Fascist experience help to explain the preference for constitutional rigidity.[23] This was in line with other constitutions approved during this period, for example the Constitution of the Federal Republic of Germany in 1949.

In the same way, the procedure for constitutional amendments and the explicit limitations imposed on them (ie the enumeration of a few 'eternal clauses', which can never be amended), outlined in Articles 138 and 139 of the Constitution, respectively, mirror the main features of the process that led to the approval of the Italian Constitution.[24] At least three elements are reminiscent of the making of the Italian Constitution.

The first is that the main and fundamental requirement for writing, as well as for amending, the Constitution must be identified by a *wide consensus* among the political parties. The procedure for amending the Constitution requires twice the number of approvals from each of the houses of Parliament as that required for passing ordinary statutes. This means that each house must vote twice on the very same bill in order to revise the Constitution. Whereas the first approval follows the ordinary rules, the second does not allow any further modification of the bill and requires higher majorities. As long as a constitutional amendment is supported in the second deliberation (to be held at least three months after the first, once the two houses have agreed on the identical text), by a two-thirds majority in each house, it is promulgated and enters into force, without any further procedural requirement.

[22] These are the words of MP Zuccarini in the Constituent Assembly (7 March 1947), quoted in L Paladin, *Per una storia costituzionale dell'Italia repubblicana* (Bologna, Il Mulino, 2004) 38; on this point, see also V Onida, 'La transizione costituzionale' (1996) 2(3) *Diritto pubblico* 571.

[23] Cf Ackerman (n 10) 142ff.

[24] The fact that the procedure for constitutional amendment tends to mirror the procedure followed for the approval of the Constitution can be deemed normal: cf T Groppi, *Federalismo e Costituzione. La Revisione Costituzionale negli Stati Federali* (Milan, Giuffrè, 2001) 26ff and R Albert, *Constitutional Amendments: Making, Breaking, and Changing Constitutions* (New York, Oxford University Press, 2019) 39ff.

The second is that the *possibility of a referendum* is envisaged, but only as a possibility, subject to several conditions. A constitutional referendum can be requested only when the two-thirds majority required in both houses has not been reached in the second deliberation, provided that at least an absolute majority in both houses has been achieved. So, in any case, the constitutional amendment must be approved by a higher majority than that required for the approval of ordinary legislation, which is a simple majority. A request for a referendum can be made within three months after the final parliamentary approval, by parliamentary minorities (one-fifth of the members of each house), citizens (500,000 voters) or the Regions (five Regional Councils). If no one requests the referendum, the text of the constitutional amendment is deemed approved and subsequently published (again), promulgated and enters into force.

In contrast to the procedure for an abrogative referendum (see Chapter 3), the Constitutional Court does not engage in any previous checks as to the compliance of the constitutional amendment with the Constitution (or, rather, as would have been the case here, with its supreme principles). The Court of Cassation undertakes formal checks on the referendum's compliance with the requirements established by legislation.

Moreover, also in contrast to the abrogative referendum, no minimum threshold of voter turnout is required to ensure the validity of a constitutional referendum. The same rule was applied to the institutional referendum of 1946, which, however, occurred simultaneously with the first democratic elections after the Fascist regime and therefore received a very high turnout, namely 89 per cent of the electorate.

The third is that the Republican outcome of the institutional referendum of 1946, obviously embedded in the new Constitution from Article 1, represents the only *explicit limitation* on constitutional amendments. According to the last provision of the constitutional text (Article 139), 'the form of Republic shall not be a matter for constitutional amendment'.

However, at a theoretical level, queries have arisen as to whether the Republic's form could be altered through a double successive constitutional amendment: the first one repealing (or greatly modifying) Article 139 and the second one redefining the form of the State (and, hypothetically, even reintroducing the Monarchy).[25] In addition to this question, other controversies also arise in relation to the interpretation of this clause. Some authors tend to interpret it as protecting the Republic

[25] See G Contini, *La revisione costituzionale in Italia* (Milan, Giuffrè, 1971) 306ff.

not only in a formal manner vis-à-vis the Monarchy, but also as a 'democratic' form of state, in which, according to the wording of Article 1, 'sovereignty belongs to the people and is exercised by the people'. This would imply a larger number of constitutional principles that cannot be the subject of constitutional amendments, including, for example, the core of many fundamental rights, such as the right to vote, the right to free elections, and many others.[26]

Most of all, the debate has concentrated on asking whether constitutional amendments face any other *'implicit' limitations*, apart from the explicit limitation of Article 139, and, if so, identifying them. The Constitutional Court responded clearly and affirmatively to the first question, while the answer to the second question is obviously more controversial.

More specifically, Judgment no 1146/1988 of the Constitutional Court stated that the Italian Constitution contains some 'supreme principles that cannot be subverted or modified in their essential content, either by laws amending the Constitution, or by other constitutional laws': principles that 'even though not expressly mentioned among those principles not subject to the procedures of constitutional amendment, belong to the essence of the supreme values upon which the Italian Constitution is founded'.

Once it recognised the existence of these supreme principles, the Italian Constitutional Court affirmed the possibility that some constitutional amendments might be declared unconstitutional:[27]

> therefore, it cannot be denied that this Court is competent to judge the compliance of laws amending the Constitution, or of other constitutional laws also with supreme principles of the constitutional legal order. Otherwise, it would lead to the absurd outcome of having a faulty and ineffective system of judicial review of the Constitution with respect to its most highly valued provisions.[28]

In so doing, the Court recalled the argument employed by the US Supreme Court in *Marbury v Madison* (1803), when it initially established the

[26] On this dispute see C Fusaro, 'Italy' in D Oliver and C Fusaro (eds), *How Constitutions Change. A Comparative Study* (Oxford, Hart Publishing, 2011) 211, 214ff; T Groppi, 'Constitutional Revision in Italy: A Marginal Instrument for Constitutional Change' in X Contiades (ed), *Engineering Constitutional Change: A Comparative Perspective on Europe, Canada and the USA* (Abingdon, Routledge, 2013) 203, 210ff.

[27] T Groppi (n 26) 210ff and Y Roznai, *Unconstitutional Constitutional Amendments: The Limits of Amendment Powers* (Oxford, Oxford University Press, 2017) 151f.

[28] For a discussion of this decision see Barsotti and others (n 15) 98ff (from which the translation of the first two excerpts from Judgment no 1146/1988 is taken).

constitutional review of legislation. This possibility is based on the distinction between the supreme principles (which represent an expression of the *pouvoir constituant*), on the one hand, and all the other constitutional provisions (amendable through the constitutional revision power, which is a *pouvoir constitué*), on the other hand.[29] In a certain way, via Judgment no 1146/1988, the Constitutional Court decided to appoint itself as the guardian of this – indeed, rather subtle – distinction (see Chapters 9 and 10).

As to the identification of the 'supreme principles', so far the Constitutional Court has explicitly recognised the paramount position of the right to a judge, provided by Article 24; however, the Court has never applied this limitation to a constitutional amendment, only to international treaties and EU law.[30]

VII. THE MOST IMPORTANT CONSTITUTIONAL AMENDMENTS

Before recalling some of the most significant constitutional amendments approved to date, a terminological clarification is necessary. The more onerous procedure envisaged by Article 138 (just described) must be followed for the approval of both *constitutional revision laws* (ie those laws that actually include amendments to the text of the Constitution) and *other constitutional laws* (ie laws that are placed at the same hierarchical level as the Constitution, but which do not, however, amend its text).

According to these procedures, 17 pieces of constitutional legislation containing constitutional amendments have been approved since 1948. They have amended 30 articles (some of them more than once) and abolished four articles (all of which had been included in the Fifth Title of the Second Part, on territorial autonomies), while no brand-new articles have been added to the text of the Constitution.[31]

[29] On the distinction between '*pouvoir constituant*' and '*pouvoir constitué*' see Sieyès, as outlined in P Pasquino, *Sieyès et l'invention de la Constitution en France* (Paris, Odile Jacob, 1998) and M Goldoni, *La dottrina costituzionale di Sieyès* (Florence, Firenze University Press, 2009).

[30] For example, Judgments nos 18/1982, 232/1989 and 238/2014. P Faraguna, 'Unamendability and Constitutional Identity in the Italian Constitutional Experience' (2019) 3 *European Journal of Law Reform* 329–44.

[31] The overall number of constitutional laws, ie of laws approved following the special procedure provided by Art 138 of the Constitution, is higher: 42 (including 15 constitutional laws modifying 'special' regional statutes and nine 'other' constitutional laws).

Constitutional referendums have been held on four occasions. The two with positive outcomes were in 2001 for the constitutional revision of territorial autonomies proposed by the centre-left majority and in 2020 to allow the reduction of members of the Chamber of Deputies and of the Senate. In the other two cases the relevant amendments were rejected: the reform of the whole second part of the Constitution proposed by the Berlusconi Government and centre-right majority in 2006 and the reform of bicameralism proposed by the Renzi Government and its centre-left majority in 2016.[32]

As has already been emphasised, in such referendums, unlike in abrogative referendums, no minimum threshold of voter turnout is required. So, in 2001 34.1 per cent of the citizens went to the polls and the constitutional revision was approved by 64.2 per cent of the votes. In 2006, the results were 52.5 per cent and 38.7 per cent respectively, so this time the reform was rejected by the people. The negative outcome in 2016 was even clearer, with a turnout of 65.5 per cent, and just 40.4 per cent of the votes in favour of the constitutional amendment. The clearest outcome was probably in 2020, when 51.1 per cent of the voters took part in the referendum and 69.9 per cent of the votes were in favour of the revision.

It is worth noting that these four referendums were requested not only by the political forces that opposed the constitutional revision, but also by those that supported it, in order to show that they were not afraid of the popular vote and to seek a more solid democratic support for the constitutional reform. Moreover, constitutional referendums have been requested not only by parliamentary minorities (by far the easiest group to persuade if one wants to ask for a constitutional referendum), but also by citizens (500,000 voters' signatures were collected both in 2006 and in 2016) and by Regional Councils (at least five, as was the case in 2006).

Several constitutional amendments have been approved without the need for a referendum, including those aimed at, *inter alia*, stabilizing the number of Members of Parliament and equalising the length of the legislative terms of the two Houses (no 2/1963); reducing the length of the tenure of Constitutional judges from 12 to 9 years (no 2/1967); abolishing the jurisdiction of the Constitutional Court with respect to 'ministerial crimes' (no 1/1989); reducing parliamentary immunities (no 3/1993); providing for direct election of the Presidents of the Regions

[32] On the first, see C Pinelli, 'The 1948 Italian Constitution and the 2006 Referendum: Food for Thought' (2006) 2(3) *European Constitutional Law Review* 329. On the second, see N Lupo, 'On the failed constitutional reform of the Italian Senate' (2019) 2 *DPCE-on line* 1595.

(no 1/1999); codifying the principles of a 'fair trial' (no 3/1999); allowing Italian citizens residing abroad to submit postal votes (nos 1/2000 and 1/2001); promoting equal opportunities for men and women in public office (no 1/2003); eliminating death penalty for military offences (no 1/2007); establishing the principle of budget balance (no 1/2012); and equalising the electorate of the Senate to that of the Chamber (no 1/2021). Not all 16 of these constitutional amendments have overcome the threshold of two-thirds of the members of each House in favour. However, a referendum was requested only in the four cases mentioned above, while in the others, after three months' delay, the constitutional laws were republished in the Official Journal and entered into force, despite having only been approved by an absolute majority in at least one House.[33]

VIII. THE EVOLUTION OF THE ITALIAN REPUBLICAN CONSTITUTION

A. The First Phase (1948–1992): A Republic Ruled by Political Parties

In order to understand the main features of Italian political institutions from the entry into force of the Constitution, on 1 January 1948, until the end of the Cold War, four decades later, it is necessary to have in mind the international framework which followed the Second World War, together with the presence in Italy of the strongest communist party in Western Europe.[34] This unusual context helps to explain, first, Italy's adoption of a proportional electoral system, which ensured a fair representation of all political parties in Parliament, irrespective of them being either in the majority or in the opposition. A second consequence was a stable, blocked political system, with lively intra-majority and often intra-party dynamics, which gives an additional explanation for the political instability of Italian governments.[35] Third, political parties were still characterised as free associations, meaning that they would not

[33] Indeed, all the constitutional amendments before 1970 needed to be approved by a two-thirds majority, as the referendum had not yet been implemented: Fusaro (n 26) 218 (see also ch 3).

[34] For a recap see P Bellucci, 'Communists' in E Jones and G Pasquino (eds), *The Oxford Handbook of Italian Politics*, (Oxford, Oxford University Press, 2015) 184.

[35] Cf J La Palombara, *Democracy Italian Style* (New Haven, Yale University Press, 1987). On the average length of tenure of the Italian Governments see also ch 5.

be obliged to respect any law regarding their own internal organisation and functioning. This legal status might seem a bit awkward as the public policies were *de facto* determined by the political parties. However, on closer inspection, it was clear that political parties' strength depended on their role within Italian society, independent from any official recognition on the part of the new State, which had actually been founded by them.[36]

The overall approach was that the Republican institutions needed to be weak and adaptable so that political parties could play, fairly freely, a major role in the political arena. The general political direction had to be determined not so much by the voters or by the Government, but by the political parties, on which the same Government depended, and which were free to form alliances in Parliament regarding the approval of legislation and supporting the Government. Elections offered citizens their only opportunity to decide the weight of every political party in Parliament, or, to use an analogy, to distribute the cards without playing the game, which was exclusively in the hands of political parties. In short, parties mattered more than institutions and, accordingly, the most central and powerful institution in the Italian consensual democracy was Parliament, not the Government.[37]

To a certain extent, this approach was even reinforced by the controversial approval and subsequent failure of a majoritarian electoral law in 1953, during the first parliamentary elections held after those of 1948 (see Chapter 3). The parliamentary process for the approval of this law, which was replete with obstacles, showed that the political culture was still far from accepting a majoritarian dynamic: the law was soon referred to as the 'swindle law' (*legge truffa*). However, the fact that the coalition, led by the Christian Democrats, did not reach the threshold for getting the majority bonus provided by this law, demonstrated that the path to be followed needed to change: maintaining the proportional system and gradually proceeding toward an enlargement of the majority to include the Socialist party, as occurred after 1963, with a government led by Aldo Moro.

The peak of this first phase of the Republic was probably represented by the so-called national solidarity governments (1976–1978). In particularly difficult years affected by the oil crisis, inflation and terrorist

[36] Cf P Scoppola, *La Repubblica dei partiti* (Bologna, Il Mulino, 1991).

[37] See S Fabbrini, 'The Institutional Odyssey of the Italian Parliamentary Republic' (2012) 17(1) *Journal of Modern Italian Studies* 10.

movements, the Communist party was also included in the parliamentary majority (although not in the Government, led by Giulio Andreotti). The end of this phase in 1978 was tragic, marred by the kidnapping and assassination of Moro, by the Red Brigades. At that time Moro was President of the Christian Democrats and the main sponsor of the progressive enlargement of the majority towards leftist parties.

During the 1980s, therefore, the political system had no clear direction for its own evolution. In order to keep their centre-left coalition (*pentapartito*: ie composed of five parties) together, for the first time in the Republic's history the Christian Democrats had to leave the premiership to leaders of other minor parties: first, the Republican party (Spadolini governments: 1981–1982; 1982) and then the Socialist party (Craxi governments: 1983–1986; 1986–1987).

It was during these years that the matter of constitutional reforms found a place on the political agenda, especially under the initiative of the Spadolini and Craxi governments. In fact, their premiers could not use the channel represented by their parties to ensure the prevalence of their political direction, and so they needed to rely on the institutional mechanisms, which at that time were almost non-existent. These initiatives led to the creation of the Bozzi bicameral committee for institutional reform (1983–1985). Its results, however, were rather limited: the approval of some important laws – on the structure and the powers of the Government (no 400/1988), on financial procedures (no 362/1988), on Italy's relationship with European Communities (no 86/1989) – and a restriction of the secret ballot in Parliament, achieved through amending the Chamber's and Senate's rules of procedures in 1988.

It was only at the turn of the decade, after the end of the Cold War – symbolised by the fall of the Berlin Wall (1989) – that the potential evolution towards a majoritarian democracy, with an alternative coalition seeking the support of the voters, looked clearer. However, the political parties were not interested in pursuing this path, and preferred to defend their own positions and revenues, as was shown by the rejection, in 1990, of the proposal aimed at introducing the popular election of mayors within the law that reformed local governments (no 142/1990).

B. The Second Phase (1993–2013): In Search of a Majoritarian Democracy

Soon after the fall of the Berlin Wall, which ended the division of the world into two blocks and, in Italy, dissolved the basis of the equilibrium which commenced in 1947, several other crucial events took place across Europe and in Italy. In Europe, the Maastricht Treaty was signed on February 1992, establishing quantitative limits on the expansion of public debt and budget deficits. In Italy, the so-called 'Bribesville' (*Tangentopoli*) scandal occurred, which exposed the system of corruption and kickbacks that characterised a large part of the political system and some of the biggest private companies. This system revealed itself to be unsustainable in the new financial climate, and was discovered by prosecutors, first in Milan and then in the rest of the country, resulting in allegations against around one-third of Members of Parliament.

As an effect of two abrogative referendums held in 1991 and in 1993, the proportional electoral system on which the main political parties relied was transformed into a mainly majoritarian electoral system, according to which three-quarters of the seats of both Houses were assigned according to a first-past-the-post rule (see Chapter 3).

In the wake of the 1994 elections, an earthquake hit the political system: none of the original political parties, on which the Republic had been established, survived. From these ruins, Silvio Berlusconi was ready to take full advantage of the situation. He founded his own party, *Forza Italia*, linked to his media and advertising businesses and was able to win the 1994 elections, the first to be held with a majoritarian system, thanks to a rather awkward alliance: in the north of the country, with the separatist Northern League; and in the rest of the country, with the right-wing party National Alliance.

In contemporary Italian politics, the following 20 years might be regarded as a prolonged and only partially accomplished quest for majoritarian democracy in order to transform a system that had been based on a proportional principle and blocked for the previous 45 years. Moreover, it was a period in which the figure of Berlusconi dominated the political arena, both while he was the President of the Council of Ministers (1994; 2001–2006; 2008–2011), but also while he was the main opposition leader.[38] While in search of an accomplishment of a majoritarian turn, the Republic experienced, in moments of difficulty and under the need to adopt economic and financial reforms required by the European Union, three examples of so-called 'technocratic governments', led by Carlo Azeglio Ciampi (1993–1994), Lamberto Dini (1995–1996) and Mario Monti (2011–2013) (see Chapter 5).

[38] See G Orsina, *Berlusconi and Italy. A Historical Interpretation* (New York, Palgrave, 2014).

The appointment of the Monti Government, in the second part of 2011, accelerated the end of the 'Berlusconi era'. After the concerns expressed by the European institutions about the risk of financial collapse of the country, a number of austerity measures of economic rebalancing were necessary. To this purpose, a new cabinet, mainly made of experts and academics, was appointed and obtained a broad parliamentary majority, until the general elections scheduled in 2013.

C. The Third Phase (2013–2021): A Republic with a De-institutionalised Party System?

The factors that, on a global scale, brought about an increased 'personalisation' of politics – that is, the internationalisation of politics, the growth of the state, the changing structures of mass communication, and the erosion of traditional political cleavages[39] – impacted the Italian political system rather dramatically, at the very moment when its features were undergoing a deep transformation, and in combination with the personal style of a media-tycoon who entered into politics in order to defend his own affairs after the disappearance of his traditional political points of reference. The concern that this mix would be explosive and that, soon after 'partitocracy', Italian politics would face a system of 'leaderocracy', was thus more than legitimate.[40]

In the aftermath of the 2013 elections, the success of a new populist party, the 5-Star Movement created a real stalemate in the political system. The way out was found in the re-election of the President of the Republic, Giorgio Napolitano (Chapter 6), and in the re-start of the process of constitutional reform. However, after several stops and starts, and the substitution of the Letta Government (2013–2014) with the Renzi Government (2014–2016), the process ended once again with the failure of the 2016 constitutional referendum mentioned earlier.

In constitutional terms, this outcome stabilised the symmetrical bicameralism and encouraged the adoption of a similar electoral system for the two Houses, namely, a proportional system for 63 per cent of the seats (law no 165/2017).

[39] These four factors are taken from T Poguntke and P Webb, 'The Presidentialization of Politics in Democratic Societies: a Framework for Analysis' in T Poguntke and P Webb (eds), *The Presidentialization of Politics: A Comparative Study of Modern Democracies* (New York, Oxford University Press, 2005) 1ff.

[40] See M Cotta, 'Partitocracy. Parties and their Critics in Italian Political Life' in Jones and Pasquino (eds) (n 34) 41ff, 48ff.

In political terms, it gave rise to a new stalemate after the 2018 elections, confirming that, since 2013, Italy's party system had been undergoing a process of 'deinstitutionalisation', characterised by instability and unpredictability in terms of partisan interactions, at all levels of competition, with considerable changes both in demand (voters' political preferences) and supply (the establishment of important new parties), and also in the nature of the competition.[41] The Republican Constitution that was founded by political parties remained, notwithstanding these parties' radical transformation, and is now being called upon to cope with the weakening and the de-institutionalisation of the party system itself.

Moreover, in this case, the stalemate following the 2018 elections led to the formation of government supported by newly forged parliamentary alliances: first, by the 5-Star Movement and the League, which abandoned its original secessionist aims (Conte 1 Government, 2018–2019); then, by the 5-Star Movement and the Democratic Party (Conte 2 Government, 2019–2021), which were more aligned with the political majority supporting the Von der Leyen Commission at the EU level, after the 2019 elections for the European Parliament.[42] After the failure of this last cabinet, within the context of the COVID-19 pandemic, the President of the Republic appointed a 'national unity government' led by Mario Draghi. Thanks to the glowing reputation and prestige of the President of the Council, a wide agreement between the political parties was reached and a new cabinet was formed based on a complex balance between political and technocratic elements. This Government, encompassing the representatives of a wide-range of political parties along with some independent experts, managed to gain very broad parliamentary support, with the only opposition party being the extreme right party (*Fratelli d'Italia*).

IX. CONCLUSION

In summarising the main lines of the evolution of the Italian Republican Constitution, it is useful to recall and discuss a distinction that has often

[41] V Emanuele and A Chiaramonte, 'Going out of the ordinary. The de-institutionalization of the Italian party system in comparative perspective' (2020) 12(1) *Contemporary Italian Politics* 4.

[42] See N Lupo, 'Intertwining "Forms of Government" Between Rome and Brussels: The Influence of EU Dynamics on the Handover from Conte I to Conte II Cabinet' (2020) 13 *Reconnect WP* 1.

been drawn between a supposed first (1948–1992) and second Republic (since 1993).

It may be argued that this distinction is very relevant for historians and political scientists, as – as just remarked – at the beginning of the 1990s there was a great degree of discontinuity concerning the main structural and functional features of the party system.

However, this distinction cannot be adopted from a strict constitutional law standpoint: the norms with respect to the form of government have not changed and even the adoption of a majoritarian electoral system, unaccompanied by a broader constitutional amendment, has not altered the main rules and principles of the Constitution or the core dynamics of the parliamentary government. This conclusion appears to have been confirmed by the Republic's latest evolution, since 2013, which has been characterised by a further transformation and 'de-institutionalisation' of the party system, but with continuity in the applicable constitutional and parliamentary rules.

FURTHER READING

Ackerman, B, 'Revolutionary Constitutions' in *Charismatic Leadership and the Rule of Law* (Cambridge, Harvard University Press, 2019).

Barbisan, B, 'The Republic of Parties: From Singular to Plural in the 1948 Italian Constitution' (2020) 39 *Giornale di Storia Costituzionale* 173.

Calabresi, SG, and M Godi, 'Italian Constitutionalism and Its Origins' (2020) 6(1) *Italian Law Journal* 23.

Cartabia, M, 'The Italian Constitution as a Revolutionary Agreement' in R Albert (ed), *Revolutionary Constitutionalism: Law, Legitimacy, Power* (Oxford, Hart Publishing, 2020) 313.

Gilmour, D, *The Pursuit of Italy: A History of a Land, its Regions and their Peoples*, Penguin, 2012.

Lupo, N, 'Two Examples of Quasi-Constitutional Amendments from the Italian Constitutional Evolution. A Response to Richard Albert' (2017) 65(5) *Buffalo Law Review* 1039.

Pasquino, P, 'The Un-Constituent Power of the People: Article 138 of the Italian Constitution and Popular Referendum' (2017) 3(1) *Italian Law Journal* 139.

Tega, D, 'The Constitution of the Italian Republic: Not revolution, but principled liberation' (2019) 17(2) *International Journal of Constitutional Law* 690.

Ziblatt, D, *Structuring the State: The Formation of Italy and Germany and the Puzzle of Federalism* (Princeton, Princeton University Press, 2006).

2

The Italian Constitution within the 'Composite' European Constitution

Internationalist Principle – International Organisations – Limitations of Sovereignty – European Union – European Convention on Human Rights – European Court of Justice – European Court of Human Rights – Counter-limits – Implementation of EU Law

I. INTRODUCTION

SINCE ITS ORIGIN, the Italian Constitution has been open to the international legal order. Indeed, its commitment to the international system is declared in its introductory provisions. In part, this is a natural consequence of the Constitution having been approved soon after the end of the Second World War, and in part it represents a rejection of the Fascist state's rhetoric, celebration of war and glorification of an outrageous form of nationalism.

In the first section of the Constitution, devoted to 'fundamental principles', Articles 10 and 11, which address relationships with the international community, grant the legislator some leeway to accept 'limitations of sovereignty' deriving from international law and to encourage Italy's participation in multi-lateral international organisations that promote 'peace and justice among nations'. It is relevant to note that the Italian Constitution was drafted and approved during the very same years as new international organisations were being developed, both at the continental and at the global levels. Over time, some constitutional amendments have introduced new provisions concerning international and European relations; however, the core principles were already established in the original text of the Constitution.

Although the Constitution does not name any specific international body, the records of the discussion which took place in the Constituent Assembly offer evidence that both the United Nations and the European Communities were at the forefront of the drafters' minds. Although no '*European clause*'[1] was included in the original text, nor was it added with subsequent amendments, the Constitution already offered a constitutional basis for the process of European integration which progressively assumed a peculiar status within the panorama of international relations. Eventually, a constitutional amendment in 2001 introduced a new principle, in Article 117.1 of the Constitution, which adds an explicit obligation for the legislator to comply with the European rules. Although the interpretation of this novel principle was a bit uncertain at the beginning, over time it has not revealed any particularly innovative potential, nor has it prompted *per se* a new course with respect to the constitutional dynamic of Italy's participation in the European Union.

As has been the case in every other EU Member State, but possibly in a more tacit and subtle way, the nature of the Italian legal order has been deeply transformed by the European integration process, although with some relevant limits. Therefore, Italy's membership of the EU entails the need to re-read the Italian Constitution in light of the principles of the European legal system. That is why this chapter devotes specific attention to the mechanisms – both implicit and explicit – through which this transformation took place and which govern the functioning, from an Italian perspective, of the so-called 'composite' European Constitution.

II. OPENNESS TO THE INTERNATIONAL ORDER AND ITS FOUNDATIONS

The '*internationalist principle*' is one of the fundamental pillars of the Italian Constitution. The basis of this openness to the international community can be explained by reference to different, although not completely divergent, phenomena.

First, the origins of the Constitution in the *Resistance* to the Fascist regime are relevant. As one of the most influential members of the Constituent Assembly, Costantino Mortati, argued, the Italian Constitution was 'born from the Resistance', and thus designed with a

[1] M Claes, 'Constitutionalizing Europe at its Source: The "European Clauses"' (2005) 24(1) *National Constitutions: Evolution and Typology, Yearbook of European Law* 81.

clear intent to reject and bypass all the 'values' (or anti-values) that had characterised the totalitarian era.[2]

A second and additional basis relates to Italy's position as a defeated power in the Second World War. It is no accident that the Japanese Constitution (promulgated in November 1946) and the German Basic Law (1949) are also characterised by their recognition of the internationalist principle. While the former seems more focused on affirming its pacifist nature,[3] the latter is mostly aimed at clarifying the effects of the internationalist principle on national sovereignty, using both the concepts of 'limitation' and 'transfer' of sovereign powers, and specifically addressing the relationship between international law and federal law.[4]

The role played by external influences during the constituent process was indeed more significant in Japan and in Germany than in Italy, where, as discussed earlier (Chapter 1), the text of the Constitution was drafted and approved by a Constituent Assembly, in which the political parties that promoted the Resistance to Fascism played a major role. However, a certain degree of external pressure was probably also brought to bear on its activity, in order to ensure that the new Constitution would leave adequate space to the international community and to those international organisations that would be established in the following years, with the aim of avoiding the excesses of nationalism. Indeed, this influence was not particularly difficult to exercise, given the universalistic approaches that characterised the foundational doctrines of the Christian Democratic and the Marxist parties, among which the constituent pact was sealed.

The Constituent Assembly was very determined to avoid the mistakes that led to the Second World War, and thus to condemn and prevent any form of nationalism and totalitarianism. Therefore, there was a rather broad consensus on following and, if possible, further advancing the trend of internationalising national constitutional law which had already commenced in Europe in the 1930s.[5]

[2] C Mortati, *Le forme di governo. Lezioni* (Padua, Cedam, 1973) 222ff (including also French Fourth Republic) and P Carrozza, 'Constitutionalism's Post-modern Opening' in M Loughlin and N Walker (eds), *The Paradox of Constitutionalism: Constituent Power and Constitutional Form* (Oxford, Oxford University Press, 2007) 169ff, 180.

[3] See Art 9 of the Japanese Constitution.

[4] See the original text of Arts 24–25 of the German Basic Law.

[5] See, among others, B Mirkine-Guetzévitch, *Les nouvelles tendances du droit constitutionnel* (Paris, Marcel Giard, 1931) 48; G Martinico, 'Constitutionalism, Resistance and Openness: Comparative Law Reflections on Constitutionalism in Postnational Governance' (2016) (35)1 *Yearbook of European Law* 318.

III. THE CONSTITUTIONAL PRINCIPLES ON INTERNATIONAL LAW

In the Italian system, a distinction must be drawn between customary international principles and international agreements as to their respective effects in the domestic order.

Article 10 of the Constitution opens with the statement 'The Italian legal system shall conform to the generally recognised principles of international law', which has ordinarily been interpreted as referring exclusively to *customary international law*. These customary rules are directly incorporated into the Italian legal order and enjoy the same rank as constitutional provisions, although even those rules are required to respect the 'supreme fundamental principles of the Constitution', as upheld by the Constitutional Court.[6]

By contrast, according to the *dualistic* approach to international law traditionally adopted by the Italian legal system,[7] international treaties must be incorporated into national law, in order to be binding within the domestic system. Articles 80 and 87 grant the power of ratification to the President of the Republic, but in some specified cases – which cover a wide spectrum of treaties – a prior act of Parliament is required.

Most international treaties become part of the Italian system through a legislative act of Parliament, which confers on the treaty provisions the same binding value of ordinary legislative statutes that are notoriously subordinate to the Constitution. As a consequence, international treaties are usually considered to be of lesser authority than constitutional law in the hierarchy of sources of law. This implies that international treaties, after ratification and transposition into domestic law, take precedence over earlier legislative acts, but can be overturned by later ordinary legislative acts according to the principle *lex posterior derogat priori* (ie the later law overcomes the earlier).

By contrast with other legal orders that normally assign this task to their constitutional courts (France, Germany, Ireland, among others),[8] in Italy there is no *ex ante* judicial check on the compatibility of international treaties with the Constitution. So, the Constitutional Court

[6] Judgments nos 48/1979, 238/2014.

[7] H Kelsen, *The Problem of Sovereignty and the Theory of International Law: A Contribution to a Pure Theory of Law* (Oxford, Oxford University Press, 2020).

[8] See M Mendez, 'Constitutional review of treaties: Lessons for comparative constitutional design and practice' (2017) 15(1) *International Journal of Constitutional Law* 84; C Closa, 'National Higher Courts and the Ratification of EU Treaties' (2013) 36(1) *West European Politics* 97.

is allowed to assess the constitutional legitimacy of any international treaty, but only *ex post*: that is, if and when the legislative act authorising the ratification and containing the order of execution either has to be applied before a judge or violates a regional competence. In these cases, through the ordinary ways of accession – *incidenter* or *principaliter* respectively (see Chapter 9) – the Constitutional Court can be called upon to decide on the constitutionality of international treaties.

A specific feature of the Italian constitutional system is provided by Article 11 of the Constitution. This provision affirms:

> Italy rejects war as an instrument of aggression against the freedom of other peoples and as a means for the settlement of international disputes. Italy shall agree, on conditions of equality with other States, to such limitations of sovereignty as may be necessary to ensure peace and justice among Nations. Italy shall promote and encourage international organisations pursuing such goals.

This provision states a very broad and ambitious principle of openness of the Italian legal order to the international community. Some expressions are worth noting: the reference to peace and war; the concept of justice applied globally; the use of the term 'world order' to identify the international community based on a premise of equality among nations; the citation of 'international organisations' in the plural; and, most of all, the use of the word 'sovereignty', in order to provide a general constitutional authorisation for the acceptance of '*limitations of sovereignty*' necessitated by participation in the international organisations.

Article 11 does not explicitly mention the European communities, nor was it framed solely with respect to European integration. Nevertheless, it has offered a solid constitutional basis for Italy's participation in European integration. By contrast with the German Basic Law, the original text of the Italian Constitution does not include any specific 'European clause'.[9] As demonstrated by reference to the preparatory works of the Constitution, the members of the Constituent Assembly were well aware and supportive of these initial attempts to pursue the goal of European integration (in view of a 'unified Europe'), and the absence of a specific reference to any form of European integration project was due entirely to the will to adopt the broadest possible approach in Article 11, including

[9] See Art 24.2 of the German Basic Law.

in its meaning the United Nations and all kinds of other international organisations.[10] Over time, the reference included in Article 11 to the 'limitations of sovereignty' has been construed as a veritable 'European clause', in particular by the case law of the Constitutional Court.

This Article has therefore provided a broad constitutional basis for the many steps of the European integration and to the numerous revisions of the founding treaties. For an extended period, thanks to the 'over-stretched' reading of Article 11, no specific constitutional amendment was required to accommodate the revisions of the European treaties, even when they entailed a major impact on a domestic constitutional principle. For example, no constitutional amendment was considered necessary for the ratification of the Maastricht Treaty, providing for the extension of electoral rights to non-Italian citizens.[11] Against this backdrop, the 2012 constitutional amendment, which changed Article 81 in order to comply with EU guidelines on balanced budgets required by the so-called 'Fiscal Compact',[12] represents quite a novelty for Italian political praxis.

However, one should not overlook the fact that, in 2001, a constitutional amendment inserted a new provision introducing the very first explicit constitutional reference to EU law. The new text of Article 117.1 of the Constitution states 'Legislative powers shall be vested in the State and the Regions in compliance with the Constitution and with the constraints deriving from EU legislation and international obligations'. This provision has been interpreted as merely codifying the obligations with which the legislator is already encumbered: namely, that national and regional legislators are constrained by the requirement to respect EU and international law while exercising their legislative function.[13]

This does not mean that the new Article 117 was without impact. It has served as a basis for recognising the special status, not only of EU law, but also of the European Convention on Human Rights (ECHR) and judgments of the European Court of Human Rights (ECtHR or the

[10] See L Chieffi and M Cartabia, 'Art. 11' in R Bifulco, A Celotto and M Olivetti (eds), *Commentario alla Costituzione* (Turin, Utet, 2006) 266f; L Gianniti, 'I costituenti e l'Europa' (2018) *Federalismi.it*.

[11] The Treaty on European Union, as signed in Maastricht on 7 February 1992. For the constitutional amendments approved in other Member States, see the European Parliament comparative study written by LFM Besselink and others, *National Constitutional Avenues for further European Integration* (Brussels, European Parliament, 2014) 147–58.

[12] Constitutional law no 1/2012.

[13] See, in particular, Judgments nos 368/2008 and 227/2010.

'Strasbourg Court'). More recently, the same special status was acknowledged with respect to the European Social Charter.[14]

Consequently, this article has strengthened the possibility of EU law and the ECHR acting as bases for the constitutional review of legislation. Indeed, if the Constitutional Court is entitled to scrutinise the compliance of statutory law with the Constitution, and the Constitution itself wants national legislation to be constrained by international obligations and European legislation, these 'external' sources can more easily enter the constitutional adjudication process. Indeed, after the constitutional amendment of Article 117.1, an increasing number of actions have been brought before the Constitutional Court to challenge national legislation for inconsistency with Article 117.1 and therefore with EU law, the ECHR and other international treaties.

IV. THE 'EUROPEAN JOURNEY' OF THE CONSTITUTIONAL COURT

Given its traditional dualistic approach to international law, during the early years of European integration the Italian legal system experienced some challenges accepting the fundamental principles of the EU legal system, namely the primacy and the direct effect of EU law. It took some decades and a '*European journey*'[15] of the Constitutional Court for the Italian legal system to ultimately align with the requirements imposed by the Court of Justice of the EU. The journey can be divided into three steps: first, the constitutional resistance to the primacy of EU law; second, the limitation of sovereignty in favour of the EU; and, third, the constitutional acceptance of the primacy of EU law.

Originally, the founding treaties of the European Communities were assimilated to every other international treaty ratified and executed by ordinary legislation. In fact, by contrast with what happened in many other EU Member States,[16] in Italy the ratification (and execution) of the international treaties founding the European Communities – as well as all their subsequent reforms enacted until the Treaty of Lisbon[17] – did

[14] See Judgment no 120/2018.

[15] For the reference to the 'European journey' of the Constitutional Court, see P Barile, 'Il cammino comunitario della Corte' (1973) *Giurisprudenza costituzionale* 2405f.

[16] See M Claes, *The National Courts' Mandate in the European Constitution* (Hart, Oxford, 2006).

[17] Signed by the EU Member States on 13 December 2007.

not require any constitutional amendment and took place through ordinary pieces of legislation.

The choice not to amend the Constitution was originally dictated by political reasons. Due to the opposition to the European project of the Communist and Socialist parties, it was practically impossible to reach the majority of two-thirds of the members of each House, then required to amend the Constitution (as the referendum was not yet implemented in the Italian legal order until 1970).[18] Thus, under the wide umbrella of Article 11, Italy's participation in the EU relied solely on ordinary legislative instruments, starting from the choice made when authorising the ratification of the first European treaties.[19]

As a result, the provisions of the European treaties, and *a fortiori* all other provisions of secondary European legislation, were designated the same rank as any other piece of ordinary legislation. They were capable of derogating from the national legislation in force, but could potentially be overturned by later ordinary laws. This position, which was rendered explicit by the Constitutional Court in Judgment no 14/1964, was clearly unsatisfactory from the perspective of the European Communities.

The Court of Justice of the European Union (hereinafter 'CJEU' or 'Luxembourg Court') instead moved on from the monistic approach, based on the well-known argument that the Communities constitute 'a new legal order of international law for the benefit of which the States have limited their sovereign rights, albeit within limited fields, and the subjects of which comprise not only Member States but also their nationals'. Consequently, EU law has direct effect within national legal orders: independently of the legislation of Member States, it 'not only imposes obligations on individuals but is also intended to confer upon them rights which become part of their legal heritage'.[20]

The contrast between the approaches of the two Courts could not have been starker, and erupted when both were required to intervene in the same proceedings, which concerned the Italian law nationalising the electricity industry. Within the context of the same judicial controversy, the Courts reached two opposite conclusions. For the Court of Justice, this represented a good occasion to affirm the primacy of EU law, noting

[18] A Barbera, 'Costituzione della Repubblica italiana' in *Enciclopedia del diritto. Annali*, VII (Milan, Giuffrè, 2015) 263–358, 352.

[19] Laws nos 766/1952 and 1203/1957.

[20] Case 26/62 *Van Gend en Loos v Netherlands Inland Revenue Administration* EU:C:1963:1.

that the Treaty establishing the European Economic Community 'has created its own legal system which, on the entry into force of the Treaty, became an integral part of the legal systems of the Member States and which their courts are bound to apply'. And that 'the executive force of Community law cannot vary from one State to another in deference to subsequent domestic laws, without jeopardizing the attainment of the objectives of the Treaty'.[21]

By way of contrast, dealing with the same legal question, the Constitutional Court affirmed that EU Treaties should be regarded as any other international treaty, given the same value as ordinary laws of the Italian Parliament, and therefore could not prevail over more recent pieces of legislation.[22]

During the following years, however, the Constitutional Court gradually changed its attitude of opposition towards the primacy of EU law and distinguished the status of EU Treaties from all other international norms. The pivot of this line of reasoning was the notion of 'limitations of sovereignty', at the core of Article 11. This idea had been already employed, together with that of 'transfers of sovereignty', in the case law of the CJEU.[23]

This new trend in the Constitutional Court's case law first appeared in the so-called *Frontini* Judgment.[24] According to the Constitutional Court the limitations of sovereignty legitimate 'the limitation of the powers of the State with respect to its legislative, executive, and judicial functions, which was necessary for the institution of a Community among the European States'. On the basis of Article 11, Italy and the other Member States 'conferred upon and recognised in the Economic Community … certain sovereign powers, constituting it as an institution characterised by an autonomous and independent legal order'. Here the Constitutional Court clearly recognised that the European integration has special features and cannot adequately be understood through the lens of the general principles of international law. Insofar as the EU institutions perform their activities within the boundaries of competences established by the Founding Treaties, their acts – regulations and directives – enjoy a special status, since they can be directly applied within the Italian legal order, with no need to be 'transplanted'

[21] Case 6/64 *Costa v ENEL* EU:C:1964:66.
[22] Judgment no 14/1994.
[23] *Van Gend en Loos* (n 20).
[24] Judgment no 183/1973.

into domestic legislation. The Constitutional Court thus paved the way for the principles of *direct effect and primacy of EU law* within the limit of competences established by the Treaties.

Once the Constitutional Court accepted the primacy of EU law on the basis of Article 11, a new problem arose: who is the guardian of the primacy of EU law within the national legal system?

On this point, the Court of Justice and the Constitutional Court once again took opposite positions from the outset. By contrast with the Italian tradition of centralised judicial review, where only the Constitutional Court is vested with the exclusive power of judging the laws, in its 1978 *Simmenthal* Judgment the Court of Justice argued that: 'every national court must, in a case within its jurisdiction, apply Community law in its entirety and protect rights which the latter confers on individuals and must accordingly set aside any provision of national law which may conflict with it, whether prior or subsequent to the Community rule'.[25]

This conferral of powers on 'every national court' to set aside national legislation was a shock to the Italian system, and brought about a period of innovation, both from a theoretical and practical standpoint. Indeed, Italy's membership of the European Union has deeply affected the model of constitutional adjudication as originally designed by the Italian Constitution of 1948. On the one hand, the principle of primacy has in fact introduced a new source of higher law, which competes with the national constitutional principles as a benchmark for judicial review of national legislation. On the other hand, the principle of direct effect entrusts all lower courts, rather than only the Constitutional Court, with the power of performing judicial review of legislation in relation to EU law.

It is no wonder, then, that it took a number of years for Italian legal scholarship and the Constitutional Court to accept the 'quiet revolution'[26] brought about by the Court of Justice in *Simmenthal*. Only in 1984, with the so-called *Granital* Judgment, did the Constitutional Court overrule its previous case law, affirming that EU law must always be applied by all judges, with the effect not of 'annulling, in the proper meaning of the term, the incompatible internal norm, but of preventing that norm from being applied for the resolution of the controversy before

[25] Case 106/77 *Amministrazione delle Finanze dello Stato v. Simmenthal SpA* EU:C:1978:49, para 21.

[26] JHH Weiler, 'A Quiet Revolution: the European Court of Justice and its Interlocutors' (1994) 26(4) *Comparative Political Studies* 510.

the national judge'.[27] Following this fundamental judgment, the task of directly applying EU law has thus been given to every national court.

More recently, the Constitutional Court has further clarified the role of the lower courts and that of the Constitutional Court itself in the field of the implementation of the EU law, in particular in the field of fundamental rights.[28] The Constitutional Court re-established its jurisdiction, alongside that of inferior courts, with respect to the judicial review of national legislation, in particular where the EU Charter was concerned. Whereas lower ordinary courts can only set aside national provisions which are inconsistent with EU law on a case-by-case basis, the Constitutional Court can invalidate with general effect all pieces of national legislation that do not comply with European obligations.[29]

The result of this new course is a sort of concurrent judicial review of national legislation when EU law is involved. The ordinary courts can set aside the national legislation which is inconsistent with a provision of the EU law having direct effect. However, if they consider it would be more appropriate to involve the Constitutional Court, in particular in the field of protection of fundamental rights, the latter maintains its jurisdiction and can decide the case with general effect, declaring the invalidity of the Italian law due to incompatibility with European rights, norms and principles.

V. THE 'COUNTER-LIMITS' DOCTRINE

Since its inception, the openness of the Constitutional Court to the legal orders of the EU and then, more cautiously, to the ECHR, has been accompanied by some reservations. In common with many other national constitutional courts – starting with the German *Bundesverfassungsgericht* (BVerfG) – it has accepted the primacy of EU law 'subject to conditions'. While in general EU law prevails over national legislation (including the Constitution, as required by the CJEU),[30] EU norms are not permitted to override the *supreme principles of the Italian*

[27] Judgment no 170/1984.

[28] See the obiter dictum in Judgment no 269/2017, later specified by Judgments nos 20, 63 and 117/2019.

[29] Judgment no 117/2019.

[30] Case 11/70 *Internationale Handelsgesellschaft mbH v Einfuhr- und Vorratsstelle für Getreide und Futtermittel* EU:C:1970:114.

Constitution and the inalienable rights of the person.[31] These core principles are considered 'counter-limits' (*controlimiti*) to the 'limitations of sovereignty' identified by Article 11.[32] As a result, EU law prevails over all national legislation, and can even derogate from the Italian Constitution, but only within the boundaries of these 'counter-limits'.

In order to understand this peculiar notion of 'counter-limits', one should consider that, when the primacy of EU law was established in the case-law of the CJEU in the 1960s and 1970s, there was no bill of rights in any European Treaty and the CJEU had declined any competence to rule on the protection of fundamental rights.[33] National constitutional courts were concerned about the lack of protection afforded to human rights, especially in cases of human rights violations resulting from acts of the European Communities. In particular, the German BVerfG firmly expressed this concern in the *Solange* Judgments of 1974 and 1986.[34]

Even before the BVerfG, the Italian Constitutional Court clearly established the doctrine of 'counter-limits' in 1973. In a famous passage, the Court argued that, on the basis of Article 11, 'limitations of sovereignty have been allowed solely for the attainment of the goals indicated there'. It must therefore be 'ruled out that those limitations concretely delineated in the Treaty of Rome – adopted by Nations with legal systems that are inspired by the rule of law and that guarantee the essential liberties of their citizens – may in any case entail for the organs of the Community an inadmissible power to violate the supreme principles of our constitutional order or the inalienable rights of the human person'.[35]

In sum, EU law must respect the supreme principles of the Italian Constitution from a substantive point of view and, in the event of a violation of those principles, the Constitutional Court claims jurisdiction. As for the consequences of the EU's violation of the supreme principles of the Italian Constitution, the Constitutional Court has maintained a cooperative stance in relation to the Court of Justice of the EU.

Departing from the BVerfG's approach, which fostered an open struggle with the Court of Justice in contemplating the possible *ultra vires*

[31] Judgment no 183/1973.

[32] For the first use of the expression 'controlimitazioni' see Barile (n 15).

[33] Case 1/58 *Stork & Cie v. High Authority* EU:C:1959:4.

[34] For good syntheses, in English, of the BVG case law, see J Kokott, 'Report on Germany' in AM Slaughter, A Stone Sweet and JHH Weiler (eds), *The European Courts and National Courts: Doctrine and Jurisprudence* (Oxford, Hart, 1997) 77–131 and J Collings, *Democracy's Guardians: A History of the German Federal Constitutional Court, 1951–2001* (Oxford, OUP, 2015).

[35] Judgment no 183/1973.

review or identity review of EU measures,[36] the Constitutional Court has been prepared to engage in dialogue. This attitude has become clear in two decisions, issued during the so-called '*Taricco saga*' concerning the principles of statutes of limitation in criminal matters.[37] As part of a productive dialogue with the CJEU, the Constitutional Court recalled its 'counter-limits' doctrine as well as the concepts of constitutional identity and common constitutional traditions.[38] This role seems entirely consistent with the so-called 'third wave' of judicial review, as identified by some scholars, which focuses, *inter alia*, on identity review.[39]

VI. THE EUROPEAN CONVENTION OF HUMAN RIGHTS IN THE ITALIAN LEGAL SYSTEM

Unlike the law of the EU, which has claimed a privileged position since the very beginning of European integration, and has demanded a uniform legal status across the Union, the ECHR leaves some room to States to define and specify the legal status assigned to the Convention within their domestic legal orders. In particular, it is up to each State to decide what its national courts should do when confronted with a piece of national legislation that conflicts with the ECHR. This means that there is a rich variety of solutions to such conflicts throughout the 47 Council of Europe Member States.[40]

In Italy, in accordance with the dualist tradition discussed earlier, for decades the ECHR was treated as a typical international convention, with the same rank as an ordinary legislative act and without any distinctive position. However, the growing relevance of the jurisprudence of the ECtHR in cases related to the protection of individual rights did not go unnoticed. Although at the outset it was mainly ordinary courts which paid attention to the jurisprudence of the Strasbourg Court, this trend

[36] See, in particular, the *Lissabon Urteil*, BVerfG 30.06.2009, 2 BvE 2/08 (*Lissabon*). See also ECJ 62/14 (*Gauweiler e a v Deutscher Bundestag*) and, more recently, BVerfG 05.05.2020, 2 BvR 859/15.

[37] Judgments nos 24/2017 and 115/2018. See also ch 10.

[38] Cf G Piccirilli, 'The "Taricco Saga": the Italian Constitutional Court Continues Its European Journey' (2018) 14(4) *European Constitutional Law Review* 814.

[39] D Lustig and JHH Weiler, 'Judicial Review in the Contemporary World. Retrospective and Prospective' (2018) 16(2) *International Journal of Constitutional Law* 315, 357ff.

[40] For an overview see H Keller and A Stone Sweet (eds), *A Europe of Rights: The Impact of the ECHR on National Legal Systems* (Oxford, Oxford University Press, 2008).

exerted pressure on the Constitutional Court to elevate the status of the Convention to a higher level of legal authority.

The Constitutional Court sanctioned the ECHR's new status within the Italian legal system with the '*twin Judgments*' nos 348 and 349/2007. The overruling was helped by the aforementioned constitutional revision adopted in 2001 (constitutional law no 3/2001). This introduced a new provision – Article 117.1 – which rendered explicit the fact that the national and regional legislators are bound to respect all European and international obligations.

The Constitutional Court argued the new wording of Article 117.1 'entails in fact a duty on Parliament to respect the said rules when enacting ordinary legislation, with the result that any national provision incompatible with the ECHR and thus with the "international law obligations" ... violates this constitutional principle'. In contrast to the position reached in relation to EU law, 'the ordinary courts do not therefore have the power to set aside ordinary legislation in contrast with the ECHR, since the alleged incompatibility between the two takes the form of a question of constitutional legitimacy due to an eventual violation of Art. 117.1, falling under the exclusive jurisdiction of the Constitutional Court'.[41] In other words, where an ordinary 'court doubts the compatibility of the national law with the "interposed" Convention provision, it must seize this court with a corresponding question concerning its constitutionality' in light of Article 117.1.[42]

However, as a result, the ECHR does not acquire the force of constitutional law. In the hierarchy of norms, it sits between the Constitution and ordinary legislation. Each of the Convention's provisions is part of the *bloc de constitutionnalité*, provided that it is compatible with the Italian Constitution. Therefore, the principles of the Convention, as interpreted by the Strasbourg Court, can be used by the Constitutional Court as a standard of judicial review of national legislation only insofar as they conform with the Constitution.[43] After all, the ECHR gives the Member States a margin of appreciation in the implementation of the principles therein protected.

In the same vein, more recently, the Italian Constitutional Court considered itself to be bound to respect the judicial decisions of the

[41] Judgment no 348/2007.
[42] Judgment no 349/2007.
[43] Judgment no 264/2012.

ECtHR only if and when the latter pronounced a 'consolidated principle' of its jurisprudence. In contrast, when a new or debated principle is at the foundation of the Strasbourg Court's decision, the Italian Court retains some leeway in the implementation of the ECHR and, in some cases, is able to overlook a specific decision of the Strasbourg Court.[44]

VII. CONSTITUTIONAL RULES AND PRACTICE OF IMPLEMENTING EU LAW

As far as the implementation of EU law is concerned, Italy was the first country to contemplate, from 1989, a specific legal instrument to ensure the timely implementation of EU law to be guaranteed by Parliament: the *Legge comunitaria* – an 'ad hoc' 'community law' to be approved each year. The specific 'European procedures' established by the Italian legislator were intended to pursue two aims: on the one hand, to involve Parliament in the processes of elaborating and implementing EU law, which otherwise remains in the hands of the Government; and on the other hand, to ensure that timely respect is afforded to all European obligations assumed by the Government.

The very first provisions were contained in law no 86/1989 (the *Legge La Pergola*), followed by law no 11/2005 (the *Legge Buttiglione*). Currently, the procedures through which the Italian Parliament interacts with the European Union are provided by law no 234/2012.[45] Law no 234/2012 introduced appropriate procedures for implementing the new forms of participation of national parliaments in the EU decision-making process outlined in the Treaty of Lisbon (including the subsidiarity check in the context of the early warning mechanism),[46] and also strengthened Parliament's ability to scrutinise and influence the Executive's activity within the EU context.

In a nutshell, these procedures are based on the following points.

[44] Judgment no 49/2015. See also ch 9.

[45] Entitled 'General rules on Italy's participation in the formation and implementation of legislation and policies of the European Union', in force since 19 January 2013.

[46] For a general overview of the Lisbon innovation related to subsidiarity and parliamentary democracy see M Cartabia, N Lupo and A Simoncini (eds), *Democracy and Subsidiarity in the EU* (Bologna, Il Mulino, 2012); A Manzella, 'The Role of Parliaments in the Democratic Life of the Union' in S Micossi and G L Tosato (eds), *The European Union in the 21st Century. Perspectives from the Lisbon Treaty* (Brussels, CEPS, 2010) 257.

A. The Government's Duty to Inform and the Parliamentary Scrutiny Reserve

The Government is bound to inform Parliament and to transmit to it a wide range of specific documents related to the framing of EU policies, such as draft legislation and other documents of the European institutions. The Government is also required to keep the two Houses informed – *ex ante and ex post* – as to the positions that Italy maintains at the 'European tables'. These Government duties to convey information are aimed at involving Parliament in the framing of EU policies and, more specifically, in elaborating the national position to be negotiated in the European arena.

Law no 234/2012 also provided for a specific instrument to ensure that Parliament is not circumvented in the delineation of Italy's national position within the European intergovernmental context: the '*parliamentary scrutiny reserve*', which can be activated in relation to any EU project or act, and which imposes on the Government a mandatory prior examination by the Chambers. Moreover, the two Houses, through a joint action, may request the Government to activate an '*emergency brake*'. Following the triggering of this procedural device, the matter is referred to the European Council, thereby delaying the final deliberation when sensitive issues are discussed within the Council of the EU. The high volume of information received by the Parliament actually enables it to engage in in-depth scrutiny of the governmental activity at the EU level. Pursuant to law no 234/2012, the President of the Council regularly appears before the Chamber and the Senate in the wake of the meetings of the European Council.[47] Moreover, the Minister (or the Under-Secretary) for EU Affairs and the Minister for the Economy and Finance have often been summoned to appear before the competent parliamentary joint committees to give evidence about the results of the Council of the EU's meetings through parliamentary hearings.[48]

[47] The European Council consists of the heads of state or government of the EU's Member States, together with its President and the European Commission President. It defines the EU's general political direction and priorities. The Council of the EU represents the Member States' governments: it is where national ministers from each EU country meet to adopt regulation and coordinate policies. The Council of the EU is a single legal entity, but it meets in 10 different 'configurations', depending on the subject being discussed: ie General Affairs, Justice and Home Affairs, Economic and Financial Affairs, etc (see www.consilium.europa.eu/en).

[48] C Fasone and D Fromage, 'Are Parliaments (More) Committed to the Trend of Open Government After the Lisbon Treaty? The Italian and the Spanish Case' in I Bouhadana and others (eds), *Parliaments in the Open Government Era* (Paris, Les éditions IMODEV, 2016) 173.

B. The Early Warning Mechanism and the Political Dialogue in the EU

The Lisbon Treaty provided that national parliaments can send reasoned opinions to the European institutions regarding EU draft legislative acts' compliance with the principle of subsidiarity in fields of shared competence with the EU (the so-called '*Early Warning Mechanism*'). Where reasoned opinions reach certain thresholds ('*yellow card*' or, when higher, '*orange card*'), the draft legislative act must be reviewed and it may be confirmed, modified or withdrawn by the European legislators.

Within the Italian Parliament, it is primarily the responsibility of the EU Affairs Committees to verify the compliance of EU draft legislative acts with the subsidiarity principle. Nevertheless, other parliamentary committees can also be involved in the process and, upon request, the subsidiarity check can be devolved to the full Assembly.[49] The Italian Parliament has presented several reasoned opinions since the entry into force of the Lisbon Treaty, with the Italian Senate being more active than the Chamber of Deputies. It can be argued that the Italian Parliament followed the trend of many other national parliaments which endorsed a broad notion of subsidiarity, including scrutiny as to the substance of the proposal, the principle of proportionality, and the choice of the legal basis for EU legislation.[50]

In September 2006, the European Commission launched the so-called '*political dialogue*', whereby its legislative proposals and consultation documents are transmitted directly to national parliaments. The parliaments are invited to express comments and opinions, to which the Commission itself has committed to reply. The Commission has maintained political dialogue even after the entry into force of the Lisbon Treaty and law no 234/2012 which codified this practice, and provided that the Chambers may submit to the European institutions, and at the same time to the Government, all the documents required to frame and develop European policies.

In practice, this procedure of political dialogue has been very successful, in the sense that many national parliaments – including the Italian Senate and Chamber – have taken advantage of this potential to entertain an informal dialogue between their committees and the European Commission.

[49] See N Lupo and G Piccirilli (eds), *The Italian Parliament in the European Union* (Oxford, Hart, 2017) 99 and 119.

[50] D Capuano, 'The role of national parliaments in the legislative process of the EU: a view from inside the Italian Parliament' in Cartabia, Lupo and Simoncini (eds) (n 46) 247.

C. The Role of the Italian Parliament in Implementing EU Measures

Law no. 234/2012 completely revisited the instruments and procedures devoted to the implementation of EU law. The annual 'Community law' (*legge comunitaria*) has been replaced by two different legislative instruments: the 'European delegation law' (*legge di delegazione europea*) and the 'European law' (*legge europea*). Via the 'European delegation law', the Parliament delegates to the Government the transposition of European directives and the implementation of other acts of the European Union. Through the 'European law', the Parliament directly adopts measures for the fulfilment of obligations arising from EU law.

The proposal of the 'European delegation law' must be presented by the Government by 28 February each year, although, if necessary, it may be submitted twice a year. Thanks also to these new instruments, the number of infringement proceedings brought against Italy, while still significant, decreased.

VIII. CONCLUSION

The European continent has become a space characterised by constitutional interdependence and, consequently, national constitutional orders are now embedded in the constitutional fabric which comprises national constitutions, EU law, European treaties and conventions. This constitutional interdependence affects all the institutional actors of the legislative, executive and judicial branches.

A review of this history demonstrates that Italy is firmly embedded within this composite European constitutional space. It has incrementally 'opened up' to the influence of EU law and the activity of the Council of Europe, and even more so to the judge-made law of the two European Courts, which has become increasingly relevant, in particular in human rights cases. There are some 'counter-limits' to this opening up to European influence, represented by the fundamental principles of the constitutional architecture. These are viewed as 'eternity clauses' by the Constitutional Court (Judgment no. 1146/1988): elements that must be respected even when amending the Constitution.

Within these limits, Italy's membership of the EU has, over time, reshaped several principles of the Italian constitutional system. It has also significantly affected the respective roles of the Government and the Parliament in the exercise of legislative function, and has had a major impact on the model of constitutional adjudication originally designed by the Italian Constitution. In fact, the decision-making process at the EU level empowers the national governments rather than parliaments. The principle of primacy of EU law has introduced a new source of higher order law, which competes with national constitutional principles. Moreover, direct effect entrusts all lower courts, rather than only the Constitutional Court, with the power of performing judicial review of legislation in relation to EU law. Italy's membership of the Council of Europe has additionally played a relevant role, by prompting the Constitutional Court to change and adapt its case law and to interpret some constitutional provisions in a different manner. The indirect or direct dialogue between national and European institutions and especially between courts has incrementally developed the interpretation of many constitutional provisions: for example, in the fields of non-discrimination, environmental protection, labour law, privacy and data protection, freedom of expression, and the right to property.

FURTHER READING

Bonelli, M, 'The Taricco Saga and the consolidation of judicial dialogue in the European Union' (2018) 25(3) *Maastricht Journal of European and Comparative Law* 357.

Fabbrini, F, and Pollicino, O, 'Constitutional Identity in Italy: Institutional Disagreements at a Time of Political Change' in E Van Der Schyff and DL Callies, *Constitutional Identity in a Europe of Multilevel Constitutionalism* (Cambridge, Cambridge University Press, 2020) 201–22.

Martinico, G, Guastaferro, B, and Pollicino, O, 'The Constitution of Italy: Axiological Continuity between the Domestic and International Levels of Governance?' in A Albi and S Bardutzky (eds), *The Role of National Constitutions in the European and Global Governance* (The Hague, TMC Asser Press, 2019).

Martinico, G, and Repetto, G, 'Fundamental Rights and Constitutional Duels in Europe: An Italian Perspective on Case 269/2017 of the Italian Constitutional Court and Its Aftermath' (2019) 15(4) *European Constitutional Law Review* 731.

Piccirilli, G, 'The "Taricco Saga": the Italian Constitutional Court Continues Its European Journey' (2018) 14(4) *European Constitutional Law Review* 814.

Tega, D, 'The Italian Way: A Blend of Cooperation and Hubris' (2019) 77(3) *The Heidelberg Journal of International Law / Zeitschrift für ausländisches öffentliches Recht und Völkerrecht* 685.

3

Popular Sovereignty and Separation of Powers

Democracy – Sovereignty – Right to vote – Citizenship – Separation of powers – Election – Electoral legislation – Majority bonus – Threshold – Single-Member Constituencies – Oversea Constituency – Referendum – Form of government – Political Direction

I. INTRODUCTION

THE ITALIAN CONSTITUTION'S first Article enounces the democratic principle: 'Italy is a democratic Republic founded on labour. Sovereignty belongs to the people and is exercised by the people in the forms and within the limits of the Constitution'. Forms and limits established by the Constitution are crucial to determining how Italian democracy works and to shaping the place for, and the relative weight of, the mechanisms of representative democracy and direct democracy.

After highlighting how the democratic principle is framed by the Italian Constitution, this chapter deals with the different formats of referendums provided for by the Constitution and their implementation, which has only taken place since 1970. The actual use of referendums is discussed in the context of the current rebalancing between representative and direct democracy, which also derives from technological innovations that have been adopted rather late within the main political institutions in Italy, while being intensively and instrumentally used by new populist parties.

The Italian Constitution provides for a representative democracy and its form of government is based upon a parliamentary system. The main instrument for the exercise of popular sovereignty is still the election of the Parliament, which must take place at least once every five years. Since its origins, the Constituent Assembly has very clearly opted in favour of a form of government that was neither presidential nor directorial, but a rationalised parliamentary one.[1] It is *parliamentary* because the Government needs the confidence of the (two Houses of) Parliament; and *rationalised* because the confidence relationship between the Parliament and Government is regulated by constitutional rules that aim to control the political forces and to stabilise the Government. In other words, the original intention of the Constituent Assembly was to adopt the parliamentary model while avoiding the risks of 'assembly government' (ie the instability of the executive and the prospect of it being held hostage by contingent parliamentary majorities).[2]

However, this rationalisation found only a very limited place in the actual constitutional text, as the main political parties, especially after the rupture of the anti-fascist coalition in May 1947 (see Chapter 1), preferred not to overly empower the future winners of political elections (first of all, those of 1948) and preferred to rely more on themselves than on institutional mechanisms to strengthen and stabilise the government.[3]

Conversely, although the Constituent Assembly took the option of a proportional electoral system for granted, it chose not to inscribe it in the text of the Constitution. This choice revealed itself to be decisive for Italian history, as it determined that the electoral system needed to be defined through ordinary legislation. In fact, the principal turning points between the different phases of the evolution of the Italian Republican Constitution (Chapter 1) were characterised by some changes in the electoral law.

In the final part of the chapter, a definition of the Italian parliamentary form of government is proposed, based on the features the chapter illustrates. That is, it analyses how the principle of the separation of powers has been adapted to the parliamentary form of government, using the concept of the 'function of political direction' (*funzione di indirizzo politico*), elaborated by Italian scholarship in the mid-twentieth century and benefiting from some notions derived, some decades later, from political science, especially regarding the role of the political parties and party system.

[1] Namely with the 'Perassi resolution', approved by the Second Subcommittee on 4 September 1946, which deemed 'unfit to the condition of Italian society both the presidential and the directorial governments and opted in favour of the parliamentary system, to be ruled, anyway, through constitutional mechanisms able to guarantee the need for the stability of Government and to avoid the degenerations of parliamentarism'.

[2] On the concept of rationalised parliamentarism see B Mirkine-Guetzevitch, *Les Constitutions de l'Europe Nouvelle* (Paris, Delagrave, 1928) 13ff and 22ff.

[3] On both these reasons see G Amato, 'Constitution' in E Jones and G Pasquino (eds), *The Oxford Handbook on Italian Politics* (Oxford, Oxford University Press, 2015) 71ff, 78.

II. THE DEMOCRATIC PRINCIPLE IN THE ITALIAN CONSTITUTION: THE RIGHT TO VOTE AND TO BE ELECTED

The Italian Constitution is clear in recognising, from its very first Article, the *democratic principle*. It characterises the Italian Republic as a 'democratic Republic' and it grants sovereignty neither to the State nor to the Nation – as would have been possible had it followed the tradition of liberal constitutions – but directly to the people.[4]

However, the people's sovereignty is to be carried out in the framework of the Constitution. Like all liberal democracies, the Italian model recognises *legal limits to political power*, even when it is exercised directly by the citizens. The Constitution, and the legislation implementing it, are therefore called upon to shape the relationship between the instruments of representative democracy and those of direct democracy.

Article 1 also refers to the fact that the democratic Republic is 'founded on labour'. Although there is a clear echo of the influences of socialist constitutions, this wording was fully accepted and supported even by the Christian Democrats, who considered it to be consistent with the social doctrine of the Catholic Church. Labour is deemed to be a means of self-fulfilment for all mankind; a duty for the State to promote active employment policies; and also an instrument for recognising the principle of equality and abolishing distinctions based on birth or blood.

This provision must therefore be interpreted in the only way in which it can coexist with the democratic principle. Indeed, consistent with that which is stated in Article 3, citizens are deemed to form part of the sovereign power not only when they exercise their own political rights but also in their private and social activities. Among these activities, a central role is to be attributed to their labour, through which they contribute to the 'the full development of the human person and the effective participation of all workers in the political, economic and social organisation of the country'.

So, it is up to the Constitution to establish the forms and limits according to which the people are entitled to exercise their own sovereign power: that is, to determine how Italian democracy works in practice and how the power of political direction is distributed among constitutional bodies.[5]

[4] On this debate, in which scholars such as Crisafulli and Mortati played a crucial role, see M Cartabia, 'The Legacy of Sovereignty in Italian Constitutional Debate' in N Walker (ed), *Sovereignty in Transition* (Oxford, Hart, 2003) 305–26.

[5] This is the most common definition of the notion of 'form of government'.

The Constitution does so by first deciding who actually comprise 'the people' and who are, therefore, entitled to exercise political rights (and duties), which are so far strictly connected to citizenship. From this standpoint, it defines who the citizens are, and the rules according to which they may obtain or lose citizenship. That is, indeed, the concrete definition of the 'demos', traditionally characterised as one of the constitutive elements of the State and seen as an essential part of the same sovereign power.

It should also not be forgotten that, following the Maastricht Treaty (1992), the attribution of Italian citizenship, as well as citizenship of other EU Member States, automatically determines the attribution of *European citizenship*. The latter was not meant to replace national citizenship but to be an additional status, conferring a second layer of rights upon the citizens of the Member States of the EU, alongside those deriving from national citizenship. For these reasons, it can be said that European citizens enjoy a dual citizenship: once they are entitled to a Member State's citizenship, they also enjoy a number of supplementary rights as European citizens, without having to perform specific duties.[6] As for electoral rights, European citizenship bestows the right to take part in local elections and the election of the European Parliament, without requiring Member States to enfranchise European citizens in national political ballots.

In common with many contemporary constitutions, the Italian Constitution does not say much on this topic, instead leaving the issue almost entirely to ordinary legislation. In this case, law no 91/1992 adopts an *ius sanguinis* centred model (ie based on the blood inherited from the parents): citizenship is maintained throughout the generations, even when residing abroad, and citizenship through residence is hard to obtain. Some proposals for reform are currently under consideration, which aim to include some *ius soli* windows, easing the naturalisation process for children of migrants living in Italy (also relying on their enculturation: the so-called *ius culturae*).[7]

However, the Constitution directly forbids the deprivation of citizenship for political reasons (Article 22) and specifies that, to be entitled to political rights, ie in order to vote and to be elected for the Chamber and the Senate, one is required to be an Italian citizen (Article 48).

[6] For a strong criticism of European citizenship, highlighting in particular its character as being derived from the Member States' citizenship, see BVG, Lissabon urteil (2009), paras 346–50.

[7] Text approved by the Chamber in October 2015 (AS, XVII Legislative term, no 2092).

In 2000 and 2001, two constitutional amendments were approved, both aimed at easing the exercise of the right to vote for the many Italians who resided abroad, allowing them to vote *in absentia*: previously, they needed to return to Italy if they wished to vote. A longstanding request led to 12 deputies and 6 senators – which became 8 and 4 respectively, following constitutional law no 1/2020 – elected by Italians living abroad within a specific 'Overseas Constituency' (*Circoscrizione Estero*), divided into four electoral districts: Europe; South America; North and Central America; Africa, Asia and Oceania. In order to do so, Article 48 as well as Articles 56 and 57 of the Constitution had to be amended (by constitutional laws nos 1/2000 and 1/2001, respectively) and then implemented by an ordinary statute (law no 459/2001).

These constitutional amendments have been strongly criticised,[8] as they give weight – which is not insignificant, especially within highly fragmented Houses – to the political preferences of citizens who are, for the most part, not connected with the Italian State through any kind of economic or social relationship, but only for the fact of having kept an Italian passport (often in addition to another citizenship) and registering with the Italian consulates via an 'ad hoc' registry (AIRE: Registry of Italians resident abroad, established by law no 470/1988). Relevant issues – sometimes even involving criminal justice – also emerged during the first concrete application of these voting mechanisms, but the right to vote seems at this point rather difficult to reverse.

III. DIRECT DEMOCRACY: THE ABROGATIVE REFERENDUM AND ITS DIFFERENT USAGES

The Italian Constitution, although clearly founding a representative democracy, provides a significant role for some instruments of direct democracy, namely through popular referendums. It took more than 20 years to activate them, essentially because, at the beginning of the Republican history, the party system was able to represent citizens and to satisfy their needs rather effectively, and thus to monopolise the channels of political representation.

The Constitution's most significant and innovative instrument of direct democracy, capable of playing a role in the ordinary life of the

[8] See, among many, E Grosso, 'Legge costituzionale 17 gennaio 2000, n 1 (Voto degli italiani all'estero)' in A Pizzorusso (ed), *Leggi costituzionali e di revisione costituzionale (1994–2005). Commentario della Costituzione* (Bologna, Zanichelli, 2006) 195–235.

country, and of repealing either entirely or partially (and thus modifying) pieces of legislation, is the *abrogative referendum*.[9] In the mid-twentieth century, there were not many countries in which forms of referendums were offered and used in practice on a national basis, and the negative experience of the Weimar Republic, whose Constitution made wide reference to the instruments of direct democracy, persuaded the drafters of the Italian Constitution to proceed very cautiously in this direction.[10] However, on 2 June 1946, Italy held an important institutional referendum selecting the Republican form of government. As mentioned earlier, this referendum was held jointly with the elections for the Constituent Assembly.

These contradictory pressures resulted in the Constituent Assembly acting with trepidation in relation to this matter. Of the many types of referendums proposed by Costantino Mortati – a constitutional law scholar who was elected as a member of the Constituent Assembly for the Christian Democrats – the final text of the Constitution excluded those that were more innovative and therefore deemed more dangerous, such as propositional, suspensive or advisory referendums. It introduced only constitutional referendums (Article 138: see Chapter 1), some referendums for territorial variations (Articles 132 and 133) and, most important of all, the abrogative referendum (Article 75).

With regards to the latter, the Constitution identifies a series of procedural features and substantive limitations. More specifically, according to Article 75, an abrogative referendum may be called for a total or partial repeal (or abrogation) of a piece of legislation if a formal request is signed by at least 500,000 voters or by five Regional Councils. International treaties, tax and budgetary legislation, and pardon and amnesty statutes may not be submitted to this kind of referendum. In order to produce effects in the legal order, the abrogative referendum should obtain a turnout of at least 50 per cent plus one of the electorate and will be determined by a simple majority of valid votes. In any case, legislation is necessary in order to ensure the implementation of these constitutional provisions, which are not self-executing.

A further important procedural limit to abrogative referendums was introduced by Article 2 of constitutional law no 1/1953, which required

[9] For a critical discussion of this point see M Luciani, *La formazione delle leggi. Art. 75. Tomo 1,2. Il referendum abrogativo* (Bologna, Zanichelli, 2005) 6ff.

[10] For a comparative analysis, see L Morel and M Qvortrup (eds), *The Routledge Handbook to Referendums and Direct Democracy* (London–New York, Routledge, 2018).

the Constitutional Court to undertake a preliminary admissibility check, aimed essentially at verifying whether the request concerned any of the objects excluded by the Constitution.[11]

These same political parties decided in 1970 to activate the device of the abrogative referendum, in order to find a compromise on a very divisive issue: the introduction of the *divorce law*, which caused an internal fracture within the majority coalition and was also met with strong opposition from the Catholic Church.[12] The Christian Democrats, the party that, since 1948, had secured the highest number of parliamentary seats, accepted having a law approved which allowed divorce, on the condition that this law be submitted to an abrogative referendum. That is why, before the approval of the divorce law (law no 898/1970), the legislation activating the abrogative referendum (and, together with it, all the other national referendums enumerated by the Constitution) needed to be approved: namely, law no 352/1970, on referendums and on popular legislative initiatives.

Law no 352/1970 provided a timeframe for requesting an abrogative referendum, including provisions on collection of signatures (from 2021 this is also possible online), and added another judicial check to that on its admissibility, which had already been entrusted to the Constitutional Court. This means that each request for an abrogative referendum also needs to survive, even before being transmitted to the Constitutional Court, a judgment on its legality; that is, on its compliance with the (mainly) procedural prerequisites outlined by ordinary legislation, attributed to an 'ad hoc' office, specialising in referendums, established within the Court of Cassation.

As noted, the first abrogative referendum was requested soon after the approval of the divorce law, and only took place in 1974 (after a parliamentary election in 1972, which caused the postponement of the referendum). The request to totally repeal the divorce law was rejected by the citizens and so the law allowing divorce was confirmed: 59.3 per cent voted no to its repeal and 40.7 per cent voted yes. The turnout was very high: 87.7 per cent of the electorate of the Chamber of Deputies went to the polls to exercise their new right for the first time.

[11] Cf R Lucifredi, 'Il controllo sulla costituzionalità sulle richieste di referendum abrogativo' (1951) 1(1) *Rivista Trimestrale Diritto Pubblico* 128f.

[12] For an overview of the positions of the different political parties see M Seymour, *Debating Divorce in Italy: Marriage and the Making of Modern Italians, 1860–1974* (New York, Palgrave Macmillan, 2006) 213ff.

Since then, the usage of abrogative referendums has evolved. During the first phase (1974–1985), all such referendums were rejected, therefore confirming the legislation in force; in the second phase (1987–1995), most of them were approved (and important abrogative effects therefore occurred, totally repealing or, more often, partially repealing many significant pieces of legislation); while in the third phase (1997–2016), in all cases but one (in 2011) the quorum was not met and therefore no abrogation took place, showing a steady decline in the popularity of the instrument.

In the first phase, referendums were mainly used in relation to specific but crucial issues, and it was noticeable that Parliament's choices were left unchanged by the citizens. The failure of the abrogative referendum in 1978 on the law granting public financing to political parties demonstrated a persistently high degree of consensus amongst the main political parties, while the confirmation of the abortion law in 1981 showed that the Catholic Church was no longer capable of obtaining State legislation that was fully compliant with its own principles.

During the second phase, all the referendums reached the quorum of 50 per cent + one of voters, with the only exception being those in 1990 regarding limitations on hunting and the use of pesticides. Almost all of the referendums were approved by the citizens, thus determining the repeal of the legislation in force. This phase began with a vote on (among others) a referendum on nuclear power plants held in 1987, one year after the Chernobyl accident, which led to the end of nuclear energy production in Italy. Maybe even more importantly, at least from an institutional viewpoint, were the results of the two referendums on electoral laws held respectively in 1991 (on the reduction to one preferential vote for the Chamber of Deputies) and in 1993 (on the transformation of the electoral system for the Senate from proportionality to mainly majoritarianism). In both cases the referendum was successfully used to trigger electoral reforms notwithstanding the opposition of the ruling political parties – whose democratic legitimacy was significantly weakened by the Bribesville scandal – thereby introducing a clear divide in the functioning of Italian institutions.

In the third phase, a structural difficulty arose in reaching a quorum, and fears of the complete failure of this constitutional device were raised. This difficulty can be attributed partly to a general decline of electoral turnout in any kind of election held in Italy, and partly to the fact that those who opposed the referendum requests realised that the easiest and more effective way to win was to campaign in favour of not showing up at the polls. The quorum was missed by just a small percentage of votes (0.4 per cent, as the turnout reached was 49.6 per cent) in another referendum on electoral law in 1999 (aimed at adopting a full majoritarian system), but the quorum was reached once, in 2011, in a referendum regarding the privatisation of water services.

An important factor in limiting the referendum requests and appropriately confining the role of direct democracy in the Italian legal order has been the *admissibility check* undertaken by the Constitutional Court. Especially since Judgment no 16/1978 (which originated from a group of eight referendums requested by the Radical Party), this check has not been confined to an external scrutiny of whether the legislation to which the referendum referred is included among the categories indicated by Article 75.2, but has extended to other implicit limitations, whose existence was discovered through a systematic analysis of the Constitution. The Constitutional Court's reasons are explicitly animated by the fact that, in a representative democracy, the promoters of a referendum are not completely free to formulate the question that they want to submit to the people. The question, therefore, must be *homogeneous, clear and unequivocal*. Furthermore, it cannot ask for the abrogation of a piece of legislation deemed to be constitutionally necessary or with a peculiar legal resistance to repeal or modification.[13] Although they are not logically impeccable, and have therefore led to some inconsistencies in the case law of the Constitutional Court in the subsequent decades,[14] these implicit limitations have overall managed to avoid a misuse of the abrogative referendum, preventing any plebiscitarian degeneration and safeguarding the primacy of representative democracy.

This explains why, out of around 140 referendum requests submitted (almost all by citizens and in just two cases by Regional Councils, in 2016 and in 2020) that have reached this stage, more than half have been declared inadmissible by the Constitutional Court. It has been a way of curbing a very powerful instrument, the political implications of which often exceed its legal binding force, because every decision taken via referendum is directly ascribed to the sovereign power.

[13] See S Bartole, 'Referendums and the Constitutional Court in Italy' in *Constitutional Justice and Democracy by Referendum: Proceedings of the UniDem Seminar Organised in Strasbourg, on 23–24 June 1995* (Strasbourg, Council of Europe Publishing, 1996) 43ff, 51ff, available at www.venice.coe.int/webforms/documents/default.aspx?pdffile=CDL-STD(1995)014-e.

[14] See A Barbera and A Morrone, *La Repubblica dei referendum* (Bologna, Il Mulino, 2003) 63ff.

IV. REPRESENTATIVE DEMOCRACY: THE ELECTORAL SYSTEM AND ITS EVOLUTION

In a representative democracy, the most important policies are designed and implemented by parliamentary means: that is, following a cycle that starts with parliamentary elections and continues in the dynamics between Government and Parliament, linked to each other by the confidence relationship. Of course, the effects and the relevance of the elections also depend on the kind of electoral system adopted.

A. An Electoral Law Written by the Parties: The Proportional System (1948–1993)

At the time of the Constituent Assembly, there was virtual consensus that the electoral system had to provide a form of proportional representation: ie that it should grant an allocation of parliamentary seats in accordance with the distribution of votes between the lists presented by the political parties. This choice was consistent both with Italy's pre-fascist history, as the proportional electoral system was the one in force – although for just two elections – since 1919, and with the preferences of the main anti-fascist political parties, as all of them clearly wanted to retain some freedom of movement after the election and, at the same time, to limit the damage in case of a defeat, avoiding the clear electoral success of only one party (see Chapter 1).

The preference for a proportional electoral system, however, although implicitly assumed by many constitutional provisions, was not codified within the text of the Constitution, which limited itself to requiring that the Senate be elected 'on a regional basis' (Article 57.1).[15] The Constituent Assembly expressed this option through several motions (*ordini del giorno*) and directly approved the two new electoral laws, for the Chamber of Deputies and for the Senate, shortly before and after the final vote on the Constitution, respectively. Indeed, there were some doubts regarding the electoral system of the Senate, as in a first motion a majoritarian system with single-member constituencies was envisaged, but then the threshold to obtain the seat was raised to 65 per cent,

[15] E Bettinelli, *All'origine della democrazia dei partiti. La formazione del nuovo ordinamento elettorale nel periodo costituente (1944–1948)* (Milan, Edizioni di Comunità, 1982) 267ff; M Luciani, *Il voto e la democrazia: La questione delle riforme elettorali in Italia* (Rome, Editori Riuniti, 1991) 19ff.

thereby making it almost impossible to assign seats directly in single-member constituencies. In fact, between 1948 and 1992 less than 50 of the 3,000 senators were elected in this way, while the other seats were all assigned according to a proportional criterion.[16]

Soon after the elections of 1948, with the success of the Christian Democrats, a change of the electoral system for the Chamber of Deputies was sought and secured by its leader, Alcide De Gasperi. A majoritarian electoral system (called 'swindle law': *legge truffa*) was approved in 1953, after a long and tough parliamentary battle: the list or the coalition of lists that obtained a majority of votes (ie at least 50 per cent of the valid votes plus one) would be able to obtain 380 of the 590 seats (ie more than 64 per cent). However, in the following elections held in that same year the centrist coalition failed (by about 40,600 votes) to reach the threshold to receive the majority bonus.

The new law was soon repealed, and for the next 30 years of Italian history the proportional rule prevailed, in part as a means for integrating the opposition parties within the parliamentary dynamics, and then – with first the Socialists and then the Communists – even in the majority supporting the Government. This process, led by non-written agreements between political parties, was characterised simultaneously as *conventio ad excludendum* (as some parties, at the extremes of the political spectrum, were excluded from the possibility of forming part of the Government) and as *conventio ad integrandum* (as the Socialist and then the Communist Parties were integrated as main actors in the legislative process).[17] This equilibrium required a bargained pluralism to survive.[18]

B. An Electoral Law Written by the People: The Majoritarian System (1993–2005)

After the end of the Cold War, the fall of the Berlin wall, and the end of the Soviet Union, the international reasons underpinning the Communist

[16] See C Fusaro, 'Party System Developments and Electoral Legislation in Italy (1948–2009)' (2009) 1 *Bulletin of Italian Politics* 49.

[17] See L Elia, 'Governo (forme di)' in *Enciclopedia del diritto*, XIX (Milan, Giuffrè, 1970). More recently, E Cheli, *Nata per unire: La Costituzione italiana tra storia e politica* (Bologna, Il Mulino, 2012) 25ff.

[18] Cf D Hine, *Governing Italy: The Politics of Bargained Pluralism* (Oxford, Oxford University Press, 1993).

Party's exclusion from the Government ceased. The collapse of international communism removed the most important factor that justified the establishment of a political system which omitted any possibility of open competition and turnover in the Government.[19]

There was indeed a movement born outside the main political parties and derived from the civil society, led by a Christian Democrat, Mario Segni and by the Radical Party of Marco Pannella, to propose an abrogative referendum aimed at abolishing the system of multiple-preferential voting (among the candidates appearing in the same party list) at the elections for the Chamber of Deputies. The referendum, which passed the admissibility check of the Constitutional Court and was then approved by the citizens in 1991, removed one of the traditional institutional supports of factional politics within the main parties, often viewed as a tool for political exchange and clientelist practice (and even as a mechanism for influencing and possibly checking packages of votes).[20]

The positive outcome of this referendum was rather surprising, as all the main political parties opposed it. The subsequent change to the electoral system partly contributed to the crisis of the political and party system. The Bribesville scandal and the Maastricht Treaty, with its stricter rules on public debt, added to the problem. This was because, at a moment of economic crisis, public funds could no longer freely be used by political parties to support themselves and some sectors of the economy.

Less surprising, although with an even deeper effect on the institutional system, was the outcome of a second abrogative referendum, held in 1993. This concerned the electoral law for the Senate. By way of a selective repeal of the legislation in force, the referendum abolished the 65 per cent threshold provided by the electoral law, transforming it into a mainly majoritarian system. It resulted in the assignment of 75 per cent of the seats according to a first-past-the-post rule in single-member constituencies and the remaining 25 per cent of the seats following a proportional criterion. Soon after the referendum, Parliament also decided to adopt the same percentages for the Chamber of Deputies (although assigning the 25 per cent proportional quota of seats based on the votes cast for lists on a second ballot) and therefore, soon after the outcome of the referendum, approved a new electoral law, called

[19] See A Brogi, *Confronting America: The Cold War between the United States and the Communists in France and Italy* (Chapel Hill, University of North Carolina Press, 2011).

[20] See M Cotta and L Verzichelli, *Political Institutions in Italy* (Oxford, Oxford University Press, 2007) 78ff.

'*Mattarellum*' (as the first promoter was Sergio Mattarella, at that time a Christian Democrat MP). Shortly after the approval of the new majoritarian electoral law, the President of the Republic, Oscar Luigi Scalfaro, decided to dissolve the Parliament – one-third of which comprised MPs subject to prosecution – thereby making the new electoral law applicable in the following elections, held in 1994.

Incidentally, during the same years, a third abrogative referendum was avoided because Parliament rendered it redundant by passing a law on the direct election of mayors (law no 81/1993) – an option that had been expressly rejected just three years earlier. The new law provided for a majoritarian electoral system at the local level too, in this case with a two-round election aimed at bipolarising the political dynamic (see Chapter 7).

The new majoritarian State electoral law was applied to the elections of 1994, 1996 and 2001. It ensured the emergence and consolidation of a bipolar pattern of electoral competition based on two dominant pre-electoral 'catch-all coalitions', coexisting with a high level of party fragmentation (notwithstanding the 4 per cent threshold for the accession to proportional quota at the Chamber of Deputies).[21] In this phase, however, Italy never became a two-party system, and the electoral coalitions revealed themselves 'fit to win, but not to govern'. After each election, in fact, both the losing and the winning coalitions struggled to survive. Usually, the former disappeared shortly after the electoral defeat, being unable to identify a common alternative strategy or to appoint a unique opposition leader, while the latter was obliged to stay together to form the Government, but soon unveiled its fragmented and conflicted nature, which was therefore unable to ensure a constant parliamentary majority supporting the Government.[22] In other words, the adoption, since 1993, of a majoritarian electoral system did not transform Italian politics into a two-party system nor did it automatically result in Executives lasting the whole legislative term, although it was gradually making the political dynamic more bipolarised at the State level, and even increasing to some extent the stabilisation of Executives supported by broad coalitions. However, the electoral system was changed again in 2005.

[21] Cf R D'Alimonte, 'Italy: A Case of Fragmented Bipolarism' in M Gallagher and P Mitchell (ed), *The Politics of Electoral Systems* (Oxford, Oxford University Press, 2005) 253ff and A Chiaramonte, 'The unfinished story of electoral reforms in Italy' (2015) 7(1) *Contemporary Italian Politics* 10.

[22] V Lippolis and G Pitruzzella, *Il bipolarismo conflittuale. Il regime politico della Seconda Repubblica* (Soveria Mannelli, Rubbettino, 2007).

C. An Electoral Law Written by the (Centre-right) Majority: The Majority Bonus (2005–2013)

Shortly before the next elections, which would have taken place in Spring 2006, the centre-right majority, without the support of the opposition, decided to change the electoral system, clearly intending to avoid or at least to reduce its defeat, which was being predicted by the polls. The approved law no 270/2005, is usually called 'Porcellum' (from the Italian '*porcata*', meaning 'unfair change' or 'dirty trick') because, as recognised by one of its authors, it aimed to avoid the victory of the centre-left coalition. It removed the single-member constituencies and instead designed an electoral system on a proportional basis, but one which had been correctly characterised as a 'majority-assuring proportional system'.[23] The core of the system was the allocation, in the Chamber of Deputies, of a majority bonus (or prize): the winning list or coalition received no less than 340 seats (out of 630), notwithstanding how many votes it actually obtained. The seats were assigned according to the order provided by fixed and long lists of candidates presented in each electoral district (with the possibility of multiple candidacies for a single person, even potentially in all districts). Single lists and coalitions had to agree on some kind of a programme (generally kept semi-clandestine) and to designate their own leader: supposedly, the future President of the Council of Ministers in the event of success, although the law stated that the President of the Republic's powers of nomination were not infringed by this provision (see Chapter 5).

In the Senate, in order not to violate the constitutional provision (Article 57) according to which the House must be elected 'on a regional basis', the same law assigned a series of majority bonuses at the regional level, ie to the winning list or coalition in each region. The outcome, therefore, was a sort of 'lottery':[24] with 17 majority bonuses, an overall majority of seats in the Senate to a winning party or coalition was far from assured, although the proportional criterion was clearly altered.

The electoral law no 270/2005 was applied in the elections of 2006, 2008 and 2013. It received significant criticism, both in relation to the

[23] Fusaro (n 16) 58, relying on the analysis in 'Conclusion. Are Mixed-Member Systems the Best of both Worlds?' in MS Shugart and MP Wattenberg (eds), *Mixed-Member Electoral Systems* (Oxford, Oxford University Press, 2001) 598.

[24] Cf R D'Alimonte, 'The Italian Elections of February 2013: The End of the Second Republic?' (2013) 5(2) *Contemporary Italian Politics* 113.

way it was approved and to its content. It was the object of many reform attempts in every legislative term, which regularly failed.

Some requests for an abrogative referendum also arose, each differently conceived. Three of them, aimed at abolishing the possibility to form coalitions and multiple candidacies, did not reach the quorum in 2008. It must be noted that the Constitutional Court, in declaring them admissible, signalled to Parliament the need to consider with due attention the problematic features of a law which did not require meeting a minimum threshold of votes and/or seats to receive the majority bonus.[25]

Two more requests for a referendum aimed at repealing the whole electoral law, proposed again four years later, were instead declared inadmissible by the Constitutional Court, as it might 'result in the absence of any "operative" legislation' for the election of the two Houses.[26] The Court denied the so-called 'revival' theory: it argued that, once a piece of legislation has been replaced (in this case, the Mattarellum electoral system), it is expunged from the legal system and does not lie dormant pending potential re-enactment in future, deriving from the repeal by abrogative referendum of a later piece of legislation.

D. An Electoral Law Written by the Constitutional Court? (2014–2017)

The 2013 election failed to deliver a decisive result and thereby added to the intensity of criticism for this method of election. For the first time under this system an election had led to stalemate, although, in part, this was because of the emergence of the new Five-Star movement, which obtained around one-third of the votes. The majority bonus attributed to the Democratic Party ensured a clear majority in the Chamber of Deputies, but not in the Senate, where, even if their seats were added to those of the centrist parties, a possible centre-left government failed to reach the majority support required. That is why a broad-coalition government, led by Enrico Letta, was formed. This represented the rupture of both the centre-left and centre-right coalitions that were on offer during the electoral campaign as alternative combinations to form the government.

In this unexpected scenario, the Court of Cassation in May 2013 decided to challenge the constitutionality of law no 270/2005

[25] Judgments nos 15 and 16/2008.
[26] Judgment no 13/2012.

(previously deemed inadmissible by many other judges). In this case, the question was upheld as well-founded by the Constitutional Court (Judgment no 1/2014), at the same time overcoming some procedural difficulties that could have blocked review.[27] The Court achieved this by relying on the argument that the electoral law is recognised as 'essential for the proper operation of a representative democratic constitution' and if this law were not regarded as constitutionally justiciable it would be 'subtracted from constitutional review'. To continue using the wording of the Court,

> any other conclusion would end up creating a free-for-all zone [*zona franca*] within the system of constitutional justice, precisely in an area which is closely related to the democratic framework as it involves the fundamental right to vote; for this reason, it would end up causing intolerable harm to the overall constitutional order.

According to the first and fundamental section of this judgment, the *majority bonus* for the Chamber provided by the legislation did not pass the proportionality test.[28] As the same Constitutional Court recalled, this test:

> requires an assessment as to whether the provision under review, along with the arrangements stipulated for its application, is necessary and capable of achieving legitimately pursued objectives by requiring that the measure chosen out of those most appropriate is the least restrictive of the rights in play and imposes burdens that are not disproportionate having regard to the pursuit of those objectives.[29]

In fact, while the majority bonus pursued 'an objective of constitutional significance, namely that of ensuring stable government for the country and efficient decision-making processes within Parliament', it did not 'comply with the requirement of the least possible sacrifice of other interests and values protected under constitutional law. It thereby violated Articles 1.2, 3, 48.2 and 67 of the Constitution' (respectively: popular sovereignty, equality, the right to vote and political representation). As it attributed the majority bonus without requiring 'the list (or coalition of lists)

[27] See E Longo and A Pin, 'Judicial Review, Election Law, and Proportionality' (2016) 6(1) *Notre Dame Journal of International & Comparative Law* 101.

[28] The importance of the proportionality scrutiny accomplished by this decision is stressed by A Pin and E Longo, 'Don't Waste Your Vote (Again!). The Italian Constitutional Court's Decision on Election Laws: An Episode of Strict Comparative Scrutiny' (2015) 10 *ICON·S Working Paper* – Conference Proceedings Series 1, available at SSRN: http://ssrn.com/abstract=2670634.

[29] Judgment no 1/2014.

with a relative majority of votes to achieve a minimum threshold or votes', law no 270/2005 was deemed 'not proportionate with regard to the objective pursued', given that it excessively limited 'the representative function of the Chamber of Deputies, as well as the equal status of each individual right to vote, in such a manner as profoundly to alter the composition of the democratic representative bodies on which the entire architecture of the prevailing constitutional order is based'.[30]

Second, the electoral legislation applicable to the Senate was also struck down by the same judgment, on the grounds that the majority bonus was irrational *per se*, and unable to achieve its own objective. In fact, there was not necessarily any relationship between the majority of seats allocated and the actual majority of votes cast nationwide, as the majority bonus was allocated for each region.

Third, the Court struck down the system of list voting on the grounds that voters were unable to express any *preferential voting* and that the lists were so large that the identities of many candidates were unknown to voters. In this way, the law deprived 'voters of any ability to choose their own representatives, which is left entirely to the parties' and thus constrained 'the freedom of choice of voters when electing their own representatives in Parliament, which is one of the principal manifestations of popular sovereignty, and thus runs contrary to the democratic principle, impairing the freedom of voting' (Article 48).[31]

Finally, the Court held that the electoral law would still be effective even after the annulment of the provisions declared unconstitutional, working as a proportional system with high thresholds. It also specified that, because of the principle of the continuity of the State, its decision would not affect the powers of the current Parliament or the acts adopted before new elections.

The impact of Judgment no 1/2014 was huge: a Constitutional Court substantially re-writing an electoral law, which is by definition the most political piece of legislation in force, and one that had already been applied in three elections, is not something which happens every day. However, the political system accepted this outcome rather smoothly, without seeking to attribute political responsibility for the past – which would, in any event, have been difficult to assign in a constantly changing political spectrum – and instead placing the debate about the new electoral system within the one on constitutional reform, which had started soon after the 2013 elections.

[30] Judgment no 1/2014.
[31] Judgment no 1/2014.

Prompted by this comprehensive decision of the Constitutional Court, Parliament under the Renzi Government approved a new electoral law for the Chamber of Deputies. In fact, it was anticipated that the constitutional reform, aimed at transforming the Senate into a territorial, indirectly elected, second chamber, would be co-ordinated with the modification of the electoral system for the Chamber of Deputies. The new electoral law no 52/2015 (called '*Italicum*') came into force from 1 July 2016 but was never applied. It introduced a two-round electoral system which guaranteed a majority in any event, as a result of a majority bonus, either in the first round or in the second round: an absolute majority (of 340 seats) was granted to the list that obtained at least 40 per cent of the votes in the first round; or to the list winning in the second round, which would be a run-off between the two most voted lists.[32]

Law no 52/2015 aimed to comply with the requirements established by the Constitutional Court in Judgment no 1/2014. There was a minimum threshold, in the first round, for obtaining the majority bonus, while in the second round this was not deemed necessary, as the winner received 50 per cent + one of the votes in any case. Furthermore, constituencies were smaller (100 instead of 27) and some place was recognised for preferential voting.[33]

The 'Italicum' reform has generated considerable controversy. According to its supporters, 'Italicum' represented an appropriate balance between the objective of promoting government stability and that of representing minorities. Essentially, it gave voters the power to choose 'directly' who would govern the country.[34] By contrast, according to its detractors, it had many technical inadequacies and was unfit for the Italian political system, in particular because of the prohibition of electoral coalitions before and after the first round of voting.[35]

However, following the rejection of the Senate reform in the constitutional referendum held on 4 December 2016 (see Chapter 1), law no 52/2015 has been partially quashed by the Constitutional Court

[32] See R D'Alimonte, 'The New Italian Electoral System: Majority-Assuring but Minority-Friendly' (2015) 7(3) *Contemporary Italian Politics* 286.

[33] Cf E Longo and A Pin, '*Chain Reaction: Constitutional Change Through Election Law Reform in Italy. Likely Scenarios After the Recent Reform of the Parliament Election Law*' (2015) *International Journal of Constitutional Law Blog*, 9 June 2015, available at www.iconnectblog.com/2015/06/chain-reaction-constitutional-change-through-election-law-reform-in-italy.

[34] D'Alimonte (n 32).

[35] G Pasquino, 'Italy Has Yet Another Electoral Law' (2015) 7(3) *Contemporary Italian Politics* 293.

(Judgment no 35/2017), on the basis of the same constitutional principles and the same proportionality scrutiny affirmed by Judgment no 1/2014. In particular, while the 40 per cent minimum threshold, in the first round, for obtaining the majority bonus was judged to be reasonable and proportionate, the second-round ballot was declared unconstitutional, as it had the effect of over-representing a list that might have received very few votes in the first round.[36]

The other provision of law no 52/2015 struck down by the Constitutional Court was a provision that made it possible for multi-elected candidates (as the law would permit a person to be a candidate in up to 10 constituencies) to choose which constituency to be elected in after the completion of the electoral process. In order to avoid any loophole in the remaining electoral legislation, the Court identified a mechanism in the regulation in force for similar cases and declared that a random draw must take place, to be held for the different constituencies that elected the same candidate, in order to determine which seat the candidate ultimately received.

In the last part of its judgment, the Court referred to the outcome of the constitutional referendum and concluded that, given the continuation of symmetrical bicameralism, two electoral systems whose results would not jeopardise the proper functioning of the parliamentary form of government were required, in order to allow the formation of a parliamentary majority in both Houses.

Following this statement, during the final months of the XVII legislative term, a new electoral law was indeed approved by a broad parliamentary majority (law no 165/2017, known as '*Rosatellum*'), which also served the purpose of avoiding elections governed by two different electoral systems, both directly resulting from the two recalled judgments of the Constitutional Court (Judgment nos 1/2014 for the Senate and 35/2017 for the Chamber). For the first time in Italian history, the same electoral system was provided for the two Houses: it could be called '*a mixed system, with one vote*'.

In greater detail, 63 per cent of the seats for both the Chamber and the Senate are assigned according to a proportional system, with blocked lists, in regional or sub-regional pluri-member constituencies; 37 per cent of the seats are assigned according to a first-past-the-post rule,

[36] P Faraguna, '"Do You Ever Have One of Those Days When Everything Seems Unconstitutional?": The Italian Constitutional Court Strikes Down the Electoral Law Once Again' (2017) 13(4) *European Constitutional Law Review* 778.

in single-member constituencies. The electoral system is open to either coalitions or single lists, with different electoral thresholds: 10 per cent for coalitions; 3 per cent for lists (but 1 per cent suffices to make their votes useful for the coalition, if they are part of it). Up to five pluri-candidatures are admitted, plus one in a single-member constituency, but a legislative criterion is determined for the multi-elected: first, the single-member constituency, then a pluri-member constituency (the one in which the candidate's list obtained fewer votes). Each list cannot have more than 60 per cent of candidates who are of the same sex.

The electoral system introduced by law no 165/2017 was applied in the 2018 elections. These elections also did not give rise to any clear parliamentary majority and required a reshuffling of political coalitions in order to form the first two Executives (Conte 1 and Conte 2 Governments). The numbers of parliamentary seats have been reduced, following the entry into force of constitutional law no 1/2020, which brought the number of members of the Chamber of Deputies down from 630 to 400, and elected senators down from 315 to 200. The effects on the electoral legislation, foreseen by law no 51/2019, were reflected in the consequent redesign of the (single-member and pluri-member) constituencies, pursuant to legislative decree no 177/2020. The political debate regarding a new electoral reform, perhaps taking a more proportional direction, is ongoing.

V. CONCLUSION

As we reflect on the content of the chapter, it is useful to define the Italian '*form of government*'. According to the traditional definition offered by most of the Italian academic commentators, by form of government we refer to the rules regarding the way in which the function of political direction is distributed among the different constitutional bodies.[37] In other words, by analysing the form of government we look at the institutional system by trying to identify the rules that govern the circuit of the political direction (*indirizzo politico*):[38] the way in which the main policies

[37] See, among many, A Barbera and C Fusaro, *Corso di diritto costituzionale* (Bologna, Il Mulino, 2020) 270, following C Mortati, *Le forme di governo. Lezioni* (Padova, Cedam, 1973) 73ff.

[38] On this notion see, among many, V Crisafulli, 'Per una teoria giuridica dell'indirizzo politico' (1939) 1–4 *Studi urbinati* 53ff; T Martines, *Contributo ad una teoria giuridica delle forze politiche* (Milan, Giuffrè, 1957); E Cheli, *Atto politico e funzione di indirizzo politico* (Milan, Giuffrè, 1961); M Dogliani, *Indirizzo politico. Riflessioni su regole e regolarità nel diritto costituzionale* (Naples, Jovene, 1985) 43ff.

are designed and implemented, namely, in the Italian case, between the Government, the Parliament and of course the citizens (relevantly in their role as voters, through the electoral system), while also taking into consideration the ultimate influence of the other constitutional bodies, ie the President of the Republic and the Constitutional Court.

The Italian Constitution envisages a parliamentary form of government, as it requires (Article 94) that 'the Government must receive the confidence of both Houses of Parliament'. The parliamentary form of government is also known as a '*monistic*' and '*fusion of power*' system. The reason for the first term is that the political direction is given first by the voters to the Parliament and then by the Parliament to the Government. By contrast, in the presidential form of government, the system is dualistic, as both the Parliament and the Government independently derive their legitimacy from a vote by the citizens, and do not necessarily have to move in the same direction. The second expression is used because the required existence of a confidence relationship between Parliament and Government lessens the separation between the Legislative and the Executive, which instead is rigorously respected and even highlighted in the presidential form of government.

As noted at the beginning of this chapter, it was the Constituent Assembly that opted in favour of a parliamentary form of government by agreeing to the Perassi resolution. However, the form of implementation was broadly defined in the Constitution, leaving a great deal for the political parties to develop. This explains, at least partially, why the type of electoral system adopted has acquired such importance in the Italian constitutional evolution. In the absence of strong constitutional mechanisms, the main institutional constraints were provided by the choice of electoral law. The original approach was to give free rein to political parties through a proportional system.

The effect of subsequent reform was to encourage and even determine changes both in the party system and in the institutional dynamics. This was especially true with respect to systems based on majoritarian principles or providing for a majority bonus (by far the strongest of the electoral mechanisms aimed at ensuring a majority). Different electoral systems encourage the parliamentary form of government to function in different ways. As will be apparent in subsequent chapters, the electoral system has the potential to affect the power of appointment of the President of the Council, the power of dissolution of the two Houses, the confidence relationship between the Government and the Parliament, the place to be assigned to counter-majoritarian institutions, and the role played by the political parties.

The importance of the electoral law and, even more so, of the party system (in both format and dynamics) in determining the concrete functioning of the Italian parliamentary form of government, in its different phases, has been highlighted. When considering these factors, it also becomes possible to explain a variety of parliamentary systems and to distinguish between different subtypes of the parliamentary form of government: namely those with 'rigid bipartitism', 'mild multipartitism' and 'extreme multipartitism' (as the Italian parliamentary system has been usually qualified).[39]

FURTHER READING

Baldini, G, 'The Different Trajectories of Italian Electoral Reforms' (2011) 34(3) *West European Politics* 644.

Chiaramonte, A, and D'Alimonte, R, 'The new Italian electoral system and its effects on strategic coordination and disproportionality' (2018) 13(1) *Italian Political Science* 8.

Pasquino, G, 'Tricks and Treats: The 2005 Italian Electoral Law and Its Consequences' (2007) 12(1) *South European Society and Politics* 79.

Passarelli, G, 'Electoral Systems in Context: Italy' in AA.VV. *The Oxford Handbook of Electoral Systems* (New York, Oxford University Press, 2018).

[39] See Elia (n 17) 12ff; G Sartori, *Parties and Party Systems: A Framework for Analysis* (Cambridge, Cambridge University Press, 1976).

4

Parliament

Symmetrical Bicameralism – Chamber of Deputies – Senate of the Republic – Parliament in Joint Session – Parliamentary Rules of Procedure – Groups – Standing Committees – Speakers – MPs' Privileges and Immunities – Legislative Process – Budgetary Process – Oversight Function

I. INTRODUCTION

THE ITALIAN CONSTITUTION established a symmetrical bicameral legislature, comprising the Chamber of Deputies and the Senate of the Republic. This chapter sets out the main characteristics and assesses the institutional effectiveness of the two Houses in relation to both the legislative process and the other parliamentary functions throughout the Republican experience. The changing features of the party system and the reforms of the electoral legislation had the effect of transforming the role of the Parliament in the institutional system as well as, to a certain extent, the balance of power between the two Houses.

The chapter first analyses the organisation of the two Houses (bicameralism, groups, committees, speakers and so on) and the prerogatives of the Members of Parliament (MPs), taking into account both constitutional provisions and the rules of procedure approved, by an absolute majority, by each House. Then, it moves to consider the main parliamentary functions, looking at the legislative and budgetary processes, and the many means through which the oversight function can be exercised. In the concluding paragraphs, some lines of continuity and of discontinuity are traced, as the role of the Italian Parliament, notwithstanding the substantial invariance of the constitutional provisions, has changed very significantly throughout the Republican experience.

II. THE ITALIAN PARLIAMENT IN THE CONSTITUTION

The first constitutional body to be regulated by the Italian Constitution, at the opening of its second part (devoted to the 'Organisation of the Republic'), is the Parliament. This position within the constitutional text is consistent both with the historical roots of constitutionalism and the architecture of the Italian Constitution.

With respect to the first element, modern constitutions and parliaments are born together, as two essential elements of the liberal state. Parliaments have been envisaged as the first and predominant limit on the King's powers, starting with the British experience, which is the paradigmatic example of parliamentarism with the principle of parliamentary sovereignty still at the center of the legal system.[1] From this perspective, Parliaments can be viewed as the fundamental core of constitutionalism, understood as a doctrine of separation and limitation of power. No (modern) constitution could be recognised as such had it not provided for a representative assembly, elected by the citizens at that time entitled to political rights. Reciprocally, no Parliament could define itself as a political representative assembly without a fundamental charter outlining its main structural and functional features, attributing to it some prerogatives, and protecting the main political rights of the citizens (including, of course, the right to vote).

Moreover, in Italian history, the *centrality of Parliament* has been a response to the marginalisation of all representative bodies during the fascist regime, when the chambers were frozen and elections became a sham, considering that the only political party admitted to the electoral competition was the fascist one. No surprise, then, if in comparative analyses, the Italian Parliament has for a long time – roughly, from 1948 to 1992 – been viewed as an example of a rather powerful and 'transformative' legislature, especially when compared with Parliaments of other European countries, operating mainly as 'arena' legislatures within the framework of a parliamentary form of government.[2] Not unexpectedly,

[1] In relation to the roots of this principle, following Dicey, see J Goldsworthy, *The Sovereignty of Parliament: History and Philosophy* (Cambridge, Cambridge University Press, 2001) and J Goldsworthy, *Parliamentary Sovereignty: Contemporary Debates* (Cambridge, Cambridge University Press, 2010).

[2] For the distinction between transformative and arena legislatures, see NW Polsby, 'Legislatures' in FI Greenstein and NW Polsby (eds), *Handbook of Political Science* (Reading Mass, Addison-Wesley, 1975).

the Italian Parliament's point of reference – both for scholars[3] and for the parliamentary administrations[4] – has often been viewed as falling within the US Congress, rather than any other parliament of the EU Member States. However, its prominence started to decline during the 1980s and has significantly decreased during the subsequent decades, partially as a consequence of the almost complete overhaul of the party system and of the passage of a majoritarian electoral law.[5]

Within the architecture of the Italian Constitution, political rights, such as the right to vote and the freedom to associate in parties, are provided for under the last title ('Political Relations') of the first part of the Constitution, immediately before the first title of the second part, dedicated to the Parliament. In this way, the close link between the political rights of the citizens and the bodies of political representation is clearly demonstrated, even in a symbolic manner.

III. A SYMMETRICAL BICAMERALISM

The Italian Parliament is designed as a *symmetrical* (often called 'perfect', although this terminology is ambiguous) bicameral system: the Chamber of Deputies and the Senate of the Republic are both directly elected by the citizens (with the only exception being a group of life senators) and exercise exactly the same powers as one another.

The decision to create such a symmetrical bicameral system, which is rather unique in the comparative landscape, was mainly the result of a compromise, within the Constituent Assembly, between three different positions. The first camp was in favour of an upper house capable of representing social and professional interests, as a sort of democratised version of the fascist 'Chamber of Fasci and Corporations' (*Camera dei fasci e delle corporazioni*, in operation from 1939 to 1943). The second proposed an upper house representative of the regions and municipalities. The third supported, as its preferred option, a unicameral

[3] For instance, see M Shaw and J Lees (eds), *Committees in Legislatures: A Comparative Analysis* (Durham, Duke University Press, 1979) 384ff.

[4] For two examples see L Elia, *Forma di governo e procedimento legislativo negli USA* (Milan, Giuffrè, 1961) and M Meschino, *Le procedure del bilancio federale negli Stati Uniti* (Rome, Camera dei deputati, 1981).

[5] See, inter alia, C Fasone, *Sistemi di commissioni parlamentari e forme di governo* (Padua, Cedam, 2012) 330ff and A Kreppel, 'Understanding the Impact of the Autonomy of National Legislatures on the EU Policy Process' in N Lupo and G Piccirilli (eds), *The Italian Parliament in the European Union* (Oxford, Hart, 2017) 267–84, 271ff.

parliament, but accepted the existence of two houses, provided that both were directly elected by the citizens.

The eventual outcome of long discussions and many rounds of votes was a compromise that was criticised even by some of the 'fathers' of the Republican Constitution,[6] as it provided for only a limited number of differences between the two Houses, without defining a clear rationale for the Italian bicameralism.

The most important difference, relating to the length of their legislative terms (five years for the Chamber and six years for the Senate), was promptly neutralised, first by institutional practice (in 1953, 1958 and 1963 the two Houses were simultaneously dissolved in order to have joint elections), and then through a constitutional amendment equalising it to five years for both the Houses (constitutional law no 2/1963, promulgated just before the third elections for a new Parliament were called).

The second important difference between the two Houses concerned the age thresholds for voting and for being elected, which are in some ways consistent with the origins of the name 'Senate'. Voters for the Chamber must be citizens aged 18 years or older, whereas the requirement for electors of the Senate was that they must have at least turned 25 (a constitutional reform approved in 2021 reduced this to 18). Similarly, candidates for the Chamber must be at least 25, while those for the Senate must be at least 40 years old.

The symmetrical bicameral system did not give rise to any significant problems so long as the two Houses were both formed according to the proportional electoral system that was in force from 1948 to 1992 (with the only exception, for the Chamber, being the 1953 elections). Neither the distribution of votes nor the distribution of seats resulted in much differentiation between the two Houses throughout this phase. Moreover, strong political parties, such as those in charge during the four decades following the entry into force of the Constitution, were actually able to ensure convergent behaviour of the Chamber and Senate, in their relationship of confidence with the Executive as well as in the legislative process, thanks also to the political parties' strict control over the intense legislative activity of the standing committees.

The downside of this kind of bicameralism became evident after the adoption, in 1993, of a predominantly majoritarian electoral system, and the crisis of the political parties upon which the Republican Constitution of 1947 had been founded. In fact, both elements together increased the

[6] See the speech held by the rapporteur, Meuccio Ruini, on 22 December 1947, just before the final vote of the Constitution by the Constituent Assembly.

risks of deadlock and of divergence between the two Houses, which were even further accentuated following the approval of a new electoral system in 2005 (see Chapter 3). Deadlocks and divergences between the Chamber and the Senate actually occurred on several occasions, thereby galvanising the attempts to achieve a constitutional reform, which had already been imagined since the mid-1980s, aimed at introducing some asymmetries to the composition of the two Houses, as well as in the distribution of functions between them.

However, these constitutional reform proposals revealed themselves to be challenging to design and ultimately impossible to pass. As already remarked (Chapter 1), a couple of reforms were indeed approved by Parliament following the special procedure provided by Article 138 (requiring a double approval by each House), proposed respectively by the Berlusconi and Renzi governments. Both were fiercely criticised, on the basis of their substance, although for opposite reasons: the first because it designed a Senate that would have been too powerful, while the second envisaged a Senate that looked too weak. They were approved, in the second vote, by parliamentary majorities of greater than 50 per cent + one of the members, but comprising less than two-thirds of the members of each House, and eventually rejected by constitutional referendums held, respectively, in 2006 and in 2016. Once more, the Italian case demonstrates all the difficulties of reforming bicameral systems.[7]

The only constitutional reforms approved regarding the structure of Parliament are thus of *punctual character*. First, constitutional law no 2/1963 made the length of the legislative terms of the two Houses equal and stabilised the number of deputies and elected senators (respectively, to 630 and 315), originally linked to the population. Second, more recently, constitutional law no 1/2020 reduced the number of deputies and senators, to 400 and 200, respectively, starting from the next elections (expected in 2023). Third, constitutional law no 1/2021 equalised the voting age to elect the two Houses.

IV. THE INTERNAL ORGANISATION OF THE CHAMBER AND THE SENATE

The organisation of the Italian Parliament clearly shows its polycentric nature. The members of the two Houses are also called upon to meet

[7] Cf M Russell and M Sandford, 'Why are Second Chambers so Difficult to Reform?' (2002) 8(3) *The Journal of Legislative Studies* 79.

all together in the Parliament in joint session (*Parlamento in seduta comune*). This body, according to the Constitution, exercises mainly elective functions, and also has the power to start a criminal trial against the President of the Republic in the event of high treason or an attempt to overthrow the Constitution (*alto tradimento* or *attentato alla Costituzione*: see Chapter 6). In all these cases, the Parliament in joint session is presided over by the Speaker of the Chamber and meets in its plenary room in Palazzo Montecitorio, which is obviously bigger than the Senate's room in Palazzo Madama.

The fundamental organisation of both the Chamber and the Senate is based on *parliamentary groups*, mainly reflecting political parties, and *standing committees*, each one responsible for a certain subject matter. Groups and committees were both introduced in 1920, shortly after the end of the First World War and the subsequent adoption of a proportional electoral system, and were capable of accommodating mass political parties such as the popular party and the socialist party. The existence of clear party cleavages resulted in the abandonment of Parliament's previous configuration as an assembly of notables, representing their territories more than the political ideas of their party. At the same time, it allowed the formation of a system of parliamentary standing committees, composed in strict proportion to parliamentary groups and with their members designated by the same groups.

Indeed, this organisational model did not last for long, as in October 1922 the Fascist regime started with the 'march on Rome' (Chapter 1) and soon abolished parliamentary groups. However, it was adopted once again at the end of the Fascist regime, as it was suitable for the mass and anti fascist political parties that founded the new Republic. The composition of parliamentary committees 'so as to reflect the proportion of the parliamentary groups' is directly foreseen by the Constitution. Although literally referred only to the committees with legislative powers (Article 72.3) and for the committees of inquiry (Article 82.2), this criterion is applied to all the standing and bicameral committees.

The requirements for establishing a parliamentary group have remained the same since 1922: that is, a certain number of MPs (at least 20 deputies or 10 senators) willing to be part of the same group. Therefore, as there were no other requirements, the traditional definition of parliamentary groups as projections of political parties within the Houses was basically true in practical terms, but not in legal terms. This was at least the case until the 2017 reform of the Senate's rules of procedure, which was triggered by the excessive number of MPs moving from one group to another and by the appearance on the scene of new groups which did not correspond to, or intend to create, any political party. This reform added to the quantitative rule a further requirement for setting up a parliamentary group, curiously enough only for the Senate: namely, the identification of the group's link with a political party that presented its own lists in the previous elections and obtained the election of senators. In both Houses, MPs not belonging to a parliamentary group are *ex officio* assigned to a mixed group, which may be internally divided into political components. Only senators for life have been permitted, since 2018, not to be part of any parliamentary group, while all the other MPs are required to be members of a group and of at least one (standing) committee.

The typology of parliamentary committees is rather rich. According to their structure, they may be unicameral or bicameral, special (also called 'ad hoc') or standing. Depending on their function, they may be mono-functional (such as bicameral advisory committees, or the committees of inquiry, which have the same powers and the same limits as the judiciary: Article 82.2) or multifunctional (when they can exercise any function related to a certain subject matter).

Both the Chamber and the Senate have a rather consolidated 'committee system', each composed of 14 multifunctional standing committees (probably to be soon diminished and reconceived, after the reduction of the number of MPs). They are established at the beginning of every legislative term – although their composition must be updated after two years – and have a specialised jurisdiction, provided by the rules of procedure, on a set of subject matters, so as to cover the whole spectrum of public policies.[8] As discussed later, when acting in a legislative capacity they even have the power to replace the plenary in the approval of legislation.

Parliamentary delegations have many elements similar to parliamentary committees: they are collegial bodies composed of MPs who are also members of parliamentary assemblies operating within international organisations (such as the Parliamentary Assembly of the Council of Europe or of the North Atlantic Treaty Organization). They are therefore parliamentary bodies which are simultaneously subject to two legal orders: national and international.

A crucial role is assigned to the *Speaker* of the Senate and the Speaker of the Chamber. The Constitution calls the Speaker of the Senate to replace the President of the Republic in the event that the President cannot perform her/his functions (Article 86), and the Speaker of the Chamber

[8] Cf C Fasone, '*The Influence of Standing Committees on the Forms of Government. The Case of France, Italy and the UK*' (2017) 1 *Rivista di Diritti Comparati*, available at www.diritticomparati.it.

to chair the Parliament in joint session (Article 63.2). Both Speakers, furthermore, have to be consulted by the President of the Republic before the President dissolves the Parliament (Article 88.1). This is a noteworthy assignation, as it is designed to be the only limit, of a procedural nature, on one of the President of the Republic's most significant powers (see Chapter 6). Moreover, expanding on from this power, the Speakers of the two Houses are also consulted by the President of the Republic before the appointment of a new Government and, more generally, every time there are difficult junctures in the institutional dynamics.

Apart from these constitutional functions, each Speaker is involved in almost every procedure taking place within the Speaker's House (as well as jointly coordinating the activity of the two Houses, wherever possible). The Speaker's powers are sometimes attributed individually, relying on the Speaker's political, yet still impartial institutional, position, while other times they are assigned to three collegial bodies chaired by the Speaker. The quasi-judicial functions of interpreting and applying the rules of procedure are exercised either by the Speaker alone or with the advice of the Committee on the rules of procedure (*Giunta per il regolamento*). The functions of programming and coordinating the activity of the House are exercised mainly within the Conference of group chairpersons (*Conferenza dei capigruppo*), whenever this body manages to reach a decision (unanimity is normally required in the Senate; while a three-quarters majority suffices in the Chamber), but by the Speaker alone when this body cannot reach a decision. The functions as guarantor of the autonomy of the House are exercised either alone or by the Bureau (*Ufficio di Presidenza*), composed of four deputy Speakers, three quaestors and at least eight secretaries.

In the Italian parliamentary experience, the overall role of the Speaker has swung between two extremes, represented by the impartiality of the Speaker of the UK House of Commons and the partisanship of the Speaker of the US House of Representatives.[9] From 1959 onwards, after the newly established Constitutional Court left entirely to the discretion of each House the task of ensuring respect for its rules of procedure – at the same time reclaiming for itself control over compliance with constitutional provisions – the Speakers increased their degree of impartiality, which probably reached its peak during the 1970s (when a constitutional convention was established according to which the Speaker of the

[9] For a parallel study, see W McKay and CW Johnson, *Parliament and Congress* (New York, Oxford University Press, 2010) 36ff.

Chamber should be a member of the main opposition party). From 1993 onwards, however, following the entry into force of the mainly majoritarian electoral system, the Speakers have become more involved in the political debate and have often been elected among the party leaders: indeed, both are from the majority parties, thereby abandoning the constitutional convention started during the 1970s.

Other parliamentary bodies that need to be mentioned are committees (*Giunte*) for elections and parliamentary immunities, whose members are formally appointed by the Speaker, but upon the advice of parliamentary groups: one in the Senate and two in the Chamber (one on elections and one for the authorisation of prosecutions), normally chaired by a member of the opposition. The chair of the bicameral Committee for the Security of the Republic, composed of a limited number of deputies and senators, is also a member of the opposition. A rotating chair is, instead, provided for the Committee on the Quality of Legislation (established in 1997 only in the Chamber): its chair has a term of 10 months and should alternate between an MP of the majority and of the opposition.

In the absence of an upper house capable of representing regions and municipalities, the task of maintaining stable relations with them is assigned to a bicameral committee on regional issues, provided for expressly by the Constitution (Article 126.1). This function would have been performed more effectively if the committee's composition had been integrated with representatives of regions and municipalities, as provided by a transitional provision of constitutional law no 3/2001, which unfortunately has not been brought into operation.

V. PRIVILEGES AND IMMUNITIES OF MPs

In line with the continental tradition, the Italian Constitution devoted specific attention to defining the privileges to which MPs are entitled to by virtue of their position. As most of them represent exceptions to the principle of equality enshrined in Article 3 of the Constitution, in particular to equality before the judiciary, these privileges need to be provided by constitutional norms as well. This means that other – sub-constitutional – sources of law are called upon to implement and procedurally develop constitutional provisions, without being permitted any integration or extension.[10]

[10] Judgment no 262/2009.

The roots and the actual justification of these privileges must be viewed in the context of the need to reduce risks of external influence and conditioning on the behaviour of MPs and thus on the decisions taken by the body they comprise: the menace comes mainly from the Executive, but possibly also from the excesses of the judiciary and, to a certain extent, even from the political parties and the citizens. That is why the principle on which these privileges are often based is the traditional freedom of the representative mandate, according to which 'each MP represents the Nation and carries out her duties *without a binding mandate*' (Article 67). They are not deemed as improper and individual exemptions because these privileges are aimed at protecting the activity of the whole body MPs are members of.

In the same vein, each House also enjoys a multifaceted form of autonomy, which constitutes a shield from the interference of other external powers: starting with the autonomy to make internal rules of procedure (article 64); to implement those rules of procedure; to organise the functioning of their bureaucratic apparatus; to manage the budget and financial resources; and even to adjudge disputes with its staff and other internal issues (the so-called *autodichia*, or system of self-justice).[11]

The MPs' most important parliamentary privileges are the so-called *immunities*, which may be traced to distinct origins. On the one hand, MPs are afforded greater protection of the freedom to speak and to vote, meaning that no kind of scrutiny or responsibility may result from the opinions expressed or votes cast. This instrument has its origins in the British Bill of Rights (1689), according to which 'the freedom of speeches and debates or proceedings in Parliament ought not to be impeached or questioned in any court or place out of Parliament'. On the other hand, MPs are afforded a degree of protection from arrest or limitation of freedom, which should not take place without a specific authorisation from the House. This protection appeared in the French Revolution and more specifically in the 1791 Constitution, according to which MPs 'for criminal matters, can be seized in the very act or in virtue of a warrant of arrest; but notice shall be given thereof without delay to the legislative body; and the prosecution can be continued only after the legislative body shall have decided that there is occasion for accusation'.

The original text of Article 68 relied upon both instruments (called *insindacabilità*, or 'unchallengeability', and *inviolabilità* or 'inviolability', respectively), stating that MPs may not be prosecuted or sued for

[11] Recognised by Judgments nos 120/2014 and 262/2017.

their expressed opinions or votes cast in the exercise of their functions (Article 68.1) and requiring an explicit authorisation from the House to which the MP belonged to start a criminal process (Article 68.2). The application of the latter provision raised multiple issues, especially when the House indefinitely delayed its decision on such authorisations, and was deemed unacceptable after the discovery of *Tangentopoli* ('Bribesville'), at the beginning of the 1990s, and the subsequent *mani pulite* ('clean hands') campaign. In this context, a constitutional amendment was approved in 1993 (constitutional law no 3/1993), which abolished this kind of authorisation for commencing criminal procedures, keeping it only *ad acta*: that is, for acts that infringe MPs' personal freedom, such as searching them or their domicile or placing them under arrest (except to enforce a final conviction, or if the MP is caught in the act of committing a crime for which arrest is mandatory). A similar parliamentary authorisation is now also required for intercepting MPs' communications.

The new text of Article 68 of the Constitution had positive outcomes with respect to avoiding abuse on the part of the Houses, but did not solve any issues, especially in the context of a very confrontational relationship between the political bodies and the judiciary.[12] According to the new constitutional rule, any member of the judiciary could initiate a criminal or civil procedure against MPs, unless the House affirms that the behaviour in question fell within the umbrella protection of Article 68.1, which provided uniquely for opinions expressed and votes cast 'in the exercise of their functions'. If the House approved such a declaration (and it did so rather often), any judge who disagreed with it could raise a dispute ('conflict of attribution') before the Constitutional Court, aimed at verifying whether the parliamentary power had been correctly exercised: following a procedure outlined for the first time by judgment no 1150/1988 and then also confirmed after the reform of Article 68, and subsequently codified by law no 140/2003.

The Constitutional Court adopted a strict interpretation of the constitutional provisions on parliamentary immunities, starting with the assumption that they are exceptions to or derogations from the general principle according to which all citizens shall be equally subject to the law and that immunities are meant to protect the Parliament and its members from prosecution by the judiciary, not to impede the due course of justice. On these bases, starting from the 'twin judgments' nos 10 and 11/2000,

[12] C Guarneri and P Peterzoli, *The Power of Judges. A Comparative Study of Courts and Democracy* (Oxford, Oxford University Press, 2012).

the Constitutional Court interpreted rather strictly the unchallengeability granted by Article 68.1, ruling that it covers opinions expressed by MPs not only inside, but also outside, the Houses, only provided that they are 'substantially reproductions of an opinion expressed in a parliamentary context'.[13] In other words, the 'functional nexus' with the activity carried out by the MPs in their capacity as parliamentarians is an essential limitation. Without this limitation, the application of the immunity 'would transform it into a personal privilege',[14] which would confer on MPs 'a sort of favored personal status with regard to the scope and the limits of their liberty of expression of thought, and would thus also lead to possible distortions of the principle of equality and of equal opportunity between citizens in the dialectic of politics'.[15]

The Constitution also overcomes the principle, affirmed by the Albertine statute (although derogated from in practice since 1912 by the Chamber and since 1920 also by the Senate), of the gratuity received by those with a parliamentary mandate, and states that MPs 'shall receive an allowance established by the law' (Article 69). The law implementing this provision (law no 1261/1965) has established a cap for the allowance in a strict sense (called *indennità*) and has left it to the internal decisions of the bureau of the Chamber and the Senate to determine the amount of another stipend, called *diaria* ('daily allowance'), which is related, although as a lump sum, to the actual expenses incurred due to the representative mandate. The pensions (called *vitalizi*) ensured to former MPs, for the rest of their lives, arise entirely from internal decisions. Originally conceded with much generosity, these pensions have now become the object of public criticism, and have therefore been transformed for the future into pensions which are effectively linked to the sums paid by MPs as contributions during their mandate.

Finally, the right of each House to adjudicate its own election may be included among the parliamentary privileges. This is also a vestige of a traditional principle, aimed at ensuring, consistently with a strict reading of the separation of powers, the independence of the electoral process from the influences of the government as well as the judiciary. At the beginnings of the Italian Republic, this right was still perceived by the political parties as a necessity, suspicious as they were, in particular, of a judiciary mainly deriving from the fascist era. This explains

[13] Judgment no 11/2000.
[14] Judgment no 375/1997.
[15] Judgment no 10/2000.

why Article 66 stated that 'Each House decides the qualifications for admissions of its members and subsequent causes of ineligibility and incompatibility'.

The implementation of this constitutional rule did not give rise to many problems so long as proportional electoral systems were in force, as the main contested issues generally concerned intra-party re-counts. The contrast between this constitutional rule and more recent constitutional decisions within Europe, according to which it is up to a judge to decide – at least on the second occasion – on issues relating to the electoral process, emerged rather clearly when the elections were held predominantly (or at least in part) on the basis of a majoritarian electoral law. In this way, the winner in a single-member constituency, or even the attribution of the majority bonus, has been determined, at the end of the day, by the (existing) parliamentary majority, in stark contrast to the principles affirmed by the Venice Commission (in its 'Code of Good Practice in Electoral Matters', established in 2002) and even in contrast to the most elementary sense of fairness.[16]

Many reform proposals of Article 66 have been conceived and discussed, with the aim of assigning, whether entirely or at least upon appeal, electoral jurisdiction either to the Constitutional Court or to a special judge. However, they have never proceeded very far, possibly because of the persistent mistrust of a relevant part of the political class with respect to the judiciary and also in connection with the very frequent changes of the electoral system (see Chapter 3).

VI. PARLIAMENTARY RULES OF PROCEDURE

As is always the case, constitutional provisions regarding Parliament are far from self-sufficient and need to be integrated and specified. The daily activity of every Parliament is governed by many procedures that require detailed regulation: the *rules and principles of parliamentary law and practice* are not ordinarily featured within the text of Constitutions and when some of them are, it is mainly with the aim of limiting parliamentary autonomy.[17] Usually, therefore, the Constitution does not specify the

[16] See C Fasone and G Piccirilli, 'Towards a Ius Commune on Elections in Europe? The Role of the Code of Good Practice in Electoral Matters in 'Harmonizing Electoral Rights'' (2017) 16(2) *Election Law Journal* 247.

[17] A good example could be the Parliaments of the German States in the nineteenth century and the 1958 French Constitution of the Fifth Republic.

details of the structure or functioning of Parliament, but leaves space for parliamentary rules of procedure, while outlining the manner in which these rules have to be approved and usually which matters are reserved to them.

In the Italian Constitution, Article 64.1 establishes, in general terms, that 'each House adopts its own Rules by an absolute majority of its members', thereby requiring a higher majority than that necessary to approve ordinary legislation and to grant or deny confidence to the Government. Other constitutional provisions explicitly remit to these rules of procedure specific subject matters, the first of which is the articulation of the legislative process (Article 72).

Indeed, immediately after the entry into force of the Republican Constitution, the new Chamber of Deputies decided to re-adopt the same rules of procedure that were in force just prior to the fascist regime, and with them the previously mentioned provisions regarding parliamentary groups and standing committees approved in 1920. The Senate, now transformed into an elective body, instead adopted new rules of procedure, but these were essentially modelled on those of the Chamber. It was not until 1971 that both Houses had entirely new rules of procedure, in the context of a new phase of constitutional implementation, and also in response to the societal transformation that took place in 1968, as well as, to a certain extent, even foreseeing the subsequent 'national solidarity' governments with the inclusion of the communist party in the parliamentary majority which supported them.

Because the constitutional provisions regarding the Parliament, as well as those on the form of government, are rather generic, the role played by parliamentary rules of procedure has indeed been rather significant. To quote just one example, the fact that they continued, until the end of the 1980s, to prioritise the secret ballot – and in the case of the Chamber, also to require the final vote on legislative bills to be a secret vote – was an essential feature of the Italian form of government for the first 40 years. It was, in fact, a procedural rule that strongly encouraged the aggregation of a legislative majority much broader than the governmental majority, in order to avoid the risk that the (hidden) dissociation of a part of the latter, through the so-called *franchi tiratori* (covert snipers), could result in the rejection of a legislative bill on its final (secret) vote.

Following the same logic, parliamentary rules of procedure contributed significantly to defining the Government's weak position in Parliament, where, similarly to what happened in the Constituent Assembly, all the parties could equally be protagonists of the legislative process.

To a certain extent, therefore, this equilibrium was a crucial part of the *conventio ad excludendum*: until the 1960s, the Communist Party was not allowed, because of Italy's international obligations, to be part of the governmental majority (see Chapter 3). At the same time, however, it was entitled to be one of the actors, often with an essential role, in the legislative process (as it had been a crucial actor of the constituent process). Moreover, in this context, it may be possible to discern an explanation as to why the 1971 parliamentary rules of procedure significantly strengthened the oversight instruments, available to all parties especially in standing committees, and required unanimity in the Conference of group chairpersons in order to determine a binding agenda for the plenary.

Once the *conventio ad excludendum* ended, after the fall of the Berlin Wall in 1989, the establishment of new parliamentary rules of procedure has been neither easy nor straightforward: the secret ballot was effectively restricted to votes regarding persons or fundamental rights and some important but partial reforms were introduced in 1997 in the Chamber and in 2017 in the Senate. Throughout the last 30 years, the predominance of the Government has therefore been achieved mostly through the very intensive use of procedural instruments conceived for different aims, in order to grant the Government a certain degree of control over the legislative agenda. The reference is mainly to decree-laws and questions of confidence (see Chapter 5).

VII. THE LEGISLATIVE PROCESS

Consistent with the symmetrical nature of Italian bicameralism are the provisions embedded in Articles 70 and 72, according to which the legislative function is collectively exercised by the two Houses. Each legislative bill may start either in the Chamber or the Senate, and in either case needs to be approved as the same final text by both Houses in order to become a law. If one or more amendments are approved by the House on the second examination, the bill must return to the first House for reconsideration, like a '*navette*' (or shuttle bus, the equivalent of the 'ping pong' in the UK).

The main features and phases of the legislative process are also provided by the Constitution. These start with those empowered to initiate legislation, which are as follows: the Government (after the approval by the Council of Ministers and the authorisation of the President of the Republic); each MP (obviously, the senators for the Senate, the deputies for the Chamber); each Regional Council; the National Council for Economy and Labour; and at least 50,000 citizens. While the subject matter and the scope of a bill ordinarily fall entirely within the discretion of the bearer of the legislative initiative, there is a series of bills which may only, and exclusively, be commenced by the Government (budget bills; conversion laws; normally also laws aimed at ratifying international treaties and at approving agreements with non-Catholic religions).[18]

In a parliamentary form of government, the legislative agenda is normally strongly influenced, if not determined, by the Government, and its bills therefore have a good chance of being approved, albeit, in the Italian tradition, often with significant amendments.

According to the Constitution, once submitted to a House a legislative bill must first be examined by a parliamentary committee and then by a plenary session, which approves it article by article and then with a final vote. This is the so-called 'regular' procedure, with the committee acting in a reporting capacity (*sede referente*). It needs to be followed for a series of bills expressly identified by the Constitution (Article 72.4): constitutional and electoral matters; delegation bills; authorisation for the ratification of international treaties; and approval of budgets and accounts. Similarly, bills aimed at converting decree-laws (see Chapter 5) and laws vetoed by the President of the Republic are required, by the parliamentary rules of procedure, to comply with this procedure.

The same Constitution, however, outlines a different option, according to which the entire procedure develops within the committee, this time acting in a legislative capacity (*sede legislativa/deliberante*), without any involvement of the plenary. This decentralised procedure has, for a long time, been exclusively an Italian feature, probably derived from the somewhat positive experience of the advisory activity of the committees of the Chamber of Fasci and Corporations. It has since been replicated in other, more recently drafted constitutions, starting with the Spanish constitution (1978).

The Constitution itself sets out restrictions with respect to permitting this decentralised option. It establishes, as already noted, a series of bills for which the decentralised procedure is not allowed and identifies some subjects which are always entitled to oppose its use, thereby requiring

[18] The legislative bills authorising the ratification of international treaties were normally considered as reserved to the Executive. However, the two Houses have also allowed, since 1999, submission of such bills by MPs (provided that they refer to the text of a treaty that has been actually signed by the Italian Government).

the resubmission of the bill to the plenary: namely, the Government; one tenth of the members of the House; and one fifth of the members of the relevant committees. Otherwise, it leaves the matter to the parliamentary rules of procedures, while also allowing some intermediate options, aimed at reserving to the plenary just the votes on the articles and on the text as a whole. Indeed, the parliamentary rules of procedure, when addressing this matter, designed a third and intermediate kind of legislative procedure, with committees acting in a drafting capacity (*sede redigente*), and introduced further requirements to allow the Committee to directly approve a bill, asking for a positive opinion also to be expressed by other committees (especially the budget and the constitutional affairs committees).

Notwithstanding all these restrictions, the decentralised procedure has been very successful, at least during its first four decades. In each of the first 10 legislative terms of the Italian Republic (1948–1992), more than 50 per cent of the laws approved by Parliament were not considered in plenary session of at least one of the two Houses. This fact led scholars to refer to sectoral 'minor laws' (*leggine*), on which it was easier to reach a high degree of consensus among the main parties within each parliamentary committee. Such agreement was also thanks to the fact that, at this time, the limits to public expenditure were not particularly strict.[19] In other words, notwithstanding the strong ideological divide between the majority and the opposition, a hidden compromise was often reached between the main political actors, in the more protected environment of the committees and thanks to the secret ballot.[20]

After 1992, the legislative process changed abruptly and there was a crisis regarding recourse to committees in their legislative capacity, while the procedure with the committees in a drafting capacity – until 2017 rather differently conceived by the rules of procedure of the Chamber and the Senate – has always been extremely limited.

The causes of this change are numerous. They can be traced back to the discontinuity in the party system following Bribesville (see Chapter 1), and also the Maastricht Treaty, which made it more difficult to use public finances to strengthen the parliamentary consensus on sectoral

[19] See G Di Palma, *Surviving without Governing: The Italian Parties in Parliament* (Berkeley, California University Press, 1977) 194ff.

[20] M Cotta and L Verzichelli, *Political Institutions in Italy* (New York, Oxford University Press, 2007) 150.

legislation, as well as making the checks undertaken by the parliamentary budget committees and by the Treasury more accurate and incisive. Institutionally speaking, a connection can be made also with the mainly majoritarian electoral system, in force since 1993, and with the subsequently increased role of the Government (and the correlative, a more adversarial role chosen by the opposition).

In any case, as a result of these changes, what had until then been the preferred channel for approving new legislation in Italy became almost completely unavailable and consequently, other channels had to be used. Among these channels, the most successful one has been, and still is, represented by decree-laws adopted by the Government (and the respective conversion laws approved by the Parliament, significantly amending the text of the decree-law) (see Chapter 5). As for Parliament, these changes, together with the entry into force of the time quota for parliamentary debates (since 1988 in the Senate; since 1997 in the Chamber), have entailed a different way of selecting legislative priorities. In fact, while until 1992 it was up to each parliamentary committee to define, within its own sector, which bills were to be effectively examined (and possibly approved directly by the same committee, in its legislative capacity), later on it was up to the Conference of group chairpersons to decide, cross-cutting the different policy sectors. This allowed a more active involvement of the Government, potentially able to set the priorities for the plenary and, indirectly, also the standing committees.

As part of the 'regular' legislative procedure, the role of the standing committees is extremely important, notwithstanding that the terminology of a 'reporting capacity' implies that they only have a limited function. Indeed, the choice and the actual drafting of the bill to be examined by the plenary, as the base text to which all amendments must refer, are left entirely to the discretion of the relevant committee (with the unique exception being conversion laws, and only within the Senate).[21] Even after the text has been transmitted to the plenary, the standing committee continues to scrutinise the bill by expressing its advice, through the rapporteur, on any amendment to be voted on and, when it deems necessary, also submitting its own amendments to the plenary.

[21] A similar power has been attributed to the committees of the French Assemblee Nationale only since the 2008 constitutional reform: see É Thiers, 'Les commissions permanentes de l'Assemblée nationale et l'élaboration de la loi depuis 2008: une révolution très discrete' (2014) 48(1) *Revue juridique Thémis* 211.

Either in committees exercising legislative capacity or in plenary, the examination of a bill follows the same stages: a general discussion, then the debate and the votes on article and amendments relating to each article, and finally the declaration of vote, and the final vote on the whole bill. Once the text has been approved by a House, it is transmitted to the other by its Speaker through an official message. If the text is exactly the same as that already approved by the other House, the Speaker instead sends it to the President of the Republic for its promulgation, which should take place within one month. Once promulgated, the law is 'immediately' published in the Official Journal (*Gazzetta Ufficiale*) and enters into force 'on the fifteenth day following publication, unless such law establishes a different deadline' (Article 73.3). According to Article 74, the President of the Republic, before promulgating the law, 'may send Parliament a reasoned opinion to request that a law scheduled for promulgation be considered anew'. However, 'if such law is passed again, it shall be promulgated' (see Chapter 6).

VIII. THE BUDGETARY PROCESS

Since their origins, Parliaments have been involved in the budgetary process. Of course, they are not the only budgetary authority (as they have to deal with the Government, especially in parliamentary systems, as well as, in the European Union, with the EU institutions), but their budgetary function is in any event deemed to be an essential one.

The Italian Constitution, in its original text, considered the budgetary process only from a national perspective and almost exclusively having regard to the approval of 'ad hoc' legislative bills. Thus, the old text of Article 81 of the Constitution specifically ruled on the law approving the budget, to be presented by the Government and passed by the Houses every year (also regulating the scenario in which the budget is not approved in a timely manner, in which case a law authorises the provisional use of the previous budget for a maximum of four months in total). The law approving the accounts must also be submitted annually by the Government (after the check and validation by the Court of Accounts). For the other laws, ie ordinary legislation, an important constitutional principle applies: namely, the need for any other law seeking new or increased expenditures to specify the means and resources for covering them (the so-called 'financial cover'). Finally, a limitation on the content of the law approving the budget was established, consistently with a traditional principle and also with the need to distinguish between decisions on the balance and those regarding new expenditure or income, as no such new taxes or new expenditure can be introduced in the law approving the budget.

All these elements, with the only exception being the last, are also repeated in the new version of Article 81, as amended by constitutional law no 1/2012. This constitutional amendment aimed to introduce the principles of the *budget balance* and of the *sustainability of public debt*, 'in accordance with the European Union', at the highest level (Articles 81, 97 and 119). Indeed, the amendment was conceived and approved, by a wide majority, coinciding with the Treaty on Stability, Coordination and Governance in the Economic and Monetary Union (the so-called Fiscal Compact), which suggested signing States should implement the budget balance rule in their national laws.[22]

The need to better harmonise Italian law with EU principles, rules and decisions, according to the Stability and Growth Pact, throughout the cycle of economic and fiscal policy coordination within the EU called the '*European Semester*', has also inspired the revision of the laws regulating the Italian budgetary procedures (see the updated texts of the 'organic law' no 243/2012 and of law no 196/2009). The outcome is a design of a euro-national parliamentary procedure, regulated by EU law and national law, involving different institutions – EU as well as Member States' bodies; political as well as technical – in the definition of the fiscal policies.

A pivotal role is assigned to a planning document, now called the Document of Economy and Finance (DEF), to be drafted by the Government and then approved, via two parallel resolutions, by the two Houses. It includes the National Reform Programme and the Stability Programme, which specify the policies to prevent/correct imbalances, and plans to comply with the EU's country-specific recommendations and fiscal rules, required by the Stability and Growth Pact to be transmitted to the EU institutions by April each year. It is usually updated in September, in view of the new economic trends and forecasts, through an update note that is also transmitted and approved by the two Houses. If these policies imply a derogation from the budget balance rule, each House, just before approving the DEF, or its update, has to vote again,

[22] The principle of budget balance should be recognised 'through provisions of binding force and permanent character, preferably constitutional, or otherwise guaranteed to be fully respected and adhered to throughout the national budgetary processes' (Article 3.2 of the Treaty signed on 2 March 2012).

this time by an *absolute majority* of the entire membership, to explicitly authorise such a derogation.

On the basis of the objectives so determined, and also taking into consideration the country specific recommendations proposed by the European Commission, discussed by the Council and finally endorsed by the European Council each July, the budget bill is then submitted by the Government and examined – starting in one House one year, then in the other the following year – by the Parliament. The Parliament, between 20 October and the end of the year, during the so-called '*budgetary session*', may amend the bill, and it usually does so extensively, but without departing from the objectives they agreed upon when approving the DEF or its update note.

The previously mentioned constitutional provision embedded in the original text of Article 81, according to which no new taxes or new expenditures may be introduced in the budget law (*legge di bilancio*), has led the legislator, since 1978, to circumvent it by creating a new kind of legislative bill, to be examined together with the budget law and approved immediately before the latter, which did exactly what the budget law was not permitted to do: that is, to introduce new taxes and new expenditure. Called first the finance law (*legge finanziaria*) and then the stability law (*legge di stabilità*), it became, particularly until 1988 (when a programmatic document was introduced), a way for the Parliament to alter, sometimes even radically, the financial policy proposed by the government. Since the 2012 constitutional amendment revoked the limitation on its content, the budget law has also been able to bear responsibility (in its first part) for the introduction of new taxes or new expenditure, although always consistently with the equilibrium already agreed in the programmatic phase and re-affirmed by the same budget law (in its second part).

IX. THE OVERSIGHT FUNCTION

The constitutional text may appear misleading in regard to parliamentary oversight, as it refers only, in the second section of the first title of the second part, to the Parliament's law-making function. However, Parliament also exercises other functions, sometimes regarded as even more important than its legislative role. It should be remembered that votes of confidence of both houses are essential for the Government to be properly in a position to exercise its own prerogatives, while a motion of no confidence approved by the Chamber or the Senate obliges the Government to resign (Article 94, on which see Chapter 5).

The main difficulty in distinguishing the functions of Parliament arises due to the fact that, very rarely, parliamentary procedures are mono-functional, ie entirely aimed at producing a certain outcome, and therefore, corresponding with the particular function that is exercised through the same act. Because Parliament, by contrast with an administrative organ, has a political nature, it is free to determine the aims of its own actions, and also to use a certain procedure to achieve, more indirectly, a different aim than the one with which it is ordinarily associated. This implies that parliamentary procedures are very often multifunctional: they pursue different aims at the same time (legislation and oversight; confidence and direction; legislation and linkage; and so on).

Even in the constitutional text, there is some overlap. For instance, the already examined budgetary procedures provided by Article 81 are exercised mainly through legislative bills, although they can be largely included within the oversight function. Or, even more clearly, the *committees of inquiry*, a typical investigative instrument, normally considered to be part of the oversight function, are provided by Article 82, always within the legislative function.

According to the Constitution, when either House – or both of them – wants to investigate an issue of public interest, it has to set up an 'ad hoc' committee, which may be unicameral or bicameral. In either case, the committee of inquiry is composed in proportion to the support for each parliamentary group. The establishment of these committees can be decided by the majority on its own (although usually they are supported by a wider consensus), and is not part of the statute of minorities/opposition as is the case in other constitutional systems (such as in Germany).

Committees of inquiry are the most powerful investigative instrument at the disposal of Parliament, as they are entitled to the same powers and the same limitations as the judiciary (Article 82.2), sharing the same powers of investigation and of searching for evidence as defined by the criminal procedural code. Unsurprisingly, the main issues which have arisen in the parliamentary experience concern the relationships with the judiciary, when there are judicial actions concerning the same facts which are subject to parliamentary inquiry. Although it is clear that their aims are radically different – applying a sanction or establishing a legal liability in the case of the judicial inquiry by contrast with expressing a political assessment in the case of the committees of inquiry – the means often overlap and rules of reciprocal collaboration need to be established, either by legislation or by a judge. In its first Judgment addressing a constitutional dispute, the Constitutional Court deemed each committee of inquiry to be a 'power of the state', as it was authorised to definitively express the will of the power of which it is a part, and was therefore capable of raising as well as defending a constitutional dispute before the same Constitutional Court.[23]

Other investigative instruments are represented by the (written and oral, either in the plenary or in committees) questions (*interrogazioni*) and (oral and necessarily in plenary, as they are deemed politically more important) interpellations (*interpellanze*), posed by the MPs to the Government. Sometimes these questions require an immediate response: that is, within 24 hours, directly by the ministers involved or by the President of the Council (called, on the basis of the UK model, 'question time' and 'Prime Minister's question time', respectively). Parliamentary hearings (*audizioni*) may be binding if they involve members of the Government. They may also be held informally or within the context of fact-finding investigations – through which parliamentary committees can acquire information and documents that are deemed useful for parliamentary business – and they can be addressed to anyone. In these cases, however, it is just an invitation and the persons sought to be heard may refuse to appear. Finally, parliamentary hearings and communications by Government representatives (when they take place at the request of the Government itself) are also among the procedures most often used to ensure some parliamentary scrutiny with respect to the EU activity of the Italian Government (see Chapter 2). For instance, it has become almost regular practice to hear – either in plenary or in joint committees of the two Houses – from the President of the Council some days before and/or after the most important meetings of the European Council and, in some committees, also from the Ministers, before taking part in a Council meeting. Some hearings of EU Commissioners and of the President of the European Central Bank have also been organised, although necessarily on a more occasional basis.

X. CONCLUSION

For the first 40 years of the Italian Republic, Parliament has played a central role in the institutional system, exercising a large and substantial part

[23] See Judgment no 231/1975.

of the legislative function, especially thanks to the standing committees in legislative capacity, and determining the life and death of Governments. In this way, it has eased the integration into the political system of parties that were originally excluded from the possibility of becoming of the majority.

In the last 30 years the picture has changed, with the Government playing its legislative role, also relying on its favourable position in the EU decision making, and with Parliament struggling to play a more significant part by contributing to scrutinise the activity of the Government.[24] In this process, further accelerated by the COVID-19 pandemic, the long-awaited and failed reform of the symmetrical bicameralism seems to have undermined the parliamentary strength and substantially blocked self-reform of the parliamentary rules of procedure. A window of opportunity is currently open, following the reduction of the number of deputies and senators determined by the constitutional law no 1/2020 and taking advantage of the digitalisation of parliamentary activity derived from the COVID-19 pandemic.

FURTHER READING

Di Palma, G, *Surviving without Governing: The Italian Parties in Parliament* (Berkeley, California University Press, 1977).

La Palombara, J, *Democracy Italian Style* (New Haven, Yale University Press, 1987).

Lupo, N, and Piccirilli, G (eds), *The Italian Parliament in the European Union* (Hart, Oxford, 2017).

Lupo, N, and Piccirilli, G, 'Omnibus Legislation and Maxi-Amendments in Italy: How to Circumvent the Constitutional Provision Requiring Approval of Bills "Article by Article"' in Ittai Bar-Siman-Tov (ed), *Comparative Multidisciplinary Perspectives on Omnibus Legislation* (Springer, Berlin, 2021) 53–71.

Vassallo, S, 'Parliament' in E Jones and G Pasquino (eds), *The Oxford Handbook of Italian Politics* (Oxford-New York, Oxford University Press, 2015).

[24] See E Griglio, *Parliamentary Oversight of the Executives: Tools and Procedures in Europe* (Oxford, Hart, 2020) 182ff.

5

The Government: Between Politics and Administration

President of the Council of Ministers – Ministers – Council of Ministers – Under-secretaries of State – Technocratic Governments – Motion of Confidence – Motion of No Confidence – Question of Confidence – Decree-Laws – Legislative Decrees – Regulations – Public Administration – Auxiliary Bodies – Independent Authorities

I. INTRODUCTION

THE 'GOVERNING FUNCTION' tends to be often overlooked by constitutional scholars as it seems to be squeezed between the executive/administrative function pressing from below (bureaucracy) and the general political direction, pressing from above (Parliament). In practice, this function is inevitably shared among several constitutional bodies. In Italy, however, there was an under-estimation with respect to the body entitled to perform the 'governing function', namely the Government,[1] although it is clearly the 'most powerful' branch, able to use the public administration, to employ the military, to levy taxes, and to exercise all powers not explicitly assigned to the other two branches. Viewed historically, the Government was often interchangeable with the King (Royal Prerogative) and tended to be referred to as 'the Executive'.

It needs to be added that, in the Italian experience, the increased role of the State in the economy, and the consequent enlargement of the Government's functions and of the dimension of the public administration, began primarily during the Fascist era but endured beyond that period. What could not endure, of course, were the mechanisms, which

[1] See G Bognetti, *La divisione dei poteri (2001)*, English Translation: *Dividing Powers: A theory of the separation of powers* (Kluwer, 2017) 60ff.

were definitely authoritarian in nature, that were employed to strengthen the Mussolini Government.[2] On the contrary, the Constituent Assembly was often said to be characterised by the *complesso del tiranno*; that is, by the fear of repeating the Fascist experience and the need to distance itself from it.[3]

II. THE STRUCTURE OF THE GOVERNMENT

A. The Essential Bodies

The Italian Government is composed of three main and essential bodies (plus some others, not required by the Constitution, as we will soon see): the *President of the Council*, the *Council of Ministers* and the *Ministers*. The hierarchy and the relationships between these bodies have not been clarified by the Constitution and are subject to the political composition of the Government.

Indeed, Article 95 contains three distinct and conflicting principles, each of which could potentially determine the internal organisation of the Government:

- The dominance of the premier, placed well above the other components of the Government, when it states that '[t]he President of the Council *conducts* and holds responsibility for the general policy of the Government'.
- The prevalence of the collegial principle, according to which all ministers are subordinated to the collegial body, when it affirms that '[t]he Ministers are *collectively responsible* for the acts of the Council of Ministers'.
- The full control of each minister with respect to that minister's own area, which lies within the affirmation that ministers 'are *individually responsible* for the acts of their own ministries' and is also consistent with the statement that '[t]he President of the Council ensures the coherence of political and administrative policies, by promoting and co-ordinating the activity of the Ministers'.

[2] S Colarizi and L Morlino, 'Italy after Fascism: An Overview of the Fascist Legacy' in SU Larsen (ed), *Modern Europe after Fascism, 1943–1980s* (New York, Columbia University Press, 1998).

[3] G Amato, *Una Repubblica da riformare: Il dibattito sulle istituzioni in Italia dal 1975 a oggi* (Bologna, Il Mulino, 1980) 37.

The latter sentence can be read as relegating the role of the President of the Council within the traditional model of a *primus inter pares* (ie first among equals) or, alternatively, as the recognition of the guidance role of the President, who, being responsible for the Government's general policy, is called upon to promote and coordinate – also using the collegial body – the activity of the other parts of Government.

The Constitution's authors were very conscious of this ambiguity and thus they left the task of actually determining the institutional balance within the Government to an 'ad hoc' piece of legislation. According to Article 95.4, 'The law establishes the organisation of the Presidency of the Council, as well as the number, competence and organisation of the ministries'. It is not a coincidence that it took at least 40 years for this piece of legislation to be put in place (law no 400/1988, regarding the Presidency of the Council, and legislative decree no 300/1999, concerning the Ministers). In the meantime, a royal decree adopted by the Zanardelli Government at the beginning of the twentieth century, regulating the functions of the Council of Ministers and designating a rather weak coordinating role to the President of the Council, was deemed to still be in force, at least with respect to most of its provisions (royal decree no 466/1901).

Indeed, in the Italian constitutional evolution, each of the three above mentioned principles has been enforced as the dominant one, in different seasons, depending on the features of the party system and the electoral legislation, which have changed a number of times over the years. Apart from the first legislative term (1948–1953), in which the strong leadership of Alcide De Gasperi made the system work similarly to a majoritarian one – although without any possibility of alternation between different political parties – the Republican Governments were characterised, in the 1950s, 1960s and 1970s, by a high degree of ministerial autonomy. Each Minister was designated and politically protected by the Minister's own party (and, in the case of a member of the Christian Democrats, by the Minister's own political faction, as there were many distinct factions within that party). Therefore, the President of the Council, who was always a Christian Democrat during that phase, could not do much more than try to use informal influence to ensure some coordination. It was during that phase that the formula of a government with multiple and scattered directions (*governo a direzione plurima dissociata*) was coined,[4]

[4] E Cheli and V Spaziante, 'Il Consiglio dei Ministri e la sua presidenza: dal disegno alla prassi' in S Ristuccia (ed) *L'istituzione Governo: Analisi e prospettive* (Milan, Comunità, 1977).

to signify the fact that each Minister could define, often together with parliamentary committees dealing with the same issues, that Minister's own political direction, and that this direction was normally unrelated, when not deliberately opposed, to that followed by the other Ministers, and even by the President of the Council. In other words, the strength and unity of governmental political direction were entirely left up to party politics, without any legal or institutional mechanisms capable of pursuing these aims.

During the 1980s, when for the first time Governments were led by Presidents of the Council who were not representatives of the Christian Democratic Party, but who were the leaders of minor parties of the majority coalition (first Giovanni Spadolini, republican, and then Bettino Craxi, socialist), they needed to rely on institutional mechanisms more than on the political strength of their own parties. Consequently, the tendency was to strengthen the collegial body and also, wherever possible, the role of the President of the Council too. Law no 400/1988, approved after almost a decade of parliamentary discussion, was probably the main outcome of this tendency.

After the entry into force of (mainly) majoritarian electoral systems, from 1993 onwards, the figure of the President of the Council started to emerge more clearly, as is natural in a more majoritarian context, although with ups and downs. According to the electoral legislation (Article 14-bis Presidential Decree no 361/1957, as inserted by law no 270/2005), each list or coalition of lists previously had to indicate its 'unique leader': in actual terms, the potential President of the Council in case of victory, although the law stated that this indication did not infringe the power of appointment assigned to the President of the Republic by Article 92.2. The unique leaders' names did not appear on the ballot papers, but only in the electoral manifestos. Nevertheless, their names then also started to be cited within the electoral symbols of the main parties ('for Prodi', 'for Berlusconi', and so on), thus sometimes even appearing on the ballot paper and giving the illusion of some kind of direct election of the President of the Council. The new electoral law no 165/2017 changed this provision, obliging each list to identify the name of its leader.

This process of personalisation of the Government was extremely clear and defined at the level of media politics, and also derived from other more structural and general factors, including the influence of the EU institutional dynamics with a more relevant role assigned to the institution composed of the Heads of Governments and of some

Heads of State, namely, the European Council.[5] It was, however, only partially and gradually mirrored at the (national) institutional level. The Government's leadership was strongly evident in public debate, but struggled to be recognised in its relationship with the other ministers. However, the Constitutional Court denied any effect of the electoral law on the internal dynamics of the Government, confirming the *primus inter pares* principle. This was on the basis of the – true, but rather formalistic – argument that the provision in question regarding the unique leader 'as a piece of ordinary legislation' was not deemed 'capable of modifying the constitutional position of the President of the Council of Ministers'.[6]

B. The Non-essential Bodies

Apart from these three essential bodies (President of the Council, Council of Ministers and Ministers), the Government also comprises other organs. Their existence is not required by the Constitution, but they have been established following a long-standing custom and are now regulated by law no 400/1988. Among them, by far the most frequent (no Government having renounced them) and the most relevant (there are some dozens of them, thus representing more than half of the Government's members) are undersecretaries of State (*Sottosegretari di Stato*). They are appointed by the President of the Republic, upon the recommendation of the President of the Council – traditionally immediately before the confidence vote in Parliament, but since 2012 some days afterwards instead – in agreement with the concerned Minister, having consulted with the Council of Ministers. In contrast to Ministers, undersecretaries may be removed, following exactly the same procedure which provided for their appointment.

Undersecretaries of State are called upon to represent the Government in Parliament, acting as substitutes for Ministers (normally in committees, but often also in plenary), and to assist and carry out tasks delegated by their Minister. One of the undersecretaries of State assisting the President

[5] On the strengthening of the President of the Council as an effect of EU dynamics see M Calise, 'Presidentialization, Italian style' in T Poguntke and P Webb (eds), *The Presidentialization of Politics: A Comparative Study of Modern Democracies* (Cambridge: Cambridge University Press, 2005) 88–106 and S Fabbrini, 'Italy and the EU: A Relationship with Uncertain Outcomes' in M Kaeding, J Pollak and P Schmidt (eds) *The Future of Europe: Views from the Capitals* (London: Palgrave Macmillan, 2018) 61–64.

[6] See Judgments nos 24/2004, 262/2009 and 23/2011.

of the Council assumes a crucial role, as the undersecretary is required to take part in the Council of Ministers' meetings – otherwise strictly reserved to Ministers – and to act as the secretary of this collegial body.

In 1999, a new category of undersecretaries was created: the '*vice-ministers*'. They are (up to 10) undersecretaries of State whose delegated tasks are of particular relevance (corresponding with either at least one ministerial department or more ministerial general directions) and are assigned not only by a ministerial decree, as normally occurs, but by the Council of Ministers, upon the proposal of the President of the Council.

According to Article 95, as already noted, each Minister should lead, and thus be responsible for, a Ministry. In addition, there have always been a number of Ministers who do not lead a whole ministerial administration, but lead a smaller administrative structure, associated with one or more departments of the Presidency of the Council. These are called 'Ministers without portfolios'. Apart from this, however, these Ministers share all the other features of their colleagues.

In some limited instances, the President of the Council has been assisted by one or even two deputies: the *Vice-President(s) of the Council*. Sometimes, the appointment of such a figure has been used to more clearly reward and, to some extent, involve the second party of the majority coalition: in these cases, the appointee has been a senior Minister and, at the same time, one of the leaders of that party. Particularly relevant, although not very successful, has been the appointment as Vice-Presidents of the leaders of the two parties composing the populist coalition at the basis of the Conte 1 Government (2018–2019).

Other non-essential governmental bodies include *High and Extraordinary Commissioners*, appointed to carry out temporary functions, in order to coordinate different State administrative structures in pursuit of a common aim. It is common to appoint such Commissioners in the event of natural calamities such as earthquakes and epidemics.

Another series of collegial bodies, called *Inter-ministerial Committees*, have been established by law. Some of them have existed for a long time, such as the Inter-ministerial Committee for Economic Planning (CIPE) – since 2021 renamed CIPESS, and including Sustainable Development – while others are more recent, such as the Inter-ministerial Committee for European Community Affairs (CIAE) and the ones for Digital Transition and for Ecological Transition (CITD and CITE, respectively). Important functions are also exercised by the Inter-ministerial Committee on Credit and Savings (CICR) and the Inter-ministerial Committee for the Security of the Republic (CISR).

C. Members of the Government, Members of Parliament

Consistently with what happens in most parliamentary forms of government, Ministers and undersecretaries of State are ordinarily selected from among the Members of Parliament, and therefore benefit from parliamentary privileges and immunities. While in office, MPs who are also members of the Government may be replaced in committees, but not in plenary, by other members of their own parliamentary group.

However, as already recalled, in recent decades, some Ministers and even three Presidents of the Council have been selected more than once from outside the Chamber or the Senate, and so have been defined as 'technocratic'. This was the case of Carlo Azeglio Ciampi (1993–1994), and Lamberto Dini (1995–1996), both coming from the highest ranks of the Bank of Italy. They were appointed upon the request of a very wide majority of political parties, following the failure of the first Governments appointed after a general election, in order to reach the next election and, in the meantime, to enact some unpopular but necessary legislative measures of fiscal policy. A very similar phenomenon took place again with the Monti Government (2011–2013), although Mario Monti, a former EU commissioner and a renowned economist, just one week before being appointed President of the Council by President Napolitano, had been also appointed by Napolitano as a life senator.[7] A similar feature seems to characterise the Draghi Government (2021–present), led by Mario Draghi, former governor of the Bank of Italy and President of the European Central Bank. In this case, in contrast to the Dini and Monti Governments, the Cabinet has a mixed composition, with a number of experts sitting alongside a number of political ministers belonging to numerous and divergent political parties.

III. THE CONFIDENCE RELATIONSHIP WITH THE TWO HOUSES OF PARLIAMENT

The main steps and features of the formation of the Government will be analysed in Chapter 6. Within this procedure, the President of the Republic is called upon to play a crucial role, while always pursuing

[7] See A Bosco and D McDonnell, 'Introduction: The Monti Government and the Downgrade of Italian Parties' in A Bosco and D McDonnell (eds), *Italian Politics: From Berlusconi to Monti* (New York, Berghahn Books, 2012) 37–56.

a unique and fundamental aim: the appointment of a Government capable of securing the confidence of a parliamentary majority in both Houses.

The foremost fundamental principle of the parliamentary form of government is enshrined in Article 94.1: 'The Government must receive the confidence of both Houses of Parliament'. As already remarked (see Chapter 3), the mechanisms to avoid a degeneration of parliamentary government into 'assembly government' which have been embedded in the Constitution are very limited, and are all included in the same Article. They consist in the provision of the two specific parliamentary procedures having the confidence relationship as their focus: the motion of confidence and the motion of no confidence.

A. The Motion of Confidence

The vote of confidence that each House must grant the Government at the beginning of its activity, within 10 days of its formation (ie according to the institutional practice, within 10 days of its oath), occurs through a specific act called a '*motion of confidence*'.

In reality, the President of the Council first appears in front of one of the two Houses and reads the official programmatic speech. Then each House – with an alternation in priority, consistently with the symmetrical nature of bicameralism – debates and, eventually, votes on the motion of confidence (a draft of which has generally been submitted by the leaders of the parliamentary groups that are soon going to compose the parliamentary majority), through which each House gives its own confidence to the newly formed Government.

There are two constitutional requirements concerning this vote. First, in order to attribute some degree of solemnity and to clarify, without any possibility of an error, how each MP positions herself – either in the majority or in the opposition – the vote should be held publicly and by roll-call. Each MP is called upon to pass on the floor, in front of the Speaker's bench, declaring their vote aloud. Second, the motion of confidence should be 'reasoned', thus requiring the members of the majority to justify why they put their confidence in that Government and which elements of its programme are deemed most essential in their view. However, the relevance of this second constitutional requirement has been significantly reduced in practice, as the motions of confidence tend to be 'reasoned *ob relationem*', that is, just generically and entirely recalling the programmatic speech given by the President of the Council, while each parliamentary group expresses its own reasons for supporting the Government during the parliamentary debate.

B. The Motion of No Confidence

The '*motion of no confidence*' is designed by the Constitution as the only parliamentary vote that legally obliges the Government to resign, once a motion of this kind is approved by either of the two Houses. Indeed, in all the other instances in which the Government is defeated in Parliament, there is no such obligation: 'An opposing vote by one or both the Houses against a Government proposal does not entail the obligation to resign' (Article 94.4).

Nevertheless, it is clear that the Government can decide to resign in any event following the outcome of any parliamentary vote, or even on the eve of a vote. In fact, this has been the dominant practice in the Italian parliamentary experience, in which almost all the governmental crises have been 'extra-parliamentary', with only two exceptions: the resignations of the Prodi Governments in 1998 and 2008, which both followed the rejection of a vote of confidence.

According to Article 94.5, 'the motion of no-confidence must be signed by at least one-tenth of the members of the House and cannot be debated earlier than three days from its presentation'. The first requirement is aimed at avoiding the too-frequent submission of such motions, although often the fear of having them boldly rejected by the assembly with an overwhelming majority is more effective in limiting their frequency. The second is meant to impede a 'surprise vote', in which the opposition could too easily prevail, thus allowing the majority to collect its forces and properly attend the sitting. Indeed, a three-day interval was conceived, in the middle of the twentieth century, in recognition of the time required to reach Rome from the different parts of the peninsula (or from Sicily and Sardinia). However, this interval still appears useful, now that the representation of Italians abroad has been granted, to enable, if necessary, even the MPs elected and resident in Australia or in South America to be summoned to vote.

C. The Motion of No Confidence in a Single Minister

In addition to the two parliamentary procedures regarding the confidence relationship with the Government provided by the Constitution, two other procedures have been set up, by institutional practice or, according to the dominant reading, by proper constitutional conventions or customs: the motion of no confidence regarding a single minister and the question of confidence.

Sticking to the letter of the Constitution, both the motion of confidence and the motion of no confidence can only refer to the Government as a whole: that is, not to the President of the Council alone, nor to individual Ministers. Therefore, the constitutionality of a motion aimed not only at severely criticising but also at revoking confidence in a single Minister, has been much debated. However, at least three factors exist in favour of admitting such motions: the already noted high degree of autonomy actually enjoyed by each Minister in determining policies; the rather clear absence, in the legal order, of any power to remove Ministers upon the proposal of the President of the Council; and the need to avoid 'concealed' motions of this kind, embedding criticisms of ministerial action so strongly as to require, not legally but politically, the resignation of the Minister in question. Indeed, it was especially this third factor which determined, since the mid-1980s, that the same procedural treatment provided for the collegial motions of no confidence should also be applied to motions requiring the dismissal of a single Minister – whether directly or indirectly, upon the judgment of the President of the Assembly.[8] This seems fully understandable, especially when considering that otherwise, at that time, these motions, which could evidently endanger the life of the (coalition) Government, altering its delicate internal political balance, would have been voted on by secret ballot.

However, the debate as to the constitutionality of individual motions of no confidence came to an end in 1996 when the Constitutional Court clarified that the 'individual' motion of no confidence represents a constitutional custom capable of integrating into the written constitutional provisions. Such a custom was deemed to be completely consistent with the features of the parliamentary form of government that require the existence of a sort of *continuum* within the political direction-responsibility-confidence relationship. As the Constitution refers to the individual responsibility of single Ministers (Article 95.2), the motion denying confidence to a single Minister aims to enforce this responsibility and thus legally oblige the Minister's resignation.[9]

[8] In the Senate, this happened through an opinion of the Rules Committee, issued on 24 October 1984.

[9] Judgment no 7/1996.

The case in question was raised by the Minister of Justice of the Dini Government, Filippo Mancuso, who first refused to follow parliamentary directives and then questioned the constitutionality of the motion of no confidence that the Senate had approved against him, after the Government had permitted the MPs freedom as to how to vote on the motion. He refused to resign but, on the basis of the parliamentary vote, he was replaced *ad interim* by the President of the Council, Lamberto Dini, by a decree of the President of the Republic. The former Minister Mancuso was defeated in the conflict of attributions he raised before the Constitutional Court (see Chapter 9).

Since this judgment, other *individual motions of no confidence* have been submitted and voted on in either of the two Houses, but none has been approved, to date, as the Government has usually covered up the behaviour of its own Ministers. So, what happened in the Mancuso case was probably due primarily to the fact that the Government was a 'technocratic Government' and the Minister of Justice – a retired high court judge himself – was acting independently not only from the parliamentary majority, but also from the other members of the Government, President of the Council included. Moreover, as already remarked, the dismissal of a Minister by the President of the Council is not deemed feasible.

D. The Question of Confidence

Much more determinant is the role played in the institutional experience by the fourth (and final) confidence procedure: the *question of confidence*. It is a procedural mechanism that exists, albeit with different features, in all parliamentary governments (except Norway),[10] and which allows the Government to pre-alert the Parliament as to the crucial effect to which a future parliamentary vote could give rise on the existence of the confidence relationship. In substance, this constitutes a sort of blackmail on the part of the Government to the Parliament, and most of all to its majority: 'on a certain issue, either you vote following my advice, or else I will resign'.

In the first years of the Italian republican experience, the procedural effects and – because of the Constitution's silence on this point – the

[10] G Tsebelis, *Veto Players. How Political Institutions Work* (New York, Russell Sage-Princeton, 2002) 100.

constitutionality of the question of confidence were strongly disputed, even causing a rift between the President of the Chamber of deputies, Gronchi, and his deputy, Leone (both leaders of the Christian Democratic party and destined to become, in the following years, Presidents of the Republic). However, a constitutional custom progressively emerged, which was partially codified first in the Chamber's (in 1971), and then in the Senate's rules of procedure (in 1988), as well as, eventually, in law no 400/1988 (in order to require an authorisation by the Council of Ministers for the question of confidence to be posed in one of the two Houses).[11]

According to this constitutional custom, the question of confidence involves three main procedural effects: first, the application of the roll-call vote, as in all the other confidence procedures; second, the chronological priority of the vote on the object on which the question of confidence has been posed; third, the unamendability and indivisibility of the text on which the Government has posed the question of confidence. These procedural effects are so relevant, especially when applied to the legislative process, that often the Government targets them and makes use of the question of confidence only instrumentally, not because it deems that vote crucial for its survival, but because it aims to accelerate the process and to avoid the many parliamentary votes otherwise required (with all the accompanying relative unknowns).

These advantages become particularly evident when the question of confidence is posed on *maxi-amendments* (ie amendments aimed at substituting the entire text of a bill). In fact, in this case, through a unique roll-call vote the Government is able to determine the text of the bill that is going to be approved by each House, obliging its parliamentary majority to accept it as a whole, without the risk of having different outcomes on each article and amendment, depending on their parliamentary support. In this way, the Government 'effectively impedes debate and eliminates all margin for negotiation' within both its majority and the opposition.[12]

The use of the question of confidence on maxi-amendments has been extremely frequent during the last 20 years, although many scholars doubt its conformity with Article 72.1 of the Constitution, when it

[11] A Manzella, *Il parlamento* (Bologna, Il Mulino, 2013) and M Olivetti, *La questione di fiducia nel sistema parlamentare italiano* (Milan, Giuffrè, 1996).

[12] S Vassallo, 'Parliament' in E Jones and G Pasquino (eds), *The Oxford Handbook of Italian Politics* (Oxford, Oxford University Press, 2015) 107–19, 114.

requires any bill to be voted on 'article by article' and then as a whole. Several official messages have been sent to the Parliament by Presidents Ciampi and Napolitano on this issue.[13] However, both the Speakers of the two Houses and the Constitutional Court) have avoided, to date, declaring an end to this practice, which has managed to ensure some kind of functioning of the legislative process and to recognise the Government's dominant role within it, to unite, although artificially, its own heterogeneous parliamentary majority.[14] Even the opposition seems to have become accustomed to this practice, as it is much easier to complain about the abuse of this instrument and to generically criticise a certain bill than to examine and contrast it article by article and amendment by amendment.

IV. THE PRIMARY AND SECONDARY NORMATIVE POWERS OF THE GOVERNMENT

The existence and the endurance of the confidence relationship between the Parliament and the Government naturally imply a strong influence of the latter on the contents and the priorities of legislation: it is mainly through legislative activity that the programme of the Government is implemented. This influence on legislation either derives from the dominant role of the Government in the drafting of the legislation approved by Parliament or from the enactment of some normative acts by the same Government.

According to Italian tradition and in compliance with the deal reached in May 1947 (see Chapter 1), the Government should not occupy a too strong role in the legislative process. Rather, all political parties were allowed to take part on an equal footing. Consequently, the other channels of governmental influence have developed to a considerable extent.

Indeed, the Constitution referred very prudently to the normative powers of the Government. First, after some hesitation, it allowed the decree-laws (*decreti-legge*, sometimes also translated as 'law decrees'), limiting them to the 'extraordinary cases of necessity and urgency', and requiring each of them to be converted into law by the Parliament within

[13] G Pistorio, *Maxi-emendamento e questione di fiducia: Contributo allo studio di una prassi illegittima* (Napoli, Editoriale Scientifica, 2018) 262ff.

[14] See Judgment no 391/1995. However, see also Judgments nos 32/2014 (striking down a provision inserted by a maxi-amendment) and 251/2014 (qualifying maxi-amendments as a 'problematic practice').

the peremptory deadline of 60 days. Second, it provided for legislative decrees (*decreti legislativi*, sometimes also known as 'delegated legislation') to be adopted by the Government, following the approval of a delegation law on the part of the Parliament. Thirdly, when dealing with the powers of the President of the Republic, it made only a reference to regulations (*regolamenti*), the name currently used to refer to all secondary normative acts, traditionally issued by the Government.

In the hierarchical system, while (governmental) regulations are placed among the secondary sources of law, and thus below primary sources (traditionally represented by ordinary laws), both decree-laws and legislative decrees are instead expressly qualified as acts having the force of law (ie as primary sources of law). That is why both categories of legislative acts need an explicit constitutional basis (Articles 77 and 76, respectively) and have to be accompanied by a proper, parliamentary law to permanently enter the legal order: either before, as the delegation law (*legge delega*) for legislative decrees, or after, as the conversion law (*legge di conversione*) for decree-laws.

A. Decree-laws

While initially drafting the Constitution the Constituent Assembly decided not to recognise any form of decree adopted by the Government in case of necessity. The experience of the First World War and especially of the years during the Fascist regime, when decree-laws had been used very intensively, and had remained in force for years, often without even being converted into law, was still at the forefront of the collective memory. At a later stage, the Assembly eventually decided to include them in the Constitution, although through a provision aimed at strictly limiting their use and at avoiding the main downfalls of this previous experience.

This approach explains why Article 77 (ie the provision allowing decree-laws) opens with a sentence that instead seems to deny them: 'The Government may not, without an enabling act from the Houses, issue a decree having force of law'. Had the provision ended here, there would have been no decree-laws at all. However, the wording of Article 77 continues and foresees circumstances in which the Government may adopt such decrees 'in extraordinary cases of necessity and urgency'. This means, at least according to the dominant reading, that such cases constitute the prerequisite for the Government to adopt decree-laws in compliance with the Constitution.

The majority of Article 77, however, aims to regulate procedural issues: requiring an immediate transmission of the decree-law to one of the two Houses (which needs to be convened, even during dissolution, within five days) and, most of all, asking for it to be converted into law by the Parliament (within 60 days of its enactment). It also specifies that, if the conversion does not happen by this deadline, the decree-law shall lapse and retrospectively lose its effect (*ex tunc*, which means 'since the beginning'). Finally, it leaves it up to the same Parliament, in this case, to regulate the legal issues which have arisen from the lapsed decree-law.

Each decree-law, therefore, once adopted by the Council of Ministers and enacted by the President of the Republic, is transmitted to one of the Houses as an attachment to a governmental bill aimed at converting it into law. The two Houses have the power to amend it and, if they want to convert it into law, they have to complete the process by approving the conversion law, in the same terms, within 60 days.

Notwithstanding the intention of the Constituent Assembly and all the limitations inserted into Article 77, the use of decree-laws has been intense even from the beginning and has progressively increased, especially since the 1970s. As has been remarked, they were often conceived (by the Government) and perceived (by the Parliament) as a kind of 'reinforced legislative initiative', open to amendments and additions.[15] This also explains why, in several cases, the two Houses did not complete the conversion within 60 days, thereby permitting the decree-law to lapse (with *ex tunc* effects, as already clarified).

This practice became even more contradictory after both the Chamber and the Senate, in 1981 and 1982 respectively, introduced into their rules of procedure further and specific scrutiny, first by the Constitutional Affairs Committee and then by the Plenary, as to whether each decree-law meets the constitutional pre-requisites of necessity and urgency. Frequently, therefore, one or even both Houses voted in favour of a decree-law (as it was very difficult for MPs, especially for majority MPs, to draw a line between an assessment on the constitutionality and on the merits of the decree-law), but then that the same decree-law, without being explicitly rejected, was not converted in time and consequently lapsed.

All these factors contribute to explaining why the Government has, most of the time, decided to systematically re-adopt the same decree-law

[15] A Predieri, 'Il Governo colegislatore' in F Cazzola, A Predieri and G Priulla, *Il decreto legge fra Governo e Parlamento* (Milan, Giuffrè, 1975).

on the very day the previous one lapsed, normally also taking into account any amendments approved during parliamentary examination. This practice, called '*reiteration*' of decree-laws, became extremely common in the 1990s. In one case the same decree-law was reiterated more than 20 times, thereby maintaining its effects for around four years. The rate of enacting decree-laws – including their reiterations – dramatically increased, reaching an average of more than one per day.

However, the practice of reiteration eventually ceased, as the Constitutional Court ruled that it was inconsistent with Article 77. According to the Court, in fact, the reiteration: (a) 'alters the provisional nature of decree-laws, *de facto* postponing the peremptory deadline'; (b) reduces the value of the extraordinary character of the pre-requisites of necessity and urgency; and (c) weakens the sanction of the retrospective lapse of the unconverted decree-law. Furthermore, from a more general perspective, the practice, 'if diffused and prolonged over time as happened in recent times, affects the institutional equilibrium, altering the same form of government and the ordinary attribution of the legislative power to the Parliament' (Article 70) and wounds 'the certainty of law in the relationship among citizens'.[16]

The end of this unconstitutional practice did not terminate the abuse of decree-laws. Their frequency reduced to around two to four per month, and almost all were converted, with several amendments, within 60 days, but their contents increased very significantly, touching upon very different subject matter. Heterogeneous decree-laws (often called '*omnibus*') are more successful, as they are moved by a stronger engine, represented by all the supporters – from different political parties and distinct ministries – of their many provisions. They tend to become even richer during the parliamentary examination and, at the conclusion of the legislative process, their conversion is often achieved thanks to a question of confidence posed by the Government, which in this way manages to unify a heterogeneous and often conflicting parliamentary majority.

The Constitutional Court also tried to limit most of these abuses. On the one hand, the Court affirmed its potential for declaring a decree-law unconstitutional, even once converted into law, in cases of 'evident lack' of the 'extraordinary cases of necessity and urgency' required by Article 77.[17] However, the Court has been very reluctant to scrutinise the

[16] Judgment no 360/1996, on which see V Barsotti and others, *Italian Constitutional Justice in Global Context* (New York, Oxford University Press, 2016) 166ff.

[17] Judgment no 29/1995.

pre-requisites of decree-laws, because it considers that the decision to adopt a decree-law falls within the margin of discretionary power of the political bodies.

On the other hand, the Court has clarified that the conversion law is not an ordinary law and therefore it can neither legalise a decree-law which was originally adopted without meeting the prerequisites of necessity and urgency, nor insert amendments devoid of any connection with the content of the decree-law. The power of conversion cannot in fact be regarded as a mere manifestation of the ordinary legislative power of the Parliament, as the conversion law is 'specialised and intended for a specific function', premised 'on the existence of a decree to be converted, and must reflect the legislative content of that decree'. Consequently, the Court struck down some provisions inserted by the Parliament while converting the decree-law that were clearly unrelated to that decree-law, as they had to be declared *ultra vires* because they did 'not respect the typical function of the conversion law', using the special procedure provided for this category of laws.[18]

B. Legislative Decrees

The succession between decree-laws and conversion laws is turned upside down in the case of delegation laws and legislative decrees. In this case, the primary act of Government (the legislative decree) must be preceded by a parliamentary law (the delegation law), aimed at delegating to the Government the exercise of the relevant legislative function.

Any delegation, however, cannot be *en blanc*: the Constitution (Article 76) requires the delegation law to specify: (a) principles and criteria; (b) time, which needs to be limited; and (c) object, which needs to be specific. In addition, Article 72.4 includes the delegation laws among those bills to be examined in accordance with the ordinary process (ie bills that cannot be approved directly by parliamentary committees: see Chapter 4). The Constitutional Court has interpreted this provision strictly, as applicable to any bill containing at least one delegation norm and even to a bill aimed at postponing the deadline for adopting legislative decrees.[19]

In addition to these limitations imposed by the Constitution, the delegation law is deemed free to provide for more constraints to the delegated

[18] See Judgment no 32/2014, quoting Judgment no 22/2012 and Order no 34/2013.
[19] Judgment no 32/1962.

legislative activity of the Government. And it usually does, through the insertion of a series of procedural steps that the draft legislative decrees have to follow before being adopted by the Council of Ministers and enacted by the President of the Republic.

Among these further procedural limitations, the most frequent is the involvement of parliamentary committees, which are called upon to issue their own preliminary opinion on the draft legislative decree: an opinion that is mandatory, but (at least normally) not legally binding. In this way, Parliament can see in advance how the Government is going to implement the delegation law, signalling where there seems to be a violation of, or some unconvincing development of the principles and criteria set by, the delegation law. The actual function exercised by parliamentary committees through these opinions may vary case by case, usually swinging between two opposite poles: the (political) control of the correct implementation of the principles and criteria, on the one hand, and collaboration as to the drafting of the legislative decree (which could be defined as a co-legislative function), on the other hand. In any case, the provision itself of the parliamentary opinion within the delegation law encourages Parliament to confer the delegation to the government, helping to overcome its natural reluctance to give away, albeit temporarily, its own legislative function.[20]

Other procedural limitations may consist in asking the Government to collect preliminary opinions of other bodies or subjects, such as EU institutions, independent authorities, the Council of State, the Court of Accounts, trade unions, other associations or confederations, the State-Region Conference, Regions or local autonomies, and so on. These procedural limitations become extremely telling of the constraints, interests and values to be effectively considered by the delegated legislator, even more so when the principles and criteria are almost absent or are present only in a generic sense.

All in all, therefore, the process of delegated legislation seems designed as a complex or dual means of decision-making, characterised by a continuous dialogue between Parliament and Government (extensible to other bodies, according to the subject matter in question). In the first phase, which concludes with the approval of the delegation law (normally, originating from a governmental initiative), the last word remains with the Parliament; in the second phase, which terminates with

[20] See BG Mattarella, *Burocrazia e riforme: L'innovazione nella pubblica amministrazione* (Bologna, Il Mulino, 2017) esp 19ff.

the adoption of the legislative decree, once the opinions of parliamentary committees and other bodies individuated by the delegation law have been collected, it is the Government, instead, which has the last word, and which defines the norms that enter into force.

A third and last phase has tended to be added to the previous two, almost systematically since the 1990s. The delegation law often delegates to the Government the power not only to adopt one legislative decree (and even more than one if the objects are multiple and articulated), but also, within a further deadline (normally one or two more years), to correct and integrate their contents, through further '*corrective*' *legislative decrees*, which need to comply with the same principles and criteria and to follow the same procedure.[21] In this way, by adopting these corrective legislative decrees, the Government can have second thoughts and revise the legal provisions set out in the first series of legislative decrees, in the light of their implementation.

The use of legislative decrees has been, generally speaking, less intensive than decree-laws and more equally distributed between different Governments and legislative terms. Legislative decrees have been used very frequently in relation to certain types of subject matter (including new codes, administrative reforms and implementation of EU directives), often characterised by a high degree of complexity, either legal or 'political'.

The advantages derive primarily from the organisation of the decision-making and its pre-defined timeframe: first, the main directions, the *ratio*; then, the provision to be applied, the *voluntas*.[22] The disadvantages relate to the fact that delegation laws may be too wide and vaguely defined and sometimes are not implemented at all by the Government. In this case, there are only political consequences, as the Government is not deemed to be legally bound to implement the delegation law.

What happens if a legislative decree fails to comply with the principles and criteria established by the delegation law? In one of its first judgments, the Constitutional Court clarified that such a legislative decree would infringe not only the delegation law, but also the constitution, albeit indirectly. Indeed, according to the Court, Articles 76 and 77.1 require that the constitutional legitimacy of the legislative

[21] See N Lupo, *Deleghe e decreti legislativi 'correttivi': esperienze, problemi, prospettive* (Milan, Giuffrè 1996); M Cartabia, 'I decreti legislativi "integrativi e correttivi": il paradosso dell'effettività?' (1997) 39(1) *Rassegna parlamentare* 45; and M Ruotolo, 'I limiti della legislazione delegata integrativa e correttiva' in *La delega legislativa* (Milan, Giuffrè, 2009).

[22] G Zagrebelsky, 'Conclusioni' in *La delega legislativa* (n 21) 319.

decree is subordinated to its conformity with the delegation law.[23] This is true for all the limitations it provides, including the procedural ones, as the violation of each of them constitutes an 'excess from the delegation' (*eccesso di delega*).

C. Regulations

While both decree-laws and legislative decrees are classified as primary sources of law, regulations (*regolamenti*) adopted by the Government are included among the secondary sources. This means that, according to the hierarchical principle, they are subordinated to laws and all other primary sources. Indeed, this principle was developed to deal with the relationship between law and regulation and then also extended and applied to the relationship between the (rigid) Constitution and law.

Originally, the typical legal denomination 'regulation' was mainly the outcome of a doctrinal and judicial elaboration. It did not appear in the Constitution, except in very specific cases, regarding the powers of the President of the Republic to enact 'decrees having the force of law and regulations' (Article 87), and regional regulations (to be adopted, according to the original constitutional text, by the Regional Councils: Article 121). It only became an official and mandatory legal denomination in 1988, when law no 400/1988 (Article 17) required the regulations to adopt this name when published in the Official Journal.[24] At the same time, law no 400/1988 also defined the procedures to be followed for the adoption of governmental regulations and ministerial regulations: the former must be approved by the Council of Ministers, while the latter – which are hierarchically subordinated to governmental regulations, being obliged not to conflict with them – are issued by the Minister, after communicating them to the President of the Council. For both governmental and ministerial regulations, the opinion of the Council of State (to be expressed within 90 days), as well as screening and registration by the Court of Accounts, are also required. All these regulations, as noted, are published in the official journal.[25]

[23] Judgment no 3/1957.

[24] See L Carlassare, 'Il ruolo del Parlamento e la nuova disciplina del potere regolamentare' (1990) 10(1) *Quaderni costituzionali* 7 and E Cheli, 'Ruolo dell'esecutivo e sviluppi recenti del potere regolamentare' (ibid) 53.

[25] N Lupo, *Dalla legge al regolamento. Lo sviluppo della potestà normativa del governo nella disciplina delle pubbliche amministrazioni* (Bologna, Il Mulino, 2003) 21ff.

Precisely in order to reduce the large number of legal norms in force, and especially of primary sources of law, of the Italian legal order (usually referred to as a high degree of 'legification'), law no 400/1988 conceived and designed a model of '*delegification*': a way of moving a certain subject matter from a primary to a secondary source of law, that is, from a law to a regulation. In order to achieve such a result, paradoxically, a new law is inevitably required: a law that repeals the legislation previously in force, postponing the effect of such repeal until the moment at which the new regulation enters into force. This is precisely the model chosen by Article 17.2 of law no 400/1988, with the addition of a couple of elements: first, similarly to how the Constitution requires the principles and criteria to be indicated by the delegation law, the law of delegification should specify the general norms regulating the subject matter; second, according to an addition made in 2009, the opinion of the parliamentary committees should also be heard, within 30 days, on every draft regulation determining a delegification. Indeed, in the institutional practice, the general norms have been rather vague, when not completely absent, and so the procedural limitations have been more relevant than the substantive ones.

V. THE DISTINCTION BETWEEN POLITICS AND ADMINISTRATION

The Italian Constitution reflects a traditional view of public administration and thus included very few provisions with respect to it within the section dedicated to the Government. According to the principle of ministerial responsibility, each minister is responsible for the activity of her/his own ministry (Article 95): it implies an administration that is subject to the direction and guidance of the Government, that is, of the parliamentary majority, in the name of political aims and choices

At the same time, the Constitution recognises the principles of impartiality and good functioning of the public administration (Article 97), which potentially conflict with the principle of ministerial responsibility: according to the former principles, administrative activity should be carried out impartially and following the good rules of administrative sciences.

One way of solving the potential conflicts among these principles has been the distinction between politics and administration. This distinction, which has been drawn by the legislation approved since the 1990s, first for local governments and then for the State and the whole public administration, assigns the responsibility for all managerial activity to civil servants, while the guidance role and the checks aimed at verifying whether the political directions have been correctly followed are granted exclusively to political figures (such as ministers, mayors and so on). In other words, a distinct separation between policy-setting powers and management responsibilities is pursued: on the one hand, political bodies 'have the power of defining the aims and programs, allocating resources, monitoring performance and results, appointing managers to carry out specific jobs and revoking appointments should they prove ineffective'; while on the other hand, managers 'are entrusted with all responsibility for management including the power to adopt administrative measures not reserved for political bodies'.[26]

During the same years, the majoritarian turn of the Italian institutional dynamics (see Chapter 3) brought about the approval of several pieces of legislation adopting a kind of '*spoils system*' in the appointment of the administrative management: in the sense of allowing the appointment of civil servants in managerial position due to their being close to the politicians winning the election and holding a public mandate (as minister, mayor or so on), substituting and dismissing the previous holders of those managerial positions.

Many of these provisions have been the subject of Constitutional Court judgments, in which the Court has dramatically reduced the potential for a spoils system and has affirmed as fully consistent with the Constitution, in general terms, 'the separation between the tasks of political leadership and administrative direction'. For instance, the Court declared unconstitutional, as infringing Articles 97 and 98, a provision of law no 145/2002 that provided 'for an automatic termination mechanism (the so-called "one-off spoils system") *ex lege* and generally applying to general level directorship appointments on expiry of the sixty-day deadline following the entry into force of the law' that introduced the mechanism. In fact, according to the Court, 'formulated in these terms and given the absence of procedural guarantees – insofar as it provides for the automatic termination of the assignment to a particular office still in existence prior to the expiry of the pre-set deadline – the above provision violates', in particular, the principle of continuity of administrative action which is closely related to that of good functioning of public administration.[27]

[26] F Bassanini, 'Overview of Administrative Reform and Implementation in Italy: Organization, Personnel, Procedures and Delivery of Public Services' (2000) 23(2/3) *International Journal of Public Administration* 229.

[27] The excerpts are taken from Judgment no 103/2007 (see also Judgments nos 104/2007, 34/2010, 304/2010).

After the clarification provided by the Constitutional Court, the spoils system is deemed permissible only with reference to the so-called 'top managers' of the administration and to the staff directly supporting ministers or mayors.

VI. THE CONSTITUTIONAL PRINCIPLES ON PUBLIC ADMINISTRATION

Notwithstanding their position, the constitutional principles established by Articles 97 and 98 are applicable not only to central government ministerial administration but also to any kind of public administration in general, including regional, local, and independent administrative authorities.[28] Furthermore, although these principles refer exclusively to the organisation design, they have also been deemed applicable to the exercise of their functions, either through authoritative instruments typical of public law or through contractual means typical of civil law. The public administration pursues a public interest as identified by the law. This is the *legality principle*, which has a twofold meaning: (a) the public administration can do only what it is authorised to do by law; and (b) the public administration is obliged to respect the law. The actual content of the legality principle is the subject of debate, in particular whether it is sufficient for the law to just offer a formal basis for the administrative activity or whether it should also define some substantive elements.[29]

In addition, from the standpoint of the Italian legal order, it is clear that EU law can also satisfy the legality principle, as has been recognised by the Constitutional Court.[30] More recently, this has been made even more explicit by a constitutional amendment adding a first paragraph to Article 97, according to which administrative bodies have to 'ensure balanced budgets and the sustainability of public debts' and

[28] See M Nigro and E Cardi, 'L'azione dei pubblici poteri. Lineamenti generali' in G Amato and A Barbera (eds), *Manuale di diritto pubblico* (Bologna, Il Mulino, 1994) esp 720ff.

[29] See N Lupo and G Piccirilli, 'The Relocation of the Legality Principle by the European Courts' Case Law: An Italian Perspective' (2015) 11(1) *European Constitutional Law Review* 55; and G Napolitano, 'The Rule of Law' in P Cane and others (eds), *The Oxford Handbook of Comparative Administrative Law* (Oxford, Oxford University Press, 2021) 421–42.

[30] *Inter alia*, Judgment no 383/1998.

must do so 'in accordance with European Union Law'. In this way, the Italian Constitution re-affirmed the *primauté* of EU law and the fact that the administration is called upon to apply and to respect EU law (see Chapter 2).

The legality principle is also developed through the rule that it is up to the law to define the areas of competence, the duties and the responsibilities of the officials (Article 97.3). Moreover, importantly, the legality principle implies the right to judicial review with respect to any decision taken by the public administration: as Article 113 specifies, 'legal action is always admissible before an ordinary or administrative court to protect one's own rights and legitimate interests'. It is on the basis of these constitutional provisions that ordinary, and especially administrative, judges have been empowered to undertake a particularly profound form of judicial adjudication on every act issued by any administration (see Chapter 8).

Article 97.2 contains the other two fundamental principles of public administration, to which all the others are connected: the principle of good functioning (*buon andamento*) and the impartiality principle.

The *principle of good functioning* includes, in rather generic terms, many of the principles that have been elaborated in administrative management and in the theories that stress the need to adapt the administration to a democratic state: namely, efficacy, efficiency, transparency, participation, simplification and timeliness. It closely links to the previously mentioned need to ensure balanced budgets and to the principle of sustainability, which explicitly refers only to public debt, but could potentially extend to any other public good. A similar principle is also stated in Article 41 of the EU's Charter of Fundamental Rights (the right to good administration: 'Every person has the right to have his or her affairs handled impartially, fairly and within a reasonable time by the institutions, bodies, offices and agencies of the Union'), with a more updated list of actual rights attributed to all citizens in their relationship with public offices (including the right to be heard and to have access to their files).

The *impartiality principle* requires the public administration to act impartially, that is, treating the same situations equally, while differentiating, reasonably, its approach in the case of different situations. The impartiality principle is applied to other (constitutional) rules relating to civil servants. For example, 'public officials are chosen through competitive evaluations, except in the cases established by law' (Article 97.4); and it is 'the duty of public officials to only serve the Nation' (Article 98.1).

VII. THE AUXILIARY BODIES AND THE INDEPENDENT AUTHORITIES

In relation to the exercise of some administrative functions, the need to ensure the impartiality principle is perceived as being particularly dominant and pressing. Consequently, the degree of independence of the bodies that are called upon to exercise such administrative functions is increased and even reaches a level which, to a certain extent, is comparable to that of a judicial body.

This is the case, first of all, with respect to some auxiliary bodies: not coincidentally, due to a constitutional choice, both the Council of State (*Consiglio di Stato*) and the Court of Accounts (*Corte dei conti*, sometimes also translated as the Court of Auditors) are concurrently administrative bodies and judicial ones (as an appeal administrative judge and a specialised judge on accounting responsibility and pensions, respectively: see Chapter 8). As these two bodies wear these 'double hats', namely advisory and judicial at the same time, this clearly means that their degree of independence, required by the law in accordance with Article 100.3, is regarded as inadequate.

In any event, the Council of State is called upon to provide advice on legal-administrative matters (Article 100.1), normally through opinions that are mandatory and preventive, but not binding, issued by its advisory sections. The Court of Accounts exercises preventive legality control of the governmental acts and subsequent control regarding the management of the State budget, and participates in the fiscal control of those bodies to which the State normally contributes. It is asked to report the results of its audits directly to the Parliament (Article 100.2), thereby assuming the role of auxiliary body in its relations both with the Government and the Parliament.

The third auxiliary body established by the Constitution (Article 99), that is, the National Council of Economy and Labour (CNEL), is rather peculiar, as it is not composed solely of experts (it includes only 10, appointed by the President of the Republic and the President of the Council of Ministers), but consists mainly of industry representatives (54 in total, representing trade unions, companies, self-employment, social promotion and volunteer organisations). It is called upon to offer advice to the Parliament and Government and is given the right to initiate legislation. Overall, while originally a sort of 'leftover' of the attempt to design an Upper House representative of social categories, the CNEL has not, to date, played a significant role and has been object of many reform attempts and even suppression (through a constitutional amendment).

A high degree of independence is granted to a series of other public bodies, normally qualified as '*independent administrative authorities*' (or, in short, 'independent authorities' or even 'authorities'), which are called upon to pursue some kind of public policies in delicate fields, where any interference by the Government or political parties would be perceived as a danger to the effectiveness of these policies.

By far the oldest of these bodies, although normally excluded from this category, is the Bank of Italy, established since 1893 (by unifying the three major banks then existing in Italy). Its independence has been increased in recent decades, before the European Central Bank (ECB) was granted the power in 1998 to issue the banknotes and to conduct the single monetary policy (to which the Bank of Italy still contributes, as a member of the European System of Central Banks (ESCB)). Its main function now consists in banking and financial supervision, in part to be exercised alone, and in part within the framework of the European Banking Union and within the Supervisory Board of the European Central Bank.

A series of independent administrative authorities were established in the 1970s (the Authority for regulation of the securities market, CONSOB, in 1974) and then, more intensively, in the 1990s, when a process of privatisation started, with the need to ensure some kind of specialised regulator for the new markets so established. This is the case of the Antitrust Authority (AGCM), established in 1990, and called upon to take care of competition and fair trading, and subsequently also repression of unfair commercial practices, misleading and unlawful comparative advertising and the application of conflicts of interest to government offices.

More sectoral approaches and jurisdictions characterise the Regulatory Authority for Energy, Networks and the Environment (ARERA), founded in 1995 and renamed in 2017 (formerly Regulation Authority for Electricity and Gas); the Communication Authority (AGCOM), founded in 1997; the Regulatory Authority for Transportation (ART), established since 2011; and the Institute for the Supervision of Insurance (IVASS), in 2012 (formerly ISVAP, since 1982), currently strictly connected to the Bank of Italy.

Due to its duty to protect certain fundamental rights, the Data Protection Authority (*Garante per la protezione dei dati personali*), set up in 1996, has some peculiar features; as do the Authority for the Supervision of Strikes in Public Services (*Commissione di garanzia dellááttuazione della legge sullo sciopero nei servizi pubblici essenziali*), in existence since 1990; and the National Anti-corruption Authority

(ANAC), which has been operating since 2014, absorbing the competences of the pre-existing Authority on Public Procurement (in existence since 1994).

This large and not always well-defined group of independent administrative authorities, although not governed by the Constitution, is characterised by some common elements. These are mainly related to the fact that in most cases their independence finds some legal basis in EU law: a law that the same authorities are often asked to apply and enforce, relying also on European networks that encompass all the national authorities of that kind. The rules regarding the appointment of their members, who should be characterised by a high level of technical expertise and obviously of independence, are rather different, including according to the phase during which the relevant piece of legislation that established each body was approved. The civil servants working for them are normally more carefully selected and better paid than those working for central and local government.

Finally, as they are still administrative authorities and not part of the judiciary, notwithstanding their rather high degree of independence, all their acts can be brought before a judge: the administrative judge, for most of them, and the ordinary judge for the Data Protection Authority. For the same reasons, they are not deemed to be qualified as judges allowed to raise, incidentally, a question of constitutionality before the Constitutional Court.[31]

VIII. CONCLUSION

In the Italian Republican experience, Governments have traditionally been characterised by their short duration: their average length being around one year, the shortest in the whole European Union).[32]

The instability of the Governments and their consequent inability to pursue a clear political and administrative agenda are at least in part due to a choice that, as has already been observed (see Chapters 1 and 3), dates back to the Constituent Assembly. At that time, given the need to

[31] In this sense, with reference to the Antitrust Authority, Judgment no 19/2019.

[32] See T Saalfeld, 'Economic Performance, Political Institutions and Cabinet Durability in 28 Parliamentary Democracies (1945–2011)' in WC Müller and HM Narud (eds), *Party Governance and Party Democracy, Festschrift to Kaare Strøm* (New York, Springer, 2013) and L Curini and L Pinto, *L'arte di fare (e disfare) i governi: Da De Gasperi a Renzi, 70 anni di politica italiana* (Milan, Egea, 2017) esp 153ff.

differentiate themselves from the preceding Fascist regime, and as no one could foresee the outcome of the first parliamentary election, to be held in 1948, all the political parties preferred to design a weak Executive and not to provide within the Constitution all the institutional mechanisms available to secure its mandate. In other words, the parties that would have lost that 1948 election obtained a kind of 'insurance', as they were granted the right to put hurdles in the path of the Government's activity and, concurrently, to be actively involved in parliamentary law-making (also thanks to the secret ballot: see Chapter 4).

It comes as no surprise, therefore, that the recurrent objectives of many constitutional amendments, as well as of electoral reforms pursued during the last 40 years, have been to stabilise the Government, thus developing the original intent of the Perassi resolution.

The mere fact that these aims are still pursued by several institutional reform projects shows that they have only been very partially achieved and that the evolution towards a more stable Executive and a majoritarian democracy has encountered many hurdles and difficulties. In fact, since 1993 the average duration of an Italian Government has significantly increased, although it remains well below the EU average. In the meantime, the need for a more stable Government has been accentuated by the dynamics of the EU institutional system, in which actors with 'longer mandates or terms of office, and more extended future time horizons are privileged'.[33] Moreover, in order to become fully effective, the transformation of the political and institutional system which commenced in 1993 would have required a different administrative apparatus, at both the central as well as the local levels. Even the recurrent experience of the so-called 'technocratic Governments' (Ciampi, 1993–94; Dini, 1995–96; Monti, 2011–13; Draghi, 2021–present) may be seen as a clear sign of a persistent difficulty in achieving Executives that are directly legitimated by the voters, while also being capable of maintaining their own parliamentary majority in the two Houses and, simultaneously, of complying with EU budgetary and policy obligations.[34]

[33] Cf K Goetz, 'Political leadership in the European Union: A Time-centred View' (2017) 16 *European Political Science* 48.

[34] See N Lupo, 'I "governi tecnici". Gli esecutivi Ciampi, Dini e Monti nel difficile equilibrio tra tecnica e politica' (2015) 1 *Rassegna parlamentare* 57 and D McDonnell and M Valbruzzi, 'Defining and Classifying Technocrat-Led and Technocratic Governments' (2014) 53(4) *European Journal of Political Research* 654.

FURTHER READING

Bassanini, F, 'Overview of Administrative Reform and Implementation in Italy: Organization, Personnel, Procedures and Delivery of Public Services' (2000) 23(2/3) *International Journal of Public Administration* 229.

Calise, M, 'Government and Prime Minister' in E Jones and G Pasquino (eds), *The Oxford Handbook of Italian Politics* (Oxford, Oxford University Press, 2015) 95–106.

Campus, D, and Pasquino, G, 'Leadership in Italy: The Changing Role of Leaders in Elections and in Government' (2006) 14(1) *Journal of Contemporary European Studies* 25.

Cotta, M, and Verzichelli, L, *Political Institutions in Italy* (Oxford, Oxford University Press, 2007) 103–36.

6

The President of the Republic

Indirect Election – Responsibility – Impeachment – High Treason – Attempt to Overthrow the Constitution – Countersignature – Presidential Acts – Pardons – Dissolution of the Parliament – Appointment of the Government – *Super partes* Institution – Political Crisis

I. INTRODUCTION

THE STRUCTURAL FEATURES and the role of the head of State may significantly vary within parliamentary forms of government. In order to show this, it suffices to look at the EU Member States.

In six cases the head of State remains, according to a hereditary principle, a monarch (namely, Belgium, Denmark, Luxembourg, the Netherlands, Spain and Sweden). The role performed by the monarch is quite definite and can be characterised as mainly symbolic and ceremonial, and therefore, consistently with the democratic principle, marginal within the political and institutional dynamic.

The remaining 21 States are called Republics and their head of State is named the President of the Republic. Only in Cyprus, where a fully presidential model is adopted, is the head of State also the head of the Government. In the other 20 Republics, it is important to identify whether there is a popular or a parliamentary election of the head of State. In the first category (comprising 13 States: namely, Austria, Bulgaria, Croatia, the Czech Republic, Finland, France, Ireland, Lithuania, Poland, Portugal, Romania, Slovakia and Slovenia), it is necessary to check whether the head of State is also directly involved in the activity of the Government: if so, qualifying them as semi-presidential systems (as is certainly the case in France, while other cases, such as Lithuania, Portugal and Romania, are more controversial). In the second category (comprising seven States: namely, Estonia, Germany, Greece, Hungary, Italy, Latvia and Malta), as the president is only indirectly elected the States are clearly parliamentary governments, but with different roles assigned to the President of the Republic, who does not always play a merely symbolic and ceremonial role. As part of the same parliamentary form of government, primarily symbolic and ceremonial actors may well co-exist with very powerful figures, who play some of the leading roles in the political and institutional arena. The office is strongly influenced by the existing political situation and its cultural and historical characteristics.

The Italian model confirms this variability: where the party system is strong and the political direction imposed by the people in a general election is clear, the President of the Republic tends to exercise less power and the converse applies when there is no clear majority and political uncertainty results.

The Italian President of the Republic, far from being confined to a ceremonial role, has played a crucial part in many turning points of Italian political and institutional history.

II. ELECTION, TERM OF OFFICE AND SUBSTITUTION

The Presidents of the Italian Republic have been elected by the Parliament in joint session with the addition of 58 regional representatives. Three representatives are elected per Region by each regional council (normally from among its own members) according to a system which allows the participation of minorities. The unique exception is the Val d'Aosta Region, which elects only one representative (Article 83). The participation of regional representatives, although quantitatively rather limited, is aimed at enlarging the President's representative basis, demonstrating that the President's role has 'represented national unity' since its genesis (Article 87.1).

The same objective is pursued by the electoral thresholds required for the President's election, which start extremely high and then diminish, in order to ensure that an election may be achieved within a reasonable timeframe. In the first three votes, two-thirds of the members are required, while 50 per cent plus one of the members are required in all the subsequent votes. There are only two cases in which the President was elected in the first vote (Cossiga in 1985; Ciampi in 1999), while on all the other occasions the election took place after the third vote: indeed, on the fourth vote in four cases (Einaudi in 1948; Gronchi in 1955; Napolitano in 2006; and Mattarella in 2015). The President who needed the highest number of votes to be elected (23) was Leone, in 1971 (obtaining the votes of 52 per cent of the members). The greatest degree of support was received by Pertini, who was elected on the sixteenth vote in 1978, by 84 per cent of the members.

In order to be elected, the President must be an Italian citizen who enjoys civil and political rights and has attained 50 years of age. Once elected, the President's mandate lasts for *seven years*. The Constitution does not specify whether the President may be re-elected for a second term. However, the fact that, for 55 years, such re-election had never occurred supported the supposition that some kind of constitutional convention existed, prohibiting a second mandate. Nevertheless, following the re-election of President Napolitano in 2013, this hypothesis was revealed to be incorrect, although Napolitano declared from the beginning that he had accepted the second mandate only in light of the very special surrounding circumstances, and that this second mandate would not last for seven years (and indeed he resigned after less than two years).

When the President of the Republic cannot perform her/his functions, either due to temporary reasons (such as travel or surgery) or due to permanent incapacity, death or resignation, these functions will be exercised by the President of the Senate, who acts as a substitute. Concurrently, where the relevant incapacity is not temporary, and in order to avoid the risk of a President of the Senate seeking to maintain this substitution for an extended period, and obstructing the election of a new President of the Republic, the President of the Chamber of Deputies, in the capacity of the President of the Parliament in joint session, is assigned the task of calling an election to replace the current President (Article 86).

III. THE RESPONSIBILITY OF THE PRESIDENT OF THE REPUBLIC

As already noted (see Chapter 1), Italy's choice of a Republic rather than a Monarchy was accomplished via a referendum, which took place at the same time as the election of the Constituent Assembly, on 2 June 1946. The outcome was clear, although divisive (the southern part of Italy having voted decisively in favour of the Monarchy). This choice was thus pre-determined, once the Constituent Assembly started taking constitutional matters into its own hands. This same Constituent Assembly, in its third sitting, elected the provisional Head of State, Enrico De Nicola: a liberal from Naples, with monarchical sympathies, who was chosen in order to represent the country in its entirety.

Given that in Italy, as in many other European States, the role of the President of the Republic is modelled after the Monarch, the rules regarding the President's responsibility are also derived from those ordinarily applied to the Monarch, which recognise the 'irresponsibility' of the position (and which are normally encapsulated by the expression 'The King can do no wrong'). This traditional principle, however, needs to be balanced against the opposing notion, which comprises one of the cornerstones of liberal and democratic states: that every power corresponds to a kind of responsibility.

This means that the President of the Republic is generally deprived of any kind of (legal) responsibility, with only two exceptions, related to very specific and grave crimes. The Constitution (Article 90.1) states that 'The President of the Republic is not responsible for the actions performed in the exercise of the presidential duties, except in the case of high treason or attempt to overthrow the Constitution'. Immediately following this statement, the Constitution (Article 90.2) establishes a special procedure which permits the prosecution of the President on charges of having committed such crimes: 'In such cases, the President may be impeached by Parliament in joint session, with an absolute majority of its members'.

Once impeached by the Parliament, the President of the Republic should then be judged by the Constitutional Court (Article 134), composed in a very special manner (Article 135.7):

> In impeachment procedures against the President of the Republic, apart from the ordinary judges of the Court, there shall also be sixteen members chosen by lot from among a list of citizens having the qualification necessary for election to the Senate, which the Parliament prepares every nine years through election using the same procedures as those followed in appointing ordinary judges.

Consequently, this very delicate task, which can result in the suspension or dismissal of the President of the Republic, is assigned to an 'ad hoc' judicial body comprising 31 members in total, the majority of whom are unknown at the time at which the Parliament in joint session decides to prosecute the President, as there is a random selection of 16 names out of 45 names of eligible people.[1]

There is an ongoing debate as to how these two crimes should be interpreted and defined. The first type of offence, namely high treason

[1] Until the constitutional amendment approved in 1989 (constitutional law no 1/1989), the Constitutional Court, in the same special composition, also had jurisdiction in cases of impeachment of the President of the Council and of Ministers for crimes committed in the exercise of their duties (and this happened only once, in the 1979 *Lockheed* case). These individuals are now prosecuted by ordinary courts, although only once the Senate or the Chamber has authorised them to proceed (Art 96 of the Constitution).

(*alto tradimento*), is traditionally viewed as seeking to encompass conspiracies with foreign and enemy States, while the second, that is, an attempt to overthrow the Constitution (*attentato alla Costituzione*), tends to be interpreted as comprising fraudulent, macroscopic and repeated violations of the basic elements of the constitutional order.[2] According to other theories, the expression should instead be read as a whole and complex type of offence, necessarily including both an external dimension (the treason) and an internal one (the aim to overthrow the Constitution).[3]

However, this is essentially a hypothetical debate, as no such impeachment process has ever been commenced by the Parliament in joint session, although some Presidents of the Republic have been forewarned that charges may be laid (and these were even formalised, in Cossiga's case).[4]

The rule is, however, that the President bears no responsibility for the acts carried out in the course of performing her/his own duties, with the exception of these two crimes, and is devoid of proper political responsibility (leaving aside some kind of diffused political responsibility, consisting in criticisms in the media or in the political debate). As the Constitutional Court has clarified, it is generally accepted that the immunity provided by Article 90 'is all-embracing, ie that it applies to acts of criminal, civil, administrative and political relevance'.[5] This also means that investigative instruments, such as telephone taps, may only be used for the purposes of ascertaining the commission of the abovementioned serious offences, in order to avoid jeopardising the 'power of persuasion' that the President of the Republic, as a 'body of influence', is called upon to exercise on a daily basis and which necessarily requires a high degree of privacy and confidentiality.

The same Constitutional Court judgment also highlighted that, in relation to offences not committed during the course of her/his duties, 'the President is subject to the same form of criminal responsibility as any other person'. However, this should arguably permit the use of more invasive tools for the collection of evidence, which should not 'cause harm to the President's communications'.[6]

[2] See, among others, G Scarlato, 'Presidente della Repubblica: II) Responsabilità penale del Presidente della Repubblica' in *Enciclopedia giuridica* XXIV (Rome, Istituto della Enciclopedia italiana, 1991).

[3] Cf R Bin and G Pitruzzella, *Diritto costituzionale* (Turin, Giappichelli, 2020) 512.

[4] See E Galavotti, 'Francesco Cossiga' in S Cassese, G Galasso and A Melloni (eds), *I Presidenti della Repubblica: Il capo dello Stato e il Quirinale nella storia della democrazia italiana* (Bologna, Il Mulino, 2018) 325–63, 350.

[5] Judgment no 1/2013.

[6] Judgment no 1/2013.

IV. THE COUNTER-SIGNATURE AND THE CLASSIFICATION OF THE ACTS OF THE PRESIDENT OF THE REPUBLIC

Closely connected with the traditional principle that 'The King can do no wrong' is the proposition that 'The King cannot act alone'. The latter principle provides the basis for the requirement of a *counter-signature*, by a member of the Government who assumes responsibility for it, of every act signed by the Monarch, who is, by definition, not responsible for her/his own acts. Entirely consistent with this tradition is the constitutional rule according to which 'No act of the President of the Republic is valid if it is not signed by the proposing Minister, who assumes responsibility for it' (Article 89.1). This is a crucial requirement, which contributes to clarifying the role and responsibilities of the President of the Republic within the Italian form of government, as well as identifying and, consequently, classifying the different kinds of acts signed by the President of the Republic (most of which are listed, without any internal hierarchy, by Article 87).

Indeed, the formulation of the constitutional provision regarding counter-signature has been regarded as too drastic, and not very precise. For example, the provision's reference to the '*proposing Minister*' is not entirely correct, as not every act of the President of the Republic actually originates from a proposal of a member of the Government. That is why the constitutional expression is ordinarily interpreted as requiring the counter-signature of the '*competent Minister*' and the respective roles and significance of the signature and counter-signatures vary, depending on the category into which the relevant presidential act falls. In other words, most of the time, the ministerial counter-signature identifies the member of the Government who is the proponent of the act in question (regarding *formally presidential, but substantively governmental, acts*). In other, less frequent cases, the counter-signature implies a mere acknowledgment of the decision reached by the President of the Republic and a kind of certification of authenticity of the President's signature (regarding *fully presidential acts*). In a couple of very special and crucial cases, the provision is interpreted as requiring an agreement or an acceptance of a decision taken jointly by the Government and the President of the Republic (regarding so-called *dual acts*).

As stated by the Constitutional Court, the counter-signature 'takes on a different value depending on the type of procedure which it completes or, more precisely, for the validity of which it is a prerequisite'. This means that 'the counter-signature plays a substantive role when the act presented for signature by the Head of State is governmental in nature and therefore an expression of the powers vested in the Executive, whilst it must be recognised as having a merely formal value where the act is an expression of the powers vested in the President of the Republic'.[7]

A. Formally Presidential, but Substantively Governmental, Acts

The most numerous category of presidential acts are the ones that are formally presidential, but in substance governmental: in other words, the content of the presidential decree is determined by the Government, which proposed it. Consequently, the counter-signature has the purpose of identifying the 'proposing Minister', while the President's signature merely serves to attest to the fact that the acts in question actually originated from the Government and appear to be compliant with the requirements established by the Constitution and, more generally, by the legal order.

As noted, the vast majority of presidential decrees (*decreti del Presidente della Repubblica*-DPR) normally form part of this category. These include, for example:

- almost all acts of appointment (of the highest levels of public servants, such as prefects and ambassadors), which usually follow the deliberation of the Council of Ministers;
- ratification of international treaties, negotiated by the Government, after Parliament's authorisation in the case of the treaties which are of a political nature, or which call for arbitration or legal settlements, or which entail changes to the national territory or financial burdens or changes to legislation (Article 80);
- dissolution of municipal councils, in cases established by legislation;[8]
- declaration of war, taking place after the Houses deliberate the state of war, conferring upon the Government the necessary powers (Article 79);
- authorisation to submit the Government's legislative initiatives to one of the Houses;
- the convening of parliamentary elections and referendums; and
- enactment of legislative decrees and decree-laws (Articles 76 and 77, respectively), following deliberation by the Council of Ministers.

[7] Judgment no 200/2006.
[8] Arts 141 and 143 Legislative Decree no 267/2000.

This category also ordinarily includes the promulgation of laws. However, in this case, there is a specific constitutional regulation, according to which laws must be promulgated by the President of the Republic, within one month of their approval (Article 73). Before doing so, the President of the Republic may request, providing justification, that the Houses deliberate again. Nevertheless, 'if the Houses pass the bill once again, then the law must be promulgated' (Article 74).

Consequently, the Constitution frames the power to deny the promulgation of laws as a suspensive veto, which can only cause a temporary delay and can be overruled by the Parliament simply by re-approving the piece of legislation, without any requirement that a greater parliamentary majority be achieved. It is debatable whether the President of the Republic can invoke, as reasons for rejection, only issues as to constitutional legitimacy or also substantive issues. The institutional practice demonstrates a moderate, although not insignificant, usage of this instrument (61 rejections in total, from 1948 to 2021), almost always motivated – *inter alia* – by doubts as to the law's constitutional legitimacy, especially in the case of insufficient financial resources (the violation of Article 81 representing more than 50 per cent of the cases).

In several other cases, especially during the last two decades, the President of the Republic has decided to promulgate a piece of legislation, declaring at the same time some doubts and critical issues (often called 'promulgation with a critical motivation'). This is normally decided after having consumed almost the entire 30 days at the President's disposal. The promulgation has been associated with a letter – addressed to the Speakers of the two Houses and to the President of the Council – in which the President raised a series of doubts regarding the constitutionality and the substance of the law's content (thereby requesting some modifications to the law just promulgated, to be passed by subsequent legislation).

Consistent with this practice, the President of the Republic has also maintained that the decision not to promulgate a piece of legislation should occur only in cases of evident constitutional violation. Otherwise, a more accurate and in-depth assessment of its compliance with the Constitution is the responsibility of the Constitutional Court.[9]

[9] See, for instance, the declaration of President Ciampi (who features among the presidents who have most intensively used the veto power) in Berlin on 27 June 2003. This argument, however, has been criticised by the majority of scholars: see I Pellizzone, *Contributo allo studio sul rinvio pregiudiziale delle leggi* (Milan, Giuffrè, 2011) 149ff.

When the President of the Republic has refused to promulgate a piece of legislation, the issues raised by the President are always taken into consideration by Parliament, either by not approving the piece of legislation again or at least by amending the provisions that have been the subject of a presidential attention. Therefore, the scenario anticipated by the Constitution, in which the President of the Republic would be obliged to promulgate a piece of legislation when it has been approved for a second time with the same text, following a suspensive veto, has never yet occurred. It is worth noting, however, that according to the most authoritative scholarship,[10] the President of the Republic might refuse the promulgation of a law despite it having been approved again in cases in which, by doing so, the President would be liable for committing high treason or attempting to overthrow the Constitution. In this way, some leeway is preserved for the President where Parliament decides to completely ignore the President's remarks.

B. Fully (Both Formally and Substantively) Presidential Acts

The category of fully presidential acts comprises a limited but distinctive series of acts, whose content is determined entirely by the President of the Republic. This means that the significance of the signature and counter-signature tends to be 'swapped' when compared with the previous category of acts: the counter-signature by the member of the Government merely attests to the fact that the act in question actually originated with the President of the Republic and seems compliant with the requirements established by the Constitution and the legislation.

Among the clearest examples of these fully presidential acts is the appointment of five life senators (Article 59.2) and of five constitutional judges (Article 135.1), as well as the power to send messages to the Houses (Article 87.2). If there were ever any doubts as to the inclusion of these acts within this category, they were rather quickly overcome, on the basis of the argument that allowing the Government to appoint life senators and constitutional judges would have risked altering the constitutional balance and encouraging a tactical use of these powers. At the time of the Republic's genesis, De Gasperi claimed for himself the

[10] See, *inter alia*, R Romboli, 'Presidente della Repubblica e Corte costituzionale' in M Luciani and M Volpi (eds), *Il Presidente della Repubblica* (Bologna, Il Mulino, 1997) 265ff, 281ff.

power to appoint the judges of the Constitutional Court, in his capacity as the Head of the Government. However, the President of the Republic Einaudi firmly denied him this power, entrenching it in the hands of the Head of State.[11]

It is even clearer that it would not make much sense to empower the Government to send (formal) messages to Parliament, given the fact that the Government has plenty of opportunities to establish a direct dialogue with the two Houses. Indeed, the President of the Republic has also gradually developed a series of other channels of communication with the political parties and public opinion at large, which are normally identified by scholars as 'powers of externalisation' (*poteri di esternazione*): official speeches, end of the year greetings, and press releases are intensively and accurately used by the President of the Republic to create a direct channel of communication with public opinion. This intense usage contributes to explaining the President's very limited deployment of the power to send formal messages to the Parliament.[12]

The classification of the *power to grant pardons and to commute punishments* has been much more controversial: that is, the power to officially forgive a person and to cancel or reduce the punishment already imposed by the judiciary (Article 87.6). Until the early twenty-first century, this was considered to be a substantively governmental power (or a dual power), which was in fact employed rather extensively, especially during the first few decades of the Republic. More recently, a disagreement between the President of the Republic and the Minister of Justice about granting a pardon to two former terrorists (Adriano Sofri and Ovidio Bompressi) brought the issue before the Constitutional Court, which resolved the dispute by establishing that the power to grant a pardon is one of the fully presidential (both formally and substantively) powers.

On the basis of an accurate historical reconstruction, recalling that the power to grant pardons was 'formerly the personal prerogative of absolute sovereigns' and 'furthers essentially humanitarian goals', the Constitutional Court stated that the substantive decision is vested exclusively in the President as 'a *super partes* institution'. This means that the President stands beyond the circuit of political direction, and

[11] A Viarengo, 'Luigi Einaudi' in Cassese, Galasso and Melloni (eds) (n 4) 117–57, 142.

[12] See MC Grisolia, 'Le esternazioni presidenziali' in A Ruggeri (ed), *Evoluzione del sistema politico-istituzionale e ruolo del Presidente della Repubblica* (Turin, Giappichelli, 2011) 177ff, 194ff.

'is called upon to assess in an impartial manner the concrete existence of the humanitarian prerequisites which justify the granting of a pardon'. According to the Court, such a conclusion has the benefit of avoiding 'the assessments of organs which form part of the executive from playing a role in the evaluation of the requirements for the adoption of a measure which has the effect of "quashing" a criminal court sentence'. Therefore, the counter-signature by the Minister of Justice is required simply in order to confirm 'the completeness and regularity of the preliminary inquiries and the procedure followed'.[13]

The Constitutional Court's judgment has been widely discussed, on the basis that the use of the power to grant pardons throughout Italian constitutional history has been far from being capable of characterisation as 'an exceptional instrument intended to satisfy extraordinary needs of a humanitarian nature'.[14] This has been particularly so after 2006, since when some cases may be identified involving the use of this power for different purposes.[15] However, the principle stated by the Constitutional Court has changed the institutional practice and reserved to the President the substantive decision as to granting pardons, after a preliminary analysis has been conducted by the Ministry of Justice (and received by an 'ad hoc' office of the President of the Republic). Consequently, today the power to grant a pardon and commute a punishment is rather uncontroversially classified as a fully presidential power.

C. Complex (or Dual) Acts: Appointment of the Government and Dissolution of the Parliament

The existence of this third category of presidential acts was initially controversial: some scholars denied its validity, assuming that all presidential acts correspond either to a substantively governmental power or to a fully presidential one.[16] However, a very limited number of acts that

[13] Judgment no 200/2006.

[14] As affirmed in Judgment no 200/2006.

[15] More critically, see L Elia, 'La sentenza sul potere di grazia; dal contesto al testo' in *Studi in onore di Nicolò Lipari: Tomo I* (Milan, Giuffrè, 2008) 877ff and A Pugiotto, 'La concessione della grazia (con particolare riferimento alla presidenza Napolitano)' in M D'Amico and B Randazzo (eds), *Alle frontiere del diritto costituzionale: Scritti in onore di Valerio Onida* (Milan, Giuffrè, 2011) 1507–44.

[16] See A Ruggeri, 'Controfirma ministeriale e teoria della Costituzione' in A Brunelli, G Pugiotto and P Veronesi (eds), *Scritti in onore di Lorenza Carlassare: Il diritto costituzionale come regola e limite al potere* (Naples, Jovene, 2009) 693–723.

are substantively co-determined by the President of the Republic and the Government has emerged and has been recognised by the majority of scholars and institutional actors: they are called 'complex' or 'dual' acts (sometimes 'duumviral'), which reflects the fact that in order to complete them, both presidential and governmental consents, roughly on an equal footing, are required.

Indeed, the acts normally comprising this category are probably those which may be considered as the two most important presidential powers within the Italian legal order: the *appointment of the Government* and the *dissolution of the Parliament*. It is through the exercise of these two powers that the President of the Republic has been developing a crucial role in the critical phases of the circuit of political direction. Needless to say, these two presidential powers are closely connected: the alternative to the resolution of a crisis through the appointment of a (new) Government is the drastic decision to dissolve Parliament and to leave the matter to the voters, thereby re-activating the circuit of political direction from scratch.

The process of forming the Government reserves a crucial role to the President of the Republic: the appointment of the President of the Council and, upon the latter's proposal, the appointment of the Ministers actually takes place via a presidential decree (Article 92.2). In order to choose a Cabinet which is potentially capable of receiving a vote of confidence from both Houses during the following 10 days (Article 94.3: see Chapter 5), a sub-process arises which is entirely ruled by non-written conventional norms, all managed by the President of the Republic and taking place primarily on Quirinale Hill in Rome, where the presidential palace is located. The parliamentary nature of the form of government helps us to understand the features of this sub-process: it may be rather quick and smooth when there is a clear majority in Parliament selecting its own leader or, conversely, extremely long and burdensome when a parliamentary majority still needs to be found and sometimes even created by the influence and initiative of the President of the Republic.

The main steps of this sub-process comprise the consultations and the mandate (*incarico*). One or more rounds of consultations, run and managed by the President of the Republic, involve the Speakers of the two Houses and the leaders of parliamentary groups, usually accompanied by the party leaders, and sometimes also former Presidents of the Republic, as well as representatives of trade unions and social organisations. The first aim of the consultations is to select a potential President of the Council to whom a mandate to form a new Cabinet may be assigned. If this outcome does not yet seem possible, the President of the Republic can request the assistance of other institutional personalities, starting from the Speakers of the two Houses. The terminology for defining this assistance can vary ('exploratory mission', 'pre-mandate' or similar), but the substance is that the President of the Republic asks someone else to verify whether any kind of parliamentary majority supporting a Government could possibly emerge and, if so, which one. However, when a mandate is eventually assigned by the President of the Republic, the President of the Council normally accepts the charge 'with reservation' (in other words, conditionally, provided that all conditions are met), and then, in her/his capacity as the President of the Council 'with a mandate' (by definition, co-existing with the outgoing President of the Council, still in charge of current affairs), commences a new series of consultations, normally only with the leaders of the parliamentary groups and the political parties that will potentially comprise the new Government or support it within Parliament.

If and when the mandate is definitely accepted by the President of the Council and the reservation is eventually raised, the more formal steps may be commenced: that is, properly appointing the President of the Council. The new President of the Council counter-signs her/his own presidential decree of appointment, for acceptance, although with a slight temporal inconsistency as she/he is not yet President at the precise time at which the decree is countersigned. Then, the President of the Republic upon the proposal of the President of the Council appoints the Ministers, who also counter-sign their own presidential appointment decrees.

Ordinarily, all signatures and counter-signatures take place during the ceremony in which all the members of the new Government are sworn in by the President of the Republic: it is from this moment that the Government may fully exercise its own functions, substituting the previous Government, although subject to the condition of receiving, within the following 10 days, the vote of confidence from the two Houses.

The classification as dual or complex act of the decree through which the President of the Republic appoints the President of the Council appears to be undisputed: the act clearly derives from the wills of both the President of the Republic and the new President of the Council. More debated is the appointment of Ministers, where the duality of the act derives from the wills of the President of the Council, who proposes the names, on the one hand, and the President of the Republic, who agrees to the proposals, on the other hand, while the new Ministers' acceptance is normally demonstrated by their counter-signature of the decrees. It is debated whether the President of the Republic might veto one or more names of Ministers proposed by the President of the Council and, if it is possible, on the basis of what reasons. Normally, these vetoes have been exercised confidentially, during the hectic hours that precede the formation of a new Government. The debate was renewed in 2018, regarding the formation of the Conte 1 Government and the proposed appointment of a Minister of Economics and Finance, Paolo Savona, who had analysed and supported the exit of Italy from the Eurozone. The President of the Republic, Sergio Mattarella, refused to appoint him as this choice would have determined 'an immediate message of confidence or alarm for economic and financial players'. Consequently, Conte declined the mandate to form a Government, declaring that the two parties would not have supported his Government with a different composition. However, five days later, he managed to propose a different composition of his Government, with a different Minister of Economics and Finance, while Savona was appointed Minister for European Affairs.[17]

The analysis of the power to dissolve Parliament is also complex. It is frequently qualified as a kind of litmus test of the parliamentary form of government, in order to distinguish, internally, between the majoritarian version (in which it is normally up to the President of the Council) and the consensual one (in which it is normally up to the Head of the State).[18] The Constitution makes reference only to the relevant procedure, requiring the President of the Republic to first heed the advice of the Speakers of the two Houses: 'The President of the Republic, having heard the Presidents of the Houses, may dissolve Parliament or even only one House' (Article 88.1).[19] The Constitution does not, however, specify any conditions or pre-requisites that should justify or even impose such a devastating option.

The Constitution demonstrates its full awareness of the saliency of this power as it forbids the President of the Republic from exercising it too close to the end of the seven-year mandate (as this power could be employed tactically as part of a re-election campaign): 'The President

[17] Among many see M Dani and AJ Menendez, 'The "Savona Affaire": Overconstitutionalization in Action?' in *Verfassungsblog*, 31 May 2018 and G Piccirilli, 'Is the institutional crisis in Italy over? Surely a storm, maybe indicating a climate change' (Part I and Part II) in blog-iacl-aidc.org, 7–8 June 2018.

[18] See, *inter alia*, A Barbera, 'Tendenze nello scioglimento delle assemblee parlamentari' (1996) 38(2) *Rassegna parlamentare* 231.

[19] The dissolution of a single House has never taken place in Italian constitutional history (except for the first dissolutions of the Senate, aimed at keeping together the elections for the two Houses: see ch 4). Therefore, the elections of the two Houses have always happened simultaneously.

of the Republic cannot exercise said right during the last six months of the presidential mandate' (Article 88.2). As the formulation of this provision was rather too radical, and risked prohibiting even a so-called 'technical' dissolution, which ordinarily takes place just a few weeks before the natural end of the five-year legislative term, a constitutional amendment (constitutional law no 1/1991, entered into force just before the President's mandate initiated its final six-month period) added the following words: 'unless said period coincides in full or in part with the last six months of Parliament'.

The content of Article 88.2 would indeed support the interpretation of the power to dissolve the Parliament as a fully presidential power. Notwithstanding this, scholars have questioned whether there are some objective elements that constrain the use of this power on the part of the President of the Republic: that is, a series of objective prerequisites, whose existence should also be assented to by the President of the Council. In other words, as the President of the Republic does not seem capable of dissolving Parliament when the same Parliament still gives its confidence to a Government, the President must reach an (informal) agreement with the President of the Council that a situation of crisis exists, and that no other Government could receive a vote of confidence from both Houses, for the dissolution to be fully compliant with the Constitution.[20]

Taking this into consideration, the counter-signature by the President of the Council of the presidential decree of Parliament's dissolution tends to assume a very peculiar character, going beyond the mere attestation of the fact that there is a will of the President of the Republic in this respect: it also confirms that the Government has resigned and that, at least *rebus sic stantibus* (things standing as they are), there is no alternative parliamentary majority in sight.

V. THE SHAPING OF THE ROLE OF THE PRESIDENT OF THE REPUBLIC THROUGHOUT THE CONSTITUTIONAL EXPERIENCE

The text of the Constitution leaves many matters unresolved as to the role of the President of the Republic. It outlines a broad list of powers, but the effective role played by the President of the Republic is open-ended.

[20] See C Fusaro, *Il Presidente della Repubblica* (Bologna, Il Mulino, 2003) 82ff and P Costanzo, 'La gestione delle crisi di governo e lo scioglimento anticipato delle Camere' in Ruggeri (n 12) 111ff, 114ff.

The practice, experience and overall history of the country have shaped the actual role of the President within the form of government.

There are different ways of interpreting this role, depending – as already noted – primarily on external elements, and first and foremost on the features of the party system, but also on the distinct personality of each holder of this office.

This explains why the role of the Italian President of the Republic, called upon to represent national unity (Article 87.1), is often described using the metaphor of a musical instrument: the '*squeeze-box*' (or 'accordion'). This characterisation signifies that, when there is a clear and stable majority in both Houses, the President's role tends to be less prominent. It never becomes merely symbolical or ceremonial but in times of a fragmented party system or when the political dynamic is in transition, thereby giving rise to a narrow and uncertain majority in at least one house of the Parliament, the President's role naturally expands. This was particularly clear, for instance, during the 'Bribesville' scandal, in 1992; at the end of the first Berlusconi Government, in 1994; in the final phase of the last Berlusconi Government, in 2011; and, even more manifestly, immediately after both the 2013 and the 2018 elections and again with the political crisis in the midst of the COVID-19 pandemic, at the beginning of 2021.

Not surprisingly, the analysis of each President of the Republic has engaged not only historians and political scientists, but also constitutional lawyers, who have attempted, on the one hand, to ascertain the particular interpretation of the role proposed by each President and whether it complies, in theoretical and in practical terms, with the constitutional norms, but also, on the other hand, whether, and how, the same norms have been developed and, in many cases, altered precisely because of the actions accomplished by each President, either alone or, more often, in collaboration with other constitutional bodies.[21]

Of course, the outcome of this kind of assessment largely derives from how scholars conceive of and theorise the role of the President of the Republic. If they opt for a Schmittian approach, according to which the Head of State is the guardian and the defender of constitutional unity and of the entirety of the people, and is the holder of the supreme power

[21] With respect to the first Presidents, see A Baldassarre and C Mezzanotte, *Gli uomini del Quirinale: Da De Nicola a Pertini* (Rome-Bari, Laterza, 1985) as well as Luciani and Volpi (n 10). On the Napolitano presidency see V Lippolis and GM Salerno, *La presidenza più lunga: I poteri del capo dello Stato e la Costituzione* (Bologna, Il Mulino, 2016). For a comprehensive and multi-disciplinary analysis see Cassese, Galasso and Melloni (n 4).

in case of crisis, it is clear that almost any increase of the political role of the President can be viewed, especially when substituting the inactivity of other institutional actors, as a kind of 'spare engine', to be activated whenever the main engine does not operate properly.[22] Conversely, if they conceive of the President of the Republic as a *super partes* institution, as an impartial guarantor of the correct application of the Constitution, any act or behaviour that gives rise to relevant effects on the political dynamic is viewed with suspicion, and its constitutional justification is thus subject to strict scrutiny.[23]

More generally, whether a strict and textual conception of the Constitution prevails, the parameter of the actions taken by the President of the Republic tends to be limited, whereas it significantly expands if the Constitution is seen as an evolving and systematic set of principles and values. Even the interaction of the Italian Constitution with EU Treaties and with EU law (see Chapter 2) plays a role, as most of the power of influence of the Presidents of the Republic has been exercised, especially during the last few decades, in order to ensure a coherence between the behaviours of the contingent majorities and the commitments and values pursued throughout the European integration process and embedded by EU institutions.

VI. CONCLUSION

The elasticity of the presidential role in Italy has led to divergent views with respect to the characterisation of its position within the constitutional system, and consequently concerning the assessment of how each President makes use of his powers. The still dominant approach, however, depicts the role as a *super partes* institution: an impartial guarantor of the correct application of the Constitution, a political figure committed to acting as a sort of arbiter or umpire, moderating the excesses of the political dynamic.

[22] As to the theories of C Schmitt (*Der Hüter der Verfassung* (Berlin, 1931)), see C Esposito, 'Capo dello Stato' in *Enciclopedia del diritto*, VI (Milan, Giuffrè, 1960) 224 and, more recently, O Chessa, *Il Presidente della Repubblica parlamentare. Un'interpretazione della forma di governo italiana* (Naples, Jovene, 2001).

[23] See, among others, G Guarino, 'Il Presidente della Repubblica italiana' (1951) *Rivista trimestrale di diritto pubblico* 942f; L Paladin, 'Presidente della Repubblica' in *Enciclopedia del diritto*, XXXV (Milan, Giuffrè, 1986) 221ff; E Cheli, 'Il Presidente della Repubblica come organo di garanzia costituzionale' in A Pace (ed), *Studi in onore di Leopoldo Elia*, I (Milan, Giuffrè, 1999) 301–15.

The metaphor of the empire was used and shared, for example, in President Sergio Mattarella's initial address:

> According to current custom, the role of the President of the Republic is normally seen as that of an umpire and the guarantor of the Constitution. It is an effective image. An umpire is in charge of strictly applying the rules. An umpire must and will be impartial. The players must do their share and play by the rules. The President of the Republic is the guarantor of the Constitution.[24]

One thing is nevertheless clear even from a plain reading of the text. As the Constitutional Court remarked, 'when describing the overall powers of the President of the Republic within the Italian constitutional system, it will become clear that he has been placed by the Constitution outside the traditional branches of state, and naturally above all political parties'.[25] The President is thus vested with powers that impinge upon each of the branches of state, with the aim of safeguarding both their separation and their equilibrium. In the light of the above, the President of the Republic 'represents national unity' (Article 87.1), 'not only in the sense of the territorial unity of the state, but also and above all in the sense of the cohesion and harmonious functioning of the powers, policies and guarantees comprising the constitutional framework of the Republic'.[26]

FURTHER READING

Clementi, F, and Bull, D, 'The Election of the President of the Republic: The Legacy of the Napolitano Presidency' (2013) 29 *Italian Politics* 160.

Fusaro, C, and Bull, D, 'The Formation of the Monti Government and the Role of the President of the Republic' (2011) 27 *Italian Politics* 78.

Grimaldi, S, 'The Role of Italian Presidents: The Subtle Boundary between Accountability and Political Action' (2011) 3(1) *Bulletin of Italial Politics* 103.

Tebaldi, M, 'From Notary to Ruler: The Role of the President of the Republic during the Italian Crisis (2010–14)' (2014) 19(4) *South European Society and Politics* 561.

[24] On 3 February 2015 (from the official translation available on www.quirinale.it).

[25] Judgment no 1/2013.

[26] Judgment no 1/2013.

7

Regional and Local Government

Autonomistic Principle – Republic of Autonomies – Special Regions – Ordinary Regions – Presidents of the Regions – Statutory Autonomy – Legislative Competences – *Principaliter* Procedure – Administrative Autonomy – Principle of Subsidiarity – Principle of Loyal Cooperation – Financial Autonomy – Local Authorities – Municipalities – Provinces

I. INTRODUCTION

> The Republic shall be composed of municipalities, provinces, metropolitan cities, regions and the State. Municipalities, provinces, metropolitan cities and regions shall be autonomous entities having their own statutes, powers and functions in accordance with the principles laid down in the Constitution (Article 114).

THE ITALIAN REPUBLIC is a plural and diverse subject: municipalities, provinces, regions and the State are all components of the unique Republic. In fact, one of the distinguishing features of the architecture of the Italian Republic is its 'institutional pluralism'.

If one considers the apportionment of powers between the centre and the peripheries, the Italian Republic can neither be characterised as a unitary and centralised state, *à la française*, nor as a federal state, as in the United States. Rather, it is a model that should be positioned somewhere between the two extremes, on the spectrum of the wide-ranging and dynamic nuances of the 'federaling process', as Carl Friedrich has described the varying experiences of federalism.[1]

That is why, within the classification of the forms of state, Italy is ordinarily grouped – together with Spain – with the so-called 'regional States', 'devolved States', 'States of Autonomies' or '*Republic of Autonomies*'.

[1] CJ Friedrich, *Trends of Federalism in Theory and Practice* (London, Pall Mall, 1968).

This latter expression appears to best suit the Italian case, given the constitutional role assigned not only to the regions, but also to sub-regional entities and particularly to municipalities.[2] The key word here is 'Autonomy', which – according to the Italian legal doctrine[3] – is neither sovereignty nor mere decentralisation.

In fact, as is explained in one of the Constitution's fundamental principles, the Italian political community is the result of an equilibrium between *unity* and *autonomy*: 'The Republic shall be one and indivisible. It shall recognise and promote local autonomies, and implements the fullest measure of administrative decentralisation of those services which are provided by the State' (Article 5).

One and indivisible: the Constitutional Court insisted on the fact that the unity of the Republic is one of the *fundamental principles of the Constitution*, 'so essential as to be protected even against the power of constitutional amendment'.[4] At the same time, the Republic is based on the *autonomy of local governments*: in the very same decision, the Court highlighted that 'the republican order is also based on principles including social and institutional pluralism and territorial autonomy'.[5]

'*Republic*' in Italy is a 'collective term', which encompasses all levels of government recognised by the Constitution. In fact, there was a discussion in March 1947 in the Plenary of the Constituent Assembly about the use of the term 'State' or 'Republic'.[6] It was made clear on that occasion that these words were not synonyms, as 'Republic comprises all the functions and activities of the State as such, but also those

[2] Notwithstanding the somewhat awkward neologism, we will make use of the English term 'autonomies' to capture both the literal word in Italian and the term of art within the Italian constitutional structure. However, see F Palermo and K Kössler, *Comparative Federalism: Constitutional Arrangements and Case Law* (Oxford, Hart, 2019) 50ff.

[3] The concept of 'autonomy' has been expounded by, among others, Santi Romano, Massimo Severo Giannini and Giorgio Berti.

[4] Judgment no 118/2015. See also ch 1.

[5] Judgment no 118/2015. In this Judgment, the Constitutional Court rejected the question of constitutionality on the regional law providing for a referendum asking the electors based in Veneto the following interrogation: 'Do you want Veneto Region to be vested with further forms and special terms of autonomy?'. See D Tega, 'Venice is not Barcelona: A Less Aggressive Regional Question gets a More Nuanced Constitutional Answer' (2015) *Int'l J Const L Blog*, available at www.iconnectblog.com/2015/07/venice-is-not-barcelona-a-less-aggressive-regional-question-gets-a-more-nuanced-constitutional-answer. On the consultative referendums that were held in Veneto and in Lombardy on 22 October 2017, see E Arban, 'The Referenda for More Autonomy in Veneto and Lombardia: Constitutional and Comparative Perspectives' (2018) 10(1) *Perspectives on Federalism* 264.

[6] Meuccio Ruini in *The Constituent Assembly*, 24 March 1947, p 2424 (our translation), with respect to Article 3 of the Constitution.

performed by the Regions and other public entities'. In theoretical terms, the name 'Republic' is used to mean the State as a legal order, while the Constitution usually employs the term 'State' to refer to the State as a subject or as a legal person.

This chapter sets out the essential features of the 'Republic of autonomies': ie the Italian system of regional and local governments, viewed against the background of their political, economic and social conditions, which, in Italy, differ depending on their territorial location, and are particularly divergent along the North–South divide. The response to the persistence of these differentiations and of the rise of political movements calling for greater autonomy, or even raising secessionist claims, has led to changes to the structure and competences of regional level institutions, requiring several amendments to the Constitution, in 1999 and 2001. And the evolution still looks far from over.

II. ORIGINS AND EVOLUTION OF THE 'REPUBLIC OF AUTONOMIES'

Within the Italian constitutional system, the distribution of powers between the central State and the 20 Regions (15 'ordinary' and five 'special' Regions) indicates that *sovereignty* is an original and exclusive attribution of the State (although it is free to limit it in favour of international organisations: see Chapter 2), whereas Regions and other local entities enjoy varying degrees of *autonomy*, framed by the Constitution. As has been remarked by the Constitutional Court, pluralism and autonomy do not permit the regions to classify themselves as sovereign bodies and do not permit their governmental organs to be treated as equivalent to the representative bodies of a nation.[7]

The Italian 'Republic of Autonomies' expresses a very original balance between State, Regions and local authorities due to historical reasons. On the one hand, cities and municipalities have a long tradition in Italy, which derives from centuries of history that can be traced back to the renaissance and even to the Middle Ages. On the other hand, at the time of the unification of the country, the centralised tradition of the liberal state prevailed. The Fascist period tended to further centralise power in the hands of the government and to suffocate all forms of local autonomy: in each and every municipality – which in Italy comprise over 8,000 – the Fascist regime introduced a delegate of the central Government,

[7] See Judgments nos 306 and 106/2002, 365/2007 and 118/2015.

the *podestà* and the *presidi*, replacing the mayors (*sindaci*) elected by the local community, in order to keep political activity under control at the local level. Against this historical background, the Constituent Assembly tended to react to, and to reject, the centralising character of the liberal and the Fascist State, and to restore the historical tradition of lively political autonomy at the local level.

As for Regions, some of them – especially the five 'special' Regions: Sicily, Sardinia, Valle D'Aosta, Trentino-Alto Adige and Friuli-Venezia Giulia – are rooted in geographical and historical special conditions, whereas the other 15 ordinary Regions, as enumerated by the Constituent Assembly, were all new and just originated from the reproduction of statistical districts framed in the nineteenth century.[8]

These roots of regionalism in Italy account for a certain asymmetry between special and ordinary regions, and help explain the delay in the implementation of constitutional provisions concerning the 15 ordinary Regions, which only started their activities in 1970. This historical background can also help clarify why some of the 'key' legislative competences, which in a federal State are typically split between the national and the local State level, are, in Italy, firmly in the hands of the central State: civil and criminal law issues, for instance, remain out of the reach of regional legislation. Moreover, the organisation of the judiciary entails the prohibition of any kind of regional judges (see Chapter 8), and functions of order and security – interpreted as functions to prevent and repress crime[9] – pertain strictly to the national State.

Another peculiar feature of the Italian regional system is its evolving character. The original system created by the 1948 Constitution is substantially different from the 'living' system which effectively existed during the 1970s and 1980s, and even more different from the regional experience which developed after 2001. The reasons for such a great variability over time are twofold. The first is that the text of the Constitution itself (Part II, Title V) was profoundly and extensively amended between 1999 and 2001. The second reason is that the 'real life' of the regional system is not determined by the constitutional rules alone. A key actor in the transformation of the constitutional principles into reality is the Constitutional Court via its judicial review of State and regional legislation: from a quantitative point of view, one of the most relevant activities

[8] Cf L Gambi, 'Le "regioni" italiane come problema storico' (1977) 34 *Quaderni Storici* 275.

[9] Judgment no 236/2020.

of the Constitutional Court is to resolve controversies between the State and the Regions, in the *principaliter* procedures for judicial review of legislation and other conflicts between the State and Regions. The most appropriate means of understanding how the relationship between the center and the peripheries really works is therefore by analysis of some leading Constitutional Court cases.

Generally speaking, since the constitutional amendments of 1999–2001, which were meant to further increase the degree of autonomy granted to the Regions and the other local communities, the Constitutional Court has played a 'centripetal' game; that is, it has used its interpretative powers in a manner that favoured the central State's competences rather than the regional and municipal ones.

Several factors may help to account for this strong 'centripetal' tendency in State–Regional relationships. First, the Italian national institutions, including the Constitutional Court, have historically shown a cultural distrust of the regional and local authorities in general, while the latter have suffered from political weakness as they have often failed to demonstrate that they can govern more effectively than the national Parliament or the Executive. More recently, the global financial and economic crisis that affected Italy from 2007 onwards increased the interference of central State powers with regional legislative authority, especially in connection with spending policies. In the last few years this trend has diminished somewhat, partly due to the more diverse composition of the Constitutional Court, which now includes sitting judges from all over the country, some of whom are very committed to the values of self-government and local autonomy.

Major reforms of this part of the Constitution have been attempted more recently, but without success. The last one, rejected by the 2016 constitutional referendum, aimed to simplify the division of powers between the State and Region, abolish the provinces (which, in the meantime, have been transformed into non-elective bodies by ordinary legislation), and establish a 'second chamber' of the national parliament, comprising representatives of the regions and municipalities. At the same time, in 2015, a process of differentiation between ordinary Regions, promoted by Veneto, Lombardy and Emilia-Romagna, commenced, with great expectations. However, the procedure for the recognition of an enhanced form of autonomy for ordinary Regions provided by Article 116.3 of the Constitution – as amended in 2001, which requires bilateral 'agreements' between the State and each of the Regions concerned, to be approved by State laws passed by an absolute majority of the members of the two Houses – has not yet even been initiated.

III. THE CONSTITUTIONAL FRAMEWORK AND ITS DELAYED IMPLEMENTATION

As already mentioned, Italy only became a unitary nation State in the second half of the nineteenth century (see Chapter 1). A latecomer on the European scene, Italy was unified due to a military expansion of the Kingdom of Piedmont and Sardinia. This historical origin helps to explain the stark differences – in terms of income, traditions, culture, language and legal systems – that existed between the different territories when the Kingdom of Italy was declared in 1861, and that have only partially been resolved by the centralised liberal state ruled by the Albertine Statute.

Furthermore, the experience of the Second World War, although foundational for the Italian Republic, was rather different in the Northern area of the peninsula, where the Resistance primarily took place, compared to the Fascist regime and the puppet state of the Republic of Salò. In Southern Italy, conversely, the war consisted mainly in the fight between the Anglo-American alliance and the Nazi armed forces, especially after the armistice became public on 8 September 1943. It was also due to these very different experiences that the 1946 referendum on the choice between the Republic and a Monarchy had the opposite outcomes in Northern and Southern Italy, with the North in favour of the Republic and the South opting for the Monarchy.

In addition, autonomist and secessionist movements were well rooted in each of the two main islands, Sicily and Sardinia, and the former even declared its own charter of autonomy by royal decree on 15 May 1946, just before the election of the Constituent Assembly,[10] and so it is clear to see that the task faced by the Constituent Assembly was far from easy. Another difficult matter was the legal status of the Italian *Südtirol*, which required an international agreement between Austria and Italy (the De Gasperi-Gruber Pact signed in Paris in 1946, in the context of the Peace Conference) and ultimately resulted in the establishment of a Special Region composed of two autonomous Provinces: Trentino and Alto Adige. As well as the eastern border, the region of Trieste remained undefined until 1963, when the Special Region of Friuli-Venezia Giulia was established.

In terms of theory, the positions held by those in the Constituent Assembly were quite distinct. On the one hand, the Christian Democrats were strongly aligned with the Catholic social doctrine, Luigi Sturzo's autonomistic ideals and the principle of subsidiarity, and thus championed

[10] According to R Leonardi, *Government and Politics of Italy* (Palgrave, London, 2017) 220ff, thanks to this, 'Italy saw the creation of the first Region in Europe'.

the primacy of society over the State when struggling for broader recognition of the political autonomy of territorial authorities. A pro-Regions attitude was also present among the Action Party and the Republican Party, both mindful of Carlo Cattaneo's and Giuseppe Mazzini's federal theories. These parties had been defeated during the nation-building process. On the other hand, the Communist and Socialist Parties were strongly in favour of the exclusivity of the political representativeness of the national Parliament and thus, in principle, against any subdivision of powers as this would lead to the consequent reduction of the political functions of the central State. The possible compromise consisted in recognising a unitary State, although clearly oriented towards the decentralisation of the State's functions and based on the recognition of regional and local autonomies.

As has been already noted, this compromise was proclaimed in Article 5: 'The Republic, one and indivisible, recognizes and promotes local autonomies; implements in those services which depend on the State the fullest measure of administrative decentralization; accords the principles and methods of its legislation to the requirements of autonomy and decentralization'. Together with its declaration of the unity and indivisibility of the State, which is correctly grouped with the Constitution's fundamental principles, this Article clearly indicates an intent to decentralise the administration and – even more importantly – recognises something that seems to even pre-date the existence of the State itself, namely regional and local autonomies. The last part of Article 5 requires the State to adapt the content and the methods of its legislation to suit the diverse and complex texture of the Republic.

The legal language of Article 5 is very carefully selected. It starts by reaffirming the unity and indivisibility of the Republic, a principle that clearly places the 'regional' system beyond the family of 'federal' systems, at least insofar as the latter are defined as comprising 'divided' States with 'shared sovereignty'. Yet, immediately after this opening, the Article uses the verb '*to recognise*' in relation to the territorial 'autonomies'. This verb has a clear meaning within Italian constitutional language, and was carefully selected by the Constituent Assembly: the very same word is also used with respect to fundamental rights in Article 2, which are 'recognised' and not established, or founded, or simply protected by the Republic (see Chapter 10). 'Re-cognise', from an etymological perspective, means to acknowledge something that pre-exists. Therefore, if the Republic 'recognises' a local entity (and does not simply guarantee, promote or protect it), this implies that the entity in question is pre-existent to the Republic and cannot be completely at the mercy of the State. In legal terms, this historical and theoretical priority of territorial bodies means that the Republic 'recognises' the autonomy of the forms of territorial government. The historical and legal precedence of territorial autonomies clearly distinguishes the Italian regional model from the family of classical 'centralised States', such as France.

The principles affirmed by Article 5 are unpacked and implemented in the Fifth Title of the Second Part of the Constitution (Articles 114–133) with some hesitations and contradictions. In this part of the Constitution, some leftovers of the rather centralised tradition of the liberal state and of the Fascist period can be identified. Moreover, the Regions were designed to be the most powerful entities among the different forms of territorial government, because they were also granted legislative power. However, in a way, unlike the municipalities and even the provinces, the regions were artificial and 'man-made', deprived of a longstanding tradition or any other historical background, with the exception of some of the five 'special regions'. In a sense, the new 'Republic of Autonomies' was designed in the Constitution as being based on the regions, but those regions did not actually exist in reality.

Indeed, right after the approval of the Constitution and after the 1948 elections, for a variety of practical reasons, political parties swiftly changed their respective positions. The Christian Democrats, once they obtained the parliamentary majority and were well established as the leading political force in the central Government, were rather reluctant to implement the constitutional design, and thus to grant political and legislative autonomy to the regions and local entities. Conversely, communist and socialist parties – which were excluded by the ruling majority – became supporters of regional and local governments, in order to govern the Regions, especially in central Italy where they could count on the majority of the votes.

This context explains why the implementation of this part of the Constitution, concerning ordinary Regions, was delayed for 22 years after the entry into force of the Constitution, meaning that the only concrete regional experience arose in relation to the special Regions, which, for different reasons – geographical, linguistic and international – required immediate recognition of their autonomy from the central Government.

IV. SPECIAL AND ORDINARY REGIONS

The Constituent Assembly recognised five 'special' Regions: Sicily, Sardinia, Valle d'Aosta, Trentino-Alto Adige and Friuli-Venezia Giulia. Each of them is regulated by its own basic law – called 'special Charter'

(*Statuto speciale*) – approved by a constitutional law of the State (Articles 116.1 and 138). These special Charters were originally approved in 1946 for Sicily, in 1948 for the other three regions, and in 1963 for the fifth, Friuli-Venezia Giulia, after the delineation of the Eastern border with the former Yugoslavia. The special Charters provide specific rules and legal principles, derogating from the general structure of the regional powers outlined by the Constitution, to be applied in each of those Regions. They partially depart from other constitutional provisions in order to provide these Regions with 'special forms and conditions of autonomy'.

The reasons underlying these five peculiar statuses relate to the Regions' particular geography and history, although their continuation is often questioned nowadays, especially by the neighbouring areas. They are the two main Italian islands (Sicily and Sardinia) and the three areas at the northern border of the peninsula, generally with a relevant presence of linguistic minorities. The status of Trentino-Alto Adige is particularly unusual. It is a special Region composed of two 'autonomous provinces', Trento and Bolzano: each one substantially comparable, in terms of powers and competences, to a special Region in itself.

By contrast, the Fifth Title of the Second Part of the Constitution (Articles 114–133) directly regulates the powers of the 15 'ordinary' Regions: Piedmont, Lombardy, Veneto, Liguria, Emilia-Romagna, Tuscany, Umbria, Marches, Latium, Abruzzi, Molise, Campania, Apulia, Basilicata and Calabria. Their territories and populations are far from homogeneous: the largest Region is Sicily (25,832 km^2), while the most populated is Lombardy (more than 10 million residents in 2019); the smallest and least populated is Val d'Aosta (125,000 residents in an area of 3.261 km^2). Even the annual GDP *per capita* of the Regions differs significantly.[11]

Following the 2001 constitutional reform, according to Article 116, additional special forms and conditions of autonomy, in some limited matters, may be attributed to other Regions by State law, approved by an absolute majority, upon the initiative of the Region concerned after consultation with the local authorities. This would be done on the basis of an agreement between the State and the Region in question. This possibility

[11] For instance, in 2019, the annual GDP *per capita* varied from an average of 39,400 euro in Lombardy (and, if one likes, from 47,560 euro in the Bolzano autonomous province) to 17,150 euro in Calabria.

(foreseeing so-called 'differentiated regionalism') has never been implemented, although some negotiations between the State and Regions are in progress.

Within each region, a number of provinces and of municipalities are recognised by the Constitution itself and entitled to undertake a series of functions. In each Region there are from 1 to 12 provinces and from 74 to 1,506 municipalities: the minimum and the maximum numbers pertain to Val d'Aosta and Lombardy respectively.

In order to divide a Region (provided that each one of the resulting regions has a minimum of one million inhabitants) or to merge two Regions, a constitutional law is required, which must be approved after consultation with the regional Council. According to Article 132.1, the request needs to originate from a number of Municipal Councils representing not less than one-third of the populations involved, and must be approved by referendum by a majority of said populations.

The process to alter regional borders is slightly easier. In this case, an ordinary law should suffice. According to Article 132.2, the provinces and municipalities which request to be detached from one Region and incorporated into another need to first pass a referendum, obtaining the majority of the populations of the province or provinces and of the municipality or municipalities concerned, and then a law of the Republic, after having consulted with the regional Councils. In recent years, a number of municipalities located on the borders between an ordinary Region and a special one have requested to be included in the special Region in order to enjoy more favourable conditions of autonomy, especially in terms of financial autonomy.

As already noted, the original text of the Fifth Title of the Second Part of the Constitution has only been implemented since 1970, and mainly in a restrictive and unsatisfying way. The State was reluctant to devolve its functions to newly created Regions, and to release to them the bodies and the civil servants that comprised its decentralised administration. For their part, regional institutions often demonstrated that they were incapable of ensuring a more stable and efficient government than the central State. This was also due to the fact that the regional form of government designed by the original text of the Constitution was parliamentary in nature (ie with the President and the Cabinet's members being elected by the regional Council, from among its members), often leaning towards an 'assemblearistic' form of government (ie giving a certain prominence to assemblies).

The result of at least the first two decades of regional institutions in Italy has been the confirmation of the ongoing significance of the historical, traditional features of the different areas of the peninsula: with the areas in which civil society has a strong civic tradition (so-called 'social capital') demonstrating a greater capacity for self-government than those areas historically characterised by a more passive attitude.[12] In other words, the implementation of ordinary Regions, since 1970, did not manage to reduce the territorial inequalities in income and infrastructure, nor to diffuse more widely the culture and experiences of democratic self-government.

V. THE DIRECT ELECTION OF THE PRESIDENTS OF THE REGIONS AND STATUTORY AUTONOMY

During the 1990s, as a consequence of the majoritarian turn of the institutional system and of the crisis of the traditional (national) political parties, and in order to respond to the electoral success – territorially concentrated in northern areas – of the Northern League, an emerging pressure was exerted in support of increasing the powers of the regions and municipalities. A first phase of expanding their powers, which could be achieved without amending the Constitution, related to both regional institutional features (essentially via an electoral law providing for a majority bonus: law no 43/1995) and to their powers (especially by law no 59/1997 and the legislative decrees that implemented it). Nevertheless, other matters required constitutional amendments. Following the failures of both the De Mita-Iotti and D'Alema bicameral committees seeking more extensive constitutional reforms, two complementary and significant constitutional amendments of the Fifth Title of the Second Part of the Constitution were approved between 1999 and 2001.[13]

Constitutional law no 1/1999 has enhanced the 'statutory autonomy' of ordinary regions and has granted broad leeway to each Region for the establishment of its own institutional organisation, albeit 'in harmony with the Constitution'. First, from a procedural point of view, the regional charter (*statuto regionale*) is now to be approved by a regional law, whereas according to the original text of the Constitution, it was to be discussed and proposed by each regional Council, but then required

[12] See RD Putnam, R Leonardi and R Nanetti, *Making Democracy Work: Civic Traditions in Modern Italy* (Princeton, Princeton University Press, 1993) 181ff.

[13] The picture is completed by constitutional law no 2/2001 (which extended similar rules to the regions enjoying special autonomy).

approval by the Chamber and the Senate via a State law. Second, as to content, the constitutional amendment permits each regional charter not merely to define some of its organisational principles, but also to choose its own 'form of government'. At the same time, the constitutional amendment suggests that the direct election of the President of the Region is the default solution, to be applied if the regional charter does not provide otherwise. The direct election of the President has indeed applied in each ordinary Region since the 2000 elections, and has now also been adopted by almost all the special Regions (with the exceptions being Valle d'Aosta and the Province of Bolzano).

According to the so-called *simul stabunt simul cadent* rule, in the event of the approval of a motion of no confidence, as well as in the case of resignation, for whatever reason, of the President, new elections must be called. This new form of government is defined by some as *premierato* (ie a prime ministerial form of government, in which the premier is directly elected and dominates the legislature, and also where the government is able to determine the dissolution of the legislature). It has ensured that the regional governments enjoy a high degree of popular legitimacy and stability. The Constitutional Court confirmed that this form of government could theoretically be abandoned in favour of a parliamentary one, but rejected the reading according to which, having opted for the direct election of the President, the regional charter would be allowed to alter the *simul stabunt simul cadent* rule (for instance by providing for a deputy President, or for a constructive motion of no confidence).[14] The greatest regional autonomy expected as a result of this reform has not been confirmed by the practical experience thus far: this is because the regional Statutes have in fact followed the model provided by the Constitution, without departing from its basic features.

VI. THE DISTRIBUTION OF LEGISLATIVE COMPETENCES BETWEEN THE STATE AND REGIONS

Two years later, constitutional law no 3/2001 strengthened the legislative, administrative and fiscal powers of regions and local authorities *vis-à-vis* the central State. The political intent of the constitutional change was to move in the direction of a more 'federal' model, designing a quasi-federal State, even if this attempt – as will be remarked in the following paragraphs – was not entirely successful.

[14] Judgment no 2/2004 on the charter of Calabria.

A symbolically strong impact in the direction of quasi-federalism resulted from the revision of the criteria for the distribution of legislative powers between the State and Regions. Indeed, since 1948, the Regions (and the Autonomous Provinces of Trento and Bolzano) have been the only authorities, other than the State, vested with legislative powers. The amendment confirms this original feature and extends their legislative powers, moving toward a federal type of system. The Constitution, as amended, identifies three different categories of law-making power: (a) the *exclusive enumerated* legislative powers of the State in relation to the matters listed under Article 117.2; (b) the *concurrent enumerated* legislative powers of both the State and Regions in relation to the matters listed under Article 117.3 (in respect of which the State is called upon to define the fundamental principles, while the rest of the legislation is regional); and, finally, (c) the *residual* legislative power of the Regions in relation to all the matters not included in the previous two lists (Article 117.4).

The reform also removed all the *ex ante* controls of the State in relation to regional acts and in particular the power of the State to challenge the constitutionality of regional laws *prior to* their promulgation and publication, in cases in which it deems that the regional law exceeds the competence of the Region. As a result of the 2001 constitutional amendment, the national Government is entitled to challenge a regional law before the Constitutional Court only *after* its entry into force, within 60 days of its publication. This makes the mechanism of the *principaliter* judgment more symmetrical with what happens in the reciprocal case, ie when a State law is brought before the Constitutional Court, on the initiative of any Region, within 60 days of its publication, when the Region deems that said State law infringes upon its competence (Article 127).

In theory, therefore, constitutional law no 3/2001 almost gave rise to a Copernican change, because it upended the notion of the enumerated powers. The original text of the Constitution enumerated the legislative powers of the Regions – the exclusive power and the concurrent ones – leaving all the residual powers to the State. In contrast, the constitutional amendments of 2001 enumerate the State legislative powers – the exclusive and the concurrent powers – while leaving the residual powers to the regions.

In practice, however, the change has been less radical, partly because the new distribution of powers is somewhat flawed, and partly because it has not been correctly and promptly implemented, either by the national Parliament (which continues to legislate more or less as it did before the entry into force of the constitutional amendment) or by the regional councils (which were not ready to assume the task and the responsibility of the main legislators, and, in the absence of a House of Parliament representing the Regions, did not even have the means to establish a regular dialogue with the State legislator).[15] As a result, the Constitutional Court was obliged to deal with an increased quantity of legislative controversies between the State and the Regions, especially those *principaliter* raised by the former (against regional legislation) or by the latter (against State legislation), and resolving them primarily by trying to justify the intervention of the State laws.

Regional legislative powers mainly concern social and economic matters. Within the long list of the Regions' concurrent legislative competencies, and the much less relevant residual ones, their competence in the field of health care towers over all the others. Within the general framework provided by the national Parliament (law no 833/1978 and legislative decree no 502/1992 as later amended), the Regions develop their own health care systems, following different models. This branch of regional activity accounts for up to 90 per cent of their resources, for hospitals and for providing other sanitary or socio-sanitary services. Many Regions in the north and center of the country have efficient health care systems, whereas many others – namely in the south – have an excess of expenditure in the field, which causes a budgetary deficit. In this case, the national government can nominate a commissioner with the task of administering the regional sanitary system in order to remove the causes of the deficit.[16] In any event, the regional autonomy in this field is always required to respect the general and fundamental principles established by the national parliament: for example, the matter of mandatory vaccination falls within the competence of the State and the Regions cannot derogate from the national legislation.[17] Moreover, it is up to the State to provide the resources and to guarantee a basic general level of services all over the country: the so-called 'basic levels of assistance' (*livelli essenziali di assistenza*), that Article 117.2, letter m, mentions among the competences of the State.[18]

The State and regional legislative competences often overlap. In this case, the Constitutional Court is required to confirm if one of the

[15] See also Judgment no 106/2002, in which the Constitutional Court denied the regional Legislatures the possibility of calling themselves 'Parliaments', recognising that the word 'Parliament' has a deontic meaning which is reserved by the Italian Constitution uniquely to the bodies that express the national political representation.

[16] Judgment no 278/2014.

[17] Judgment no 5/2018.

[18] See Judgment no 62/2020.

competing competences prevails, to the exclusion of the other, or if they are strictly intertwined: if this is the case, the Court requires the State and Regions to collaborate in relation to the drafting of the legislation in question, according to the principle of loyal cooperation.[19]

However, there are some State competences that tend to trump regional competences. This is the case in relation to '*horizontal*' *or* '*cross-cutting*' *matters*, which appear on the lists of exclusive State legislative powers and which are intrinsically capable of having an effect on and interfering with other legislative powers accorded to the Regions. The list of such powers is rather long and includes: 'protection of the environment'; 'competition'; 'civil and criminal law'; and 'determination of the basic level of benefits relating to civil and social entitlements to be guaranteed throughout the national territory'.

For example, with respect to the authority over environmental protection – reserved exclusively to the State under Article 117.2, letter s – the Constitutional Court has said that it 'cannot be described in the technical sense as a "matter reserved to the power of the State", since it amounts to a constitutionally protected value', and, therefore, entitles the State to 'establish a uniform standard of protection throughout the entire Nation'.[20] Another example is competition and antitrust regulation (Article 117.2, letter e). In this respect, the Court affirmed that 'the protection of competition has a cross-cutting character, which implies that, since its object is to regulate the market surrounding economic activities, it may also encompass matters, concurrent or residual, attributed to the regional legislatures'.[21]

Another technique used by the Constitutional Court consists in identifying and widening the scope of some 'catch-all' competences, ie powers that can be invoked by the State to permit its intervention in every possible regional area. The classical example is the coordination of public finances, which is included within the concurrent legislative powers but is used very intensively by the State). The inversion of the criterion for the distribution of legislative functions is also mirrored at the level of secondary sources of law (ie regulations: see also Chapter 5). According to Article 117.6, 'The State shall have regulatory powers in its areas of exclusive legislation', but it is also possible for the State to delegate such powers to the Regions. As for the rest, 'regulatory powers shall

[19] Judgment no 1/2016.
[20] Judgment no 108/2005.
[21] Judgment no 420/2007.

be vested in the regions in all other subject matters', with the exception of the functions attributed to municipalities, provinces and metropolitan cities, whose implementation occurs via their regulatory powers. In theory, therefore, regulatory powers should be exercised mainly by the Regions – which are more or less free to attribute this power to the regional council or to the regional executive.[22] In reality, however, after some initial hesitations, this has moved in a different direction. The State, as just remarked, has more and more often invoked its so-called 'horizontal competences', which primarily appear on the lists of exclusive State legislative powers, and this choice, in accordance with the distribution criterion set by Article 117.6, has allowed it to intervene not only through legislation but also through regulations.

VII. ADMINISTRATIVE AUTONOMY AND THE PRINCIPLES OF SUBSIDIARITY AND LOYAL COOPERATION

The criteria for the distribution of administrative powers, as redesigned by constitutional law no 3/2001, also represented a remarkable change, if compared with the original text of the Constitution. Initially, the criterion for the distribution of administrative powers between the State and the Regions was the so-called 'paralleling' doctrine, which established that whenever regions were attributed legislative power, they also had administrative powers. The central State could only intervene in these regional competences in cases of 'strictly local interests', in order to delegate administrative functions to more local authorities (municipalities or provinces). The new Article 118 begins from a totally different principle: 'Administrative functions shall be vested into municipalities, unless they are attributed to provinces, metropolitan cities and regions or the State, pursuant to the principles of subsidiarity, differentiation and proportionality, in order to ensure uniform implementation.' Therefore, the level of public authority of the Republic that is, in the first instance, generally endowed with administrative powers is the Municipality, with the exception of those functions that, for reasons of subsidiarity, differentiation or proportionality, need to be assigned to a higher authority (ie a province, metropolitan city, Region or the State). Here, the subsidiarity

[22] Judgment no 313/2003.

principle operates – to borrow imagery from the scholarship – as a kind of 'elevator':[23] that is, as a mechanism that lifts administrative functions up from the local level towards higher levels (up to the central State), only when necessary 'to ensure their uniform implementation'.

Unsurprisingly, this construction of the principle of subsidiarity, according to which all administrative functions are to be allocated to the level of public authority closest to the citizens, unless those functions can be better performed, in terms of either efficiency or territorial range, by a higher-level authority, is also called '*vertical subsidiarity*'.

Conversely, '*horizontal subsidiarity*', as specified in Article 118.4, means that 'the State, regions, metropolitan cities, provinces and municipalities shall promote the autonomous initiatives of citizens, both as individuals and as members of associations, relating to activities of general interest, on the basis of the principle of subsidiarity'. The horizontal notion of subsidiarity does not relate to the distribution of functions among the different levels of public authorities forming the Republic, but between public powers and private citizens or civil society associations. Here, the principle is more connected to its original meaning – deriving from Catholic social thought – as a limitation on public power according to which the State and all public authorities should not unnecessarily substitute themselves for civil society in carrying out 'activities of general interest'. In other words, the Constitution recognises that not all administrative functions need to be performed by the State or some other public authority of the Republic. On the contrary, there are 'public' functions (ie, of general interest) that can be appropriately and effectively carried out directly by civil society, 'as individuals and as members of associations'.

Indeed, in this case too, the new constitutional design would have required a great deal of activity on the part of the State legislator to re-distribute administrative functions consistently with these new principles. Not only was this activity mostly neglected by the legislator, but the new criteria were used, in substantial continuation of the original 'paralleling doctrine', to bring a degree of flexibility to, and greater protection of unitary interests in, the distribution of legislative competences.

In this respect, reference must be made to a particularly renowned ruling of the Constitutional Court, which has been characterised by some scholars as a sort of rewriting of the content of constitutional

[23] See R Bin and G Pitruzzella, *Diritto costituzionale* (Turin, Giappichelli, 2020) 105.

law no 3/2001,[24] applied the principle of subsidiarity, and the flexibility it entails, to the allocation not only of administrative powers, but also of legislative ones. According to the Constitutional Court, the State, invoking the 'vertical' principle of subsidiarity provided by Article 118.1 (a '*subsidiarity call*', as it has been defined), can elevate an administrative function, and simultaneously bring with it, thanks to the legality principle and the parallelism it requires between administration and legislation, the accompanying legislative function.

To use the Judgment's words, Article 118.1 'explicitly refers to the administrative functions, but introduces a dynamic mechanism for them', which renders the distribution of legislative powers less rigid. It is 'consistent with the theoretical matrix as well as the practical meaning of subsidiarity that the distribution should effect a *subsidium* when a particular level of government is inadequate to achieve the intended purpose'. This ascension of the function at a higher level 'cannot but have consequences for the exercise of the legislative function, since the principle of legality, which dictates that functions assumed under the subsidiarity principle, must also be organized and regulated by law, logically results in preventing the individual regions, with different regulations, from organizing and regulating administrative functions drawn up to the national level and confirming that only the State may do so'. The result is that 'the State, through this "subsidiarity call", can assume a lower authority's administrative functions on the basis of "subsidiarity, differentiation and adequacy" and to that extent can consequently legislate on this issue as well.'[25]

According to this Judgment, the State's legislative measures adopted on this legal basis, representing an exception to the distribution called for in Article 117, need to be proportionate, not unreasonable and agreed to by the regions. However, in this way, the principle of subsidiarity could be called upon to act as a 'Trojan horse';[26] even more so as the requirements established by this Judgment were gradually weakened by subsequent case law.

The State must also respect the principle of subsidiarity, together with the principle of loyal cooperation, in the exercise of its *substitutive*

[24] The reference is to Judgment no 303/2003 and to A Morrone, 'La Corte costituzionale riscrive il titolo V' (2003) 23(4) *Quaderni costituzionali* 818.

[25] See Judgment no 303/2003.

[26] Cf G Martinico 'The Impact of "Regional Blindness" on the Italian Regional State' (2011) *EUI Working Papers*, 6, available at https://cadmus.eui.eu/handle/1814/18337.

power: more precisely, when the Government 'can subsume the authority of a region, metropolitan city, province and municipality if it fails to comply with international rules and treaties or EU legislation, or in case of grave danger for public safety and security, or whenever such action is necessary in order to preserve legal or economic unity and in particular to ensure the minimum level of benefits relating to civil and social entitlements, regardless of the geographic borders of a local authority' (Article 120.2). According to the provisions of the implementing legislation (Article 8 of law no 131/2003), a deadline must ordinarily be assigned to the region by the President of the Council and, in the event of persistent inactivity, the Council of Ministers should adopt the necessary measures: either directly or through the appointment of an 'ad hoc' commissioner.

The *principle of loyal cooperation*, the existence of which has been affirmed by the Constitutional Court since the 1950s with respect to the relationships between the State and the special Regions, and then gradually extended to ordinary Regions and also to local governments,[27] is explicitly recognised by the Constitution (in Article 120.2, as just seen).

This principle underpins the establishment, since the 1980s, of a system of inter-governmental joint Conferences involving the State Government, on the one side, and the regional and/or local Executives, on the other. There are currently three such joint inter-governmental Conferences: the State-Regions Conference (*Conferenza Stato-Regioni*), which is the oldest (established in 1982) and still the most important; the State-Municipalities Conference (*Conferenza Stato-città ed enti locali*); and the unified Conference (*Conferenza unificata*), which combines the former two.[28]

All these inter-governmental Conferences are presided over by the President of the Council, or by a Minister upon the President's delegation (usually, the Ministers for regional affairs). They are composed of the ministers responsible for the matters on the agenda and of the presidents of the regions and/or the mayor, and are usually preceded by meetings at the regional or local level, aimed at coordinating – wherever possible – the positions of the different Regions and municipalities. The Conferences are asked to provide advice (*parere*) and sometimes an agreement (*accordo*) or an understanding (*intesa*) on draft normative

[27] Cf S Bartole, 'Supremazia e collaborazione nei rapporti tra Stato e Regioni' (1971) 21(1) *Rivista Trimestrale di Diritto Pubblico* 84ff.

[28] Legislative decree no 281/1997.

and administrative acts of the State that have effects on regional and local competences. The provision of their advice, and sometimes even of an understanding, regarding State administrative acts is often viewed by the Constitutional Court as being a necessary condition of the constitutionality of State legislation dealing (also) with regional and local competences.[29]

The system of inter-governmental Conferences has, until now, been the main channel of communication between the central, regional and local levels. They have worked well when the most significant cleavage to be addressed has arisen between different territorial levels and their respective administrations. However, their limits have become evident when asked to deal with sharp political or territorial cleavages relating, for example, to issues of transparency and participation of minorities, as, in these cases, it is increasingly unlikely that a common position will be reached amongst the executives of different regions or local autonomies. This explains why the absence of a House of Parliament capable of representing territories has been particularly keenly felt, for example, in relation to the attempts to implement the 'differentiated regionalism' foreseen by Article 116.3.

VIII. FINANCIAL AUTONOMY

Other very important changes were also introduced by the constitutional law no 3/2001. The financial autonomy of the Regions and local governments has been re-designed, via a complete replacement of Article 119. This reform was aimed at abandoning the tradition of almost complete regional 'derived finance', ie devolved or assigned by the State, and subsequent political irresponsibility, while ensuring financial autonomy – with respect to both revenues and expenditures – to municipalities, provinces, metropolitan cities and Regions. Constitutional law no 1/2012 has added the obligation for Regions and local governments to balance their budgets and to comply with economic and financial constraints deriving from EU law.

However, the manifold principles and rules affirmed by the following paragraph of that constitutional provision appear to be contradictory and rather ambiguous, leaving the main tasks to the State laws: either

[29] For example, Judgments nos 211/2016 and 261/2017.

in the exercise of their exclusive legislative competence regarding the harmonisation of public budgets (Article 117.2, letter e, as amended by constitutional law no 1/2012) or through the specific definition of the principles for the coordination of public finance and the taxation system (Article 117.3: as already remarked, this has been very broadly interpreted by the Constitutional Court).

The main implementation of these constitutional principles and rules is still a work in progress and every budget bill redefines the framework and sets new rules for public finance. Law no 42/2009 represented a general attempt, aimed directly at implementing the so-called '*fiscal federalism*' designed by the new Article 119.[30] As it was primarily formulated as a delegation law, it required a series of nine legislative decrees and other acts in order to be fully implemented. Notwithstanding the adoption of these implementing measures, the objective of creating more responsible Regions and local governments seems far from being achieved, and their financial autonomy is still very limited, especially with respect to the revenues (while the expenditures have been rather severely cut due to the financial crisis).

Therefore, in this case too, the Constitutional Court has been responsible for extracting from Article 119 some of the rules to be respected. The following are some of the many such rules: (a) regional laws cannot levy taxes, without the previous approval of a coordinating State law;[31] (b) State laws cannot establish specific and conditional funds in favour of regional or local governments in relation to matters that are of regional exclusive or concurrent competence;[32] and (c) State laws can determine the objectives of public finance for the Regions and can also set some more specific limits to regional and local expenditures, wherever strictly necessary to achieve these objectives.[33]

In any case, special Regions have been granted broader financial autonomy, and are capable of representing themselves more effectively during the law-making process (also through the insertion of specific 'safeguard clauses', aimed at preventing or minimising the application of new State legislation in their territories and deferring the matter to specific bilateral agreements between each special Region and the State) and defending

[30] N Rodean, 'Fiscal Federalism in Italy: Between Necessity and Sustainability' (2012) 95 *Revista Española de Derecho Constitucional* 215.

[31] Judgment no 37/2004.

[32] Judgments nos 16/2004 and 320/2004.

[33] Judgments nos 151/2012 and 173/2012.

their autonomy before the Constitutional Court. However, especially in the last decade, the Court has denied that the method of entering into bilateral agreements with special regions is constitutionalised[34] and has affirmed that also special regions are subject to the State laws coordinating public finance and limiting regional expenditure.[35]).

IX. LOCAL AUTHORITIES

In Italy, there are almost 8,000 municipalities (*comuni*: slowly but gradually reducing in number, due to mergers taking place because of incentives offered by recent legislation), 13 metropolitan cities (*città metropolitane*: Bari, Bologna, Cagliari, Catania, Firenze, Genova, Messina, Milano, Napoli, Palermo, Reggio Calabria, Torino and Venezia), plus 'Roma Capitale' (which has had a special status since 2010), and 80 provinces. The term 'local government' will be used to refer to all these entities collectively.

As already mentioned, according to Article 114, local government, together with the Regions and the State, constitutes the Republic of Italy. Their features and powers have always been defined by different legal sources: the Constitution, State legislation and regional legislation. By contrast with sub-state entities in federal systems, which normally depend entirely on their member state's rules, in Italy – even more clearly since constitutional law no 3/2001 – local government's features and powers tend to be defined primarily at the central level, even by several constitutional provisions.

According to this logic, the Constitution, as amended in 2001, recognises the power of each local entity to approve its own charter (Article 114.1) and its own regulations (Article 117.6), through which it exercises its administrative autonomy. A certain degree of financial autonomy is also granted (Article 119).

On the basis of the subsidiarity principle (Article 118.1), the smallest territorial units of representation of the political community, ie municipalities, are the public authority that are entitled, 'by default', to exercise all the administrative functions, unless they need to be elevated to a higher level of government. While it is an important principle, it needs to

[34] Judgments nos 23/2014 and 19/2015.
[35] Judgments nos 54/2014 and 77/2015.

be mitigated by the adequacy principle (also affirmed by Article 118.1), especially when considering that by far the majority of Italian municipalities are classified as 'small municipalities', with a population of less than 5,000 inhabitants.[36] This explains why Italian legislation encourages the merger of municipalities and also the formation of common entities, in order to jointly exercise some administrative functions: their generic denomination is 'unions of municipalities' (*unioni di comuni*); they are called 'mountainous communities' (*comunità montane*), when they join municipalities in mountainous areas or 'island communities' (*comunità isolane*), when they are instituted on one or more islands, with the exception of Sicily and Sardinia.

The municipalities' form of government is characterised by a mayor, who is directly elected by the citizens (since 1993), according to a plurality system in minor municipalities (up to 15,000 inhabitants) and according to a majority system with a run-off in larger municipalities. The mayor's mandate lasts five years, and the mayor cannot be re-elected after serving two consecutive terms (or after serving three terms in municipalities with up to 3,000 inhabitants). The mayor appoints and dismisses the assessors (*assessori*), ie the members of the municipal executive (*giunta comunale*), each of whom bears responsibility for a single policy. In the major municipalities (over 15,000 inhabitants) this mandate is incompatible with that of elected member of the municipal council. The functions of political direction and oversight are attributed to the municipal council, comprising between 10 and 48 members, all directly elected by the citizens at the same time as the mayor. The municipal council can approve, by absolute majority of members, a motion of no confidence in relation to the mayor and its executive, which would necessitate new elections. Similarly, the resignation of the mayor, for whatever reason, also entails new elections, according to the *simul stabunt simul cadent* rule, as already discussed in relation to the regional form of government.

The features of provinces and metropolitan cities have been very uncertain throughout the last 30 years. Traditionally, provinces corresponded to the territories of decentralised entities of the central State (usually coordinated by the 'prefect', according to the French model) and were gradually transformed into territorial elective bodies. Since the times of the Constituent Assembly until the (failed) 2016 constitutional

[36] L Castelli, 'The Territory of Local Authorities in Italy: Characteristics, Dimensions, Transformations' in S Mangiameli (ed), *Federalism, Regionalism and Territory* (Milan, Giuffrè, 2013) 357–89, 368 ff.

referendum, there were often proposals for the suppression of provinces, but these were never brought to a conclusion. According to the current legislation, provinces, when not transformed into metropolitan cities, are run by bodies that are no longer directly elected and are composed of members elected by and chosen from among the mayors and the municipal councilors of the municipalities included within their territory. Provinces and metropolitan cities exercise the so-called 'functions of ample area' (*funzioni di area vasta*), mainly regarding transport, some types of schools and other functions that municipalities decide to attribute to them.

X. CONCLUSION

The Italian State comprises an original balance between the State, Regions and local authorities (encompassing municipalities, provinces and metropolitan cities), that – as already remarked – can be encapsulated in the expression 'State of Autonomies' or, even better, 'Republic of Autonomies'.

This means that the central State uniquely expresses the 'sovereign power' of the Italian people, while the Regions and other local authorities are expressions of the 'Autonomy' of their respective populations. To recap what this distinction means, it is possible to refer, in conclusion, to a leading case of the Constitutional Court. Probably the most relevant is Judgment no 365/2007.

This case was brought before the Court by the State against a law of the Sardinia Region, establishing a 'Special Committee for the new regional Charter of Autonomy and Sovereignty of the People of Sardinia'. The problem was the use of the term 'sovereignty' in reference to the people of the Sardinia Region. Unlike some federal systems, such as in the United States, for example – where several entities can still be said to retain and share (a limited form of) 'sovereignty' – in Italy sovereignty belongs exclusively to the central State. Accordingly, the Constitutional Court declared the Sardinian regional law to be unconstitutional:

> Through the use of the term 'sovereignty', the law attempts to attribute a structure to the Region that differs profoundly from the existing one and is characterized by institutions more appropriate and suitable for a federal model, which is normally the result of historical processes in which the territorial entities that comprise the federal State retain forms and institutions that are marked by their prior condition of sovereignty.

The Court conceded that the absolute nature of State sovereignty today is intensely challenged, mainly by international and supranational legal orders, but at the same time it strongly reaffirmed that 'the internal sovereignty of the State keeps its essential structure intact, undamaged even by the significant expansion of the many functions attributed to the Regions and territorial entities by the Constitution'. For that reason, the Court confirmed the significance of the constitutional distinction between 'sovereignty' and 'autonomy'.[37]

FURTHER READING

Arban, E, Martinico, G, and Palermo F (eds), *Federalism and Constitutional Law: The Italian Contribution to Comparative Regionalism* (Abingdon, Routledge, 2021).

Desideri, C, 'Regionalism and Territorial Politics in Italy' in S Mangiameli (ed), *Federalism, Regionalism and Territory* (Milan, Giuffrè, 2013) 149–96.

Mangiameli, S (ed), *Italian Regionalism: Between Unitary Traditions and Federal Processes: Investigating Italy's Form of State* (Cham, Springer, 2014).

[37] All these expressions are taken from Judgment no 365/2007.

8

The Judiciary

Judicial Function – Separation of Powers – Judicial independence – High Council of the Judiciary – Unity of Jurisdiction – Supreme Court of Cassation – Special Judges – Administrative Courts – Council of State – Regional Administrative Courts – Public Prosecutors – Natural Judge – Impartiality – Fair Trial – Judicial Responsibility

I. INTRODUCTION

'JUDGES SHALL BE subject only to the law' reads Article 101.2 of the Constitution. This is the core constitutional principle that depicts the position of courts within the overall constitutional architecture of powers, and reveals the understanding of the judicial function entrenched in the Italian Constitution.

On the one hand, this constitutional principle proclaims the independence of judicial bodies and aims to protect the judiciary from all external pressures and interference, especially from the political branches, in contrast with the previous practice, notably during the fascist era, when judges were officials subject to the government and bound by its political directives. As it has been rightly observed, 'There is no liberty, if the judiciary power be not separated from the legislative and executive'.[1]

On the other hand, Article 101 endorses an understanding of the judiciary as a neutral power, whose mission is to enforce with virtually no discretionary power the legislation adopted by Parliament. This understanding echoes Montesquieu's definition of the judge as the *bouche de la loi* and suggests that the judicial function is that of simply implementing the legislation passed by Parliament in the context

[1] CL de Montesquieu, *De l'esprit des lois* (1748), English translation: AM Cohler, BC Myller and HS Stone (eds), *The Spirit of Laws* (Cambridge, Cambridge University Press, 1989) 2nd Part, Book 11.

of actual controversies, drawing a clear-cut line between *legis-latio* and *juris-dictio*. That is why the Constitution does not characterise the judiciary as a 'power', but as a 'branch' (*ordine*). In fact, Article 104 contrasts the judiciary with the 'powers' of the State and defines the judiciary as 'a branch that is autonomous and independent of all other powers'.

II. THE EVOLUTION OF THE JUDICIAL FUNCTION

Today, the judicial function can hardly be reductively defined as a simple activity of pronouncing what the law is, as the etymological meaning of the word *juris-dictio* would suggest: *jus-dicere*. In truth, the image of the judge as the *bouche de la loi*, which was already a myth in the nineteenth century, does not accurately correspond to the contemporary reality even in a country, such as Italy, which ascribes to the continental tradition based on parliamentary legislation.[2]

Since the Second World War, even 'civil law' countries have been the theatre of the 'rise of the judiciary' within the constitutional system.[3] A number of factors have broadened the judicial discretion[4] and have brought the judiciary's role to prominence within contemporary public life: including the constitutional culture and the related new methods of interpretation, the role of national courts in the EU and Council of Europe legal systems, the rights revolution, and the judicialisation of political issues.

First, the interpretative powers of judicial bodies have become increasingly creative, thanks to a methodological approach that is being used more frequently by the Italian courts, namely the interpretation of the law 'according to the Constitution'. In this regard, the twelfth national congress of the National Association of Judges (*Associazione nazionale magistrati*), held in September 1965, was a turning point.[5] On that occasion, the judiciary unanimously stated its intention to abandon its formalistic understanding of the interpretative activity of courts in order to promote a canon of interpretation 'in conformity with the principles of the Constitution'. Since then, a robust constitutional culture has

[2] N Zanon and F Biondi, *Il sistema costituzionale della magistratura* (Bologna, Zanichelli, 2019) 3ff.

[3] See M Cappelletti, *Giudici legislatori?* (Milan, Giuffrè, 1984).

[4] A Barak, *Judicial Discretion* (New Haven, Yale University Press, 1989).

[5] A Meniconi, *Storia della magistratura italiana* (Bologna, Il Mulino, 2012) 310ff.

permeated the mentality of all judges, and since the 1970s, a dynamic judicial activism has shaped the stance of the Italian judiciary, including first-instance judges (*pretori*).[6] This constitutional mindset is strongly cultivated within the legal education at the university level and in the ongoing training of judges conducted by the 'school of the judiciary' (Scuola superiore della magistratura), which was introduced in Italy by legislative decree no 26/2006.[7] Instead of uncritically executing any legislative command, judges may either trigger the process of judicial review of legislation before the Constitutional Court, if they have doubts as to the constitutionality of the legislation at stake (see Chapter 9), or interpret it in such a way as to ensure a rule which is consistent with the principles of the Constitution.

The Constitutional Court itself encourages such an approach, when it says that 'as a matter of principle, laws are not to be declared unconstitutional because they are susceptible to being interpreted in contrast with the Constitution (and some judges choose such an unconstitutional interpretation), but only if it is impossible to interpret them in conformity with the Constitution'.[8] Over time, this methodological approach has contributed to the dissemination of a robust constitutional culture within the judiciary. By means of this canon, judges are encouraged to make use of a broad discretionary power in order to avoid any construction of the law which could lead to results that conflict with higher norms: considering the poor quality of parliamentary legislation, the interpretative power of judges has expanded enormously, in the form of value-oriented interpretation.

Second, the Court of Justice of the European Union (CJEU) has very much contributed to the empowerment of the national judiciary, in affirming, since the *Simmenthal* case (1978), that every national court has to apply EU law (see Chapter 2). This ruling has encouraged judges who previously considered themselves strictly 'subject to the law' (Article 101.1) to disregard the national law, and even to dis-apply it, in order to ensure the direct effect of the EU law. Indeed, the aforementioned principle applies only in those cases where an EU provision with direct effect is at stake. However, one cannot overstate the spill-over effect of the *Simmenthal* doctrine on the general position of the judiciary, which

[6] E Bruti Liberati, 'La ANM e le correnti della magistratura' in S Merlini (ed), *Magistratura e politica* (Florence, Passigli, 2016) 112ff.

[7] V Onida, 'La cultura e la formazione dei magistrati' in Merlini (n 6) 109ff.

[8] Judgment no 56/1996.

over time has become more prone to challenging the law made by higher sources – be they constitutional or transnational – rather than perceiving themselves to be strictly 'subject' to it.

Third, a similar reinforcement of the judicial power of national courts was also prompted by the European Court of Human Rights (ECtHR) in the context of a more general development of a legal culture of individual rights. The 'rights revolution', which was originally triggered in the late 1960s and 1970s in the United States, has little by little expanded at a global level, so that 'constitutionalism 2.0' is centred upon individual rights and courts.[9] Most of the new legal issues are framed in terms of individual rights stemming from the right to private life, the right to self-determination, and the right to non-discrimination. New claims concerning social needs, bioethical issues, family relationships, multicultural concerns, new technologies, law and religion, and immigration are part and parcel of the everyday work of courts. These cases are governed by a number of different and overlapping sets of principles of national and international origin. In the European context, a crucial role is played by the ECtHR in Strasbourg, which has been enforcing the European Convention on Human Rights as a 'living instrument'. The enforcement of the European Convention and its rights – as developed by the Strasbourg Court via a dynamic interpretation – falls within the jurisdiction of the national judges, who are therefore provided with another canon of rights-oriented interpretation, to be added to the above-mentioned instruments that expand the role of the judiciary within the constitutional system.

Fourth, and closely connected with the previous elements, is the judicialisation of political issues,[10] which shows that an increasing number of divisive political issues are being brought before the courts.

During his visit to America, the French aristocrat Alexis de Tocqueville was struck by the powerful position of the judiciary within that country's legal and political system. Among other things, he noticed that, 'there is almost no political question in the United States that is not resolved, sooner or later, into a judicial question'.[11] Nowadays, his remark could

[9] D Lustig and JHH Weiler, 'Judicial Review in Contemporary World: Retrospective and Perspective' (2018) 16(2) *International Journal of Constitutional Law* 315.

[10] M Shapiro and A Stone Sweet, *On Law, Politics and Judicialization* (Oxford, Oxford University Press 2002). On the 'montée en puissance des juges' see also M Delmas-Marty, *Les forces imaginantes du droit, III. La refondation des pouvoirs* (Paris, Seuil, 2007), part I, ch 1.

[11] A de Tocqueville, *Democracy in America* (New York, Adlard & Saunders, 1838) Book 2, 8.

easily be applied to many legal orders across Europe, including Italy. By way of illustration, it suffices to recall the two major judgments of the Italian Constitutional Court on electoral laws,[12] in which the Court incisively corrected, and practically re-wrote, pieces of electoral legislation that for a long time were viewed as the 'domain of politics' (see Chapter 3).

Over time, the judiciary has gained great relevance in public life and in Italian society. This relevance dramatically emerged at a pivotal point in Italian history, namely, the Bribesville criminal investigation (*Tangentopoli*) in 1992: conducted by the prosecutors of Milan, the investigation resulted in a high number of indictments of famous politicians for corruption, and eventually brought the political system into disrepute in the public's opinion, and finally led to the collapse of the traditional political parties (see Chapter 1). Since then, the relations between the sphere of politics and the judiciary have been tense and occasionally conflictual.[13]

The judiciary in Italy is certainly no longer perceived as the 'least dangerous branch', as Alexander Hamilton said in *Federalist* no 78, or as a 'null power', as Montesquieu suggested. On the contrary, the Italian judiciary is an influential branch and the Italian case confirms the trend of an 'ever accelerating reliance on courts and judicial means for addressing core moral predicaments, public policy and political controversies'.[14] It is in this context that the core values of the separation of powers and judicial independence are to be preserved and developed according to new lines that mirror contemporary reality.

III. THE SEPARATION OF POWERS AND JUDICIAL INDEPENDENCE

The fundamental values of the separation of powers and judicial independence are considered central tenets of all liberal democracies, everywhere and at all times. Separation of powers is not only a matter of constitutional architecture, intended to secure the rational organisation of powers, it is also a matter of liberty for each individual and for society as a whole. It is a basic condition for the effective protection of individual rights and liberties, in order to guarantee to each individual an

[12] Judgments nos 1/2014 and 35/2017.
[13] S Merlini, 'Magistratura e politica. Una introduzione' in Merlini (n 6).
[14] R Hirschl, *Towards Juristocracy* (Cambridge, Harvard University Press, 2004) 12ff.

effective remedy against any breach of her rights. It is no surprise, then, that since the totalitarian regime, special emphasis has been given by the Constitution to the independence of the judiciary, the actions of which had been blatantly directed by the authoritarian, Fascist Government. Today, the independence of the judiciary is under attack in a variety of ways in many countries.[15]

The Italian Constitution ensures the independence of judges in two ways: the *external* independence of the judiciary as a whole from outside pressures by any other State organ, especially by the Government; and the *internal* independence of every single judge within the judicial system, namely from any interference by other judicial bodies.

A. External Independence: The High Council of the Judiciary

As to the judiciary's 'external independence', the primary dividing line which is sought to be preserved has always been between political institutions, on the one hand, and guarantee institutions, on the other. The historical dichotomy between *gubernaculum* (the government) and *iurisdictio* (the judicial branch) is once again topical today: judicial independence is put at risk when the clear division between *gubernaculum* and *iurisdictio* is blurred.

The Italian Constitution requires judges to maintain a neutral stance with respect to political associations. In fact, Article 98 provides that limitations may be put in place for judges (as well as other classes of public servants, such as military staff and diplomatic or consular representatives) with respect to their rights to be members of political parties. In accordance with this constitutional directive, the law prohibits judges from being enrolled in political parties and participating on a regular basis in their activities, as well as in the activity of bodies operating in financial and economic sectors, as that may impair their independence and impartiality or undermine the perception of their independence and impartiality.[16] This does not imply that a member of the judiciary cannot run for political elections: in fact, it is not unusual for a judge to become a member of the national parliament or of the regional council and therefore to become suspended from judicial functions until the end of

[15] G Pitruzzella, O Pollicino and M Bassini (eds), *Corti europee e democrazia. Rule of law, indipendenza e accountability* (Milan, Bocconi, 2019).

[16] Article 3 of Legislative Decree no 109/2006, as interpreted by Constitutional Court (Judgment no 170/2018).

that mandate. However, so long as the judge is an active member of the judiciary, the judge is required to refrain from any active participation in political activities, in order to preserve the judge's independence as well as the public perception of independence from political forces.

The overarching principle of the independence of the judiciary is outlined in Article 104, which provides that the judicial branch 'shall be autonomous and independent of all other powers'. The Constituent Assembly decided that judges should be shielded from all interference from the Government and the Ministry of Justice, as well as from any other political authority. In particular, the executive branch was stripped of all powers to direct judges, as well as all powers regarding the careers of ordinary judges, including matters such as transfers, promotions and disciplinary measures. The Constituent Assembly considered that decisions regarding the professional position of the members of the judiciary might influence their autonomy and, as a direct or indirect consequence, their independence. Consequently, it decided to entrust these functions to a 'governing body of the judiciary' – the High Council of the Judiciary (*Consiglio Superiore della Magistratura* (CSM)) – composed mainly, though not exclusively, of judges. For similar reasons, the Constituent Assembly decided that public prosecutors should not answer to the Minister of Justice, but should be entrenched within the Judiciary, along with all other judges.

In actual fact, the idea of a 'Council for the judiciary' predates the Constitution and was initially instituted by law no 511/1907, at the initiative of Vittorio Emanuele Orlando, acting as Minister of Justice at the time. However, during the years of the Fascist regime, the judiciary was subjected to the will of the Government. In order to prevent history from repeating itself, the Constituent Assembly decided to re-establish a judicial council and to entrench the new body within the Constitutional framework in order to safeguard against future threats to its existence and to its powers.

The High Council of the Judiciary, established by Article 104, is chaired by the President of the Republic. It is not a judicial body (except when it delivers disciplinary measures), as it mainly carries out administrative functions concerning the professional career of the judges. It was first instituted in 1958 (10 years after the entry into force of the Constitution) and was originally regulated by law no 195/1958, which was eventually amended a number of times. The members of the Council are divided in two categories: two thirds of them are the 'gowned members', who are elected by the ordinary judges, while one third are the 'lay members', who are elected by the Parliament in joint session.

According to the present legislation (law no 44/2002), the High Council of the Judiciary is composed of 27 members; 16 are judges elected from and amongst their own ranks, while the remaining eight are either university law professors or senior lawyers, elected by the Parliament in joint session. The First President and the Prosecutor General of the Court of Cassation are *ex officio* members of the High Council.

The 16 ordinary judges of the High Council are elected by judges themselves 'belonging to the various categories' (Article 104.4). Candidates are elected in three national electoral constituencies, reflecting different categories of judges: judges, public prosecutors and members of the Court of Cassation. Candidates are chosen from various lists, normally representing the different organised groups (*correnti*), with different cultural and political orientations, into which the National Association of Judges is traditionally divided.[17] The role of these organised groups is a matter for discussion and reform proposals of have been presented in Parliament in order to contrast the risks of 'politicisation' of the election for the representatives of the judiciary in the High Council. The other members of the High Council are elected by the Parliament in joint session, by secret ballot and the majority of three-fifths of the members of the two Houses (or the majority of three-fifths of the voters after the second counting).

Owing to the numerical superiority of members elected by judges, the High Council is often defined as a 'self-governing body' of the judiciary. It is not, however, a true form of self-government, due to the presence of members who are neither chosen from among judges, nor by the judges themselves. It is a presence conceived in order to prevent the judiciary from being totally detached from the other powers and also to prevent the independent judiciary from turning into a 'caste', detached and isolated from the rest of the constitutional organisation.[18]

All the members of the High Council hold office for four years and are not immediately eligible for re-election.

As to its functions, Article 105 assigns the High Council a series of competences previously delegated to the Minister of Justice, including 'jurisdiction on recruitment, posting and transfer, promotion and disciplinary measures of member of the Judiciary'. The High Council rules on the careers and legal status of judges in order to guarantee their institutional independence.

[17] E Bruti Liberati, 'La ANM e le correnti della magistratura' in Merlini (n 6) 139ff.

[18] S Bartole, *Autonomia e indipendenza dell'ordine giudiziario* (Padua, Cedam, 1964).

As a result, the role of the Minister of Justice was diminished. The Minister of Justice maintains some organisational powers, as outlined in Article 110: 'Without prejudice to the authority of the High Council of the Judiciary, the Minister of Justice shall have responsibility for the organisation and implementation of services relating to the administration of justice'. The Minister is allowed to cooperate with the High Council, including to make requests, asking for and providing information and advice on a number of issues, but the final say is reserved for the High Council.[19]

Moreover, according to Article 107, the Minister of Justice can initiate disciplinary action against any member of the judiciary, but these disciplinary procedures take place before, and are decided by, the High Council (more precisely by its dedicated section).

In the last decade a number of scandals – including the *Palamara* case, regarding a former president of the National Association of Judges and member of the High Council, who was indicted for corruption and struck off as a judge in 2021 – have affected some components of the judiciary, especially those elected in the High Council for their connections with politicians and for their power to influence appointments to the highest positions of the judicial offices. Therefore, a project of reform of the High Council is under discussion and a few abrogative referendums concerning the judiciary have been proposed by some political forces.

B. Internal Independence: Appointment, Tenure and Absence of Hierarchy

In order to ensure the full independence of the judiciary, the Constitution outlines a set of principles aimed at shielding each judge from pressure and influences deriving from within the judicial branch too. This objective is pursued by constitutional provisions concerning: (i) the appointment of judges; (ii) their security of tenure; and (iii) the absence of hierarchy within the judiciary.

i. Appointment of Judges

With respect to the appointments of judges, Italy follows the bureaucratic model of a judiciary composed of professional judges. Entry to

[19] Judgments nos 379/1992 and 380 /2003 of the Constitutional Court.

the judiciary is by competitive public examination (Article 106.1), ie a selection, traditionally open to every person who has been awarded a degree in law, based on meritocratic criteria. This choice is based on the conviction that the criteria for selecting members of the judiciary should be based exclusively on candidates' legal expertise.

Rules regarding access to the profession of judges and prosecutors have been changed over the last few years, in order to promote the development of a cultural basis common to all the members of the legal world: judges, prosecutors, notaries and lawyers.[20] The legislator has constituted post-graduate schools within universities for law graduate students who wish to enter the legal profession. Graduate students who aspire to enter the judiciary are invited to either attend the post-graduate school for the legal profession or to undertake an 18-month traineeship before applying for the competitive public examination.

It is noteworthy that, until 1963, women were not admitted to the judiciary, despite Article 51 providing that 'any citizen of either sex is eligible for public offices and elected positions on equal terms'. The Constitutional Court paved the way for the Parliament to reform the previous legislation and remove all legal obstacles that prevented women from participating in the public selection for entry to the judiciary.[21] The percentage of female judges has gradually increased and is currently around 55 per cent of the total, which is slightly below 10,000 individuals.

The Constitution itself provides a few exceptions to the general rule established by Article 106, which states that 'Judges shall be recruited through competitive examinations'.

First, honorary magistrates can be appointed to perform judicial functions while not officially being members of the profession. These magistrates are presently the *giudici di pace* and they have jurisdiction regarding minor civil and criminal cases (law no 374/1991). The rationale for this exception is to lighten the case load of the judiciary, and to speed up the resolution of minor controversies.

The second exception relates to the members of juries, who are required for some criminal trials. Juries are composed of ordinary citizens with secondary school qualifications who are selected by drawing lots to sit on the *Corte d'Assise*, both at first instance and on appeal.

[20] Legislative decree no 398/1997.

[21] Judgment no 33/1960 and Law no 66/1963. Cf M Cartabia, 'Il principio di pari opportunità nella giurisprudenza costituzionale' in M D'Amico, CM Lendaro and C Siccardi (eds), *Eguaglianza di genere in Magistratura. Quanto ancora dobbiamo aspettare?* (Milan, Franco Angeli, 2017).

This is the only implementation of citizens' direct participation in the administration of justice provided for by Article 102. In the Italian tradition, there is no separation between the fact-finding phase, the outcome of which is a verdict, and the legal phase, which is the responsibility of the court and the result of which is the judgment. On the contrary, jury members share with professional judges all the judicial functions in the process in which they are called upon to participate, and they act as a unique body.

The third and last exception is represented by the appointment as judges of the Court of Cassation of law professors and lawyers, upon the recommendation of the High Council of the Judiciary. Article 106.3 justifies such appointments on the basis of the candidates' 'outstanding merits'. The rationale is to improve the professional expertise of the Court of Cassation, although this provision has not been used very often until recently.

ii. Security of Tenure

Pursuant to Article 107.1, judges cannot be removed from office, nor transferred, without their consent. They can be dismissed or suspended from their duties or transferred to other courts or given other duties only by means of a decision of the High Council of the Judiciary, reached in relation to disciplinary, or pre-determined organisational, reasons. The rationale underlying this principle is to guarantee security of tenure to each judge, which is an essential component of the protection of their independence.

This means that judges' locations can only be altered on a voluntary basis or for disciplinary reasons,[22] although transfers can also be imposed by the High Council for objective reasons related to the 'environmental incompatibility' of an individual judge.

iii. Absence of Hierarchy within the Judiciary

There is no hierarchical relationship between judges: the judiciary is not organised through a hierarchical or a pyramidal structure, but it should instead be regarded as a diffuse power.[23] Members of the superior courts cannot be considered to be 'higher' judges vis-à-vis members of courts of first instance. Moreover, senior judges are not permitted

[22] Article 13 of Legislative Decree no 196/2006.
[23] Judgments nos 228/1975 and 229/1975.

to instruct junior judges as to their preferred methods of issuing judgments.[24] Pursuant to Article 107.3, 'Judges shall be distinguished only by their different functions'. The Constitution provides that the powers of each justice department should never interfere with the powers of higher courts.[25]

There are, however, different degrees of adjudication: that is, decisions reached at first instance can be appealed and be quashed, in whole or in part, by courts of appeal and may be further appealed to the Supreme Court of Cassation. This does not mean, however, that courts of first instance are hierarchically subordinate to courts of appeal, nor the latter to the Court of Cassation: judges are completely independent in the exercise of their functions and no *stare decisis* rule (ie binding judicial precedent) applies. This is why the judicial branch is defined as a 'diffused' power and every single judge is considered to be a 'power of the State' so that the judge can raise or resist a dispute before the Constitutional Court in the event of a conflict between different branches of Government (see Chapter 9).

Of course, internal independence does not mean that judges can completely and deliberately ignore previous judgments, especially when decided by the Court of Cassation: they are free to decide differently, although always expressly articulating why they do not agree with the principle previously affirmed or why they think that the principle is inapplicable to the dispute before them. In a civil law system, judicial precedents serve a persuasive role. The Court of Cassation relies upon this persuasive role, in order to exercise its function of ensuring the uniform interpretation of legal provisions. This is a demanding function, consistent with ensuring 'the exact observance and uniform interpretation of the law, the unity of the national objective law', and referred to by the traditional expression, *nomofilachia*.[26] The exercise of this function appears extremely demanding in contemporary pluralistic society, especially by a body, the Court of Cassation, composed of more than 350 judges. However, the most important and controversial questions are assigned to the United Sections, either civil or penal, each of which is composed of nine judges.

The Court of Cassation is also assigned the task of establishing jurisdiction (ie indicating, when there is a conflict between the ordinary courts and the special, Italian or foreign courts, which body possesses

[24] Judgment no 40/1964.
[25] Judgment no 143/1973.
[26] Article 65 of the Basic Law on the Judiciary no 12/1941.

the power to resolve the matter) and competence (ie resolving a conflict between two lower courts).[27]

IV. THE ORGANISATION OF THE JUDICIARY

The Constitution provides individuals with a number of rights before the judiciary. These include access to justice and the right to a defence (Article 24), the right to be processed by a natural judge predetermined by the law (Article 25) and the right to a fair trial (Article 111, as amended in 1999). Although in Italy the judiciary is a strong branch and a prominent protagonist in the public sphere – always at the forefront in the implementation of constitutional rights and values – a continuing issue is the excessive length of the judicial proceedings. The ECtHR has pronounced some 2,000 decisions condemning Italy for violation of the right to a reasonable duration of judicial proceedings. This difficulty is becoming more and more relevant, because citizens, as well as economic actors, feel unsecure about the system's capacity of effectively protecting their rights. The actual guarantee of individual rights depends on how the judiciary is organised and on how prompt and effective is the judicial response. It is not by chance that the Strasbourg Court requires the member states to provide an 'effective judicial remedy' for the protection of individual rights. Therefore, some reforms concerning the judicial organisation in Italy are under examination in order to fix this endemic issue. For example, alongside with the reform of the criminal and civil procedure, decree-law no 80/2021, as converted by law no 113/2021, has introduced the 'office for the process': young judicial assistants who can help the judges in discharging their duties. Moreover, new recruitments of judges and staff are underway in order to support the judicial offices and reduce the backlog.

A. The Principle of Unity of Jurisdiction and Special Judges

Article 102 of the Constitution establishes the unity of jurisdiction when it states that 'Judicial proceedings shall be exercised by ordinary judges empowered and regulated by the provisions concerning the Judiciary'. This principle implies that all the judicial functions are performed by a single judicial body. The primary objective in establishing this provision

[27] The Court of Cassation also performs some non-judicial but administrative functions relating to elections and abrogative referendums (see ch 3).

was to better secure the full independence of all courts. The principle, however, is not without exceptions.

During the debates in the Constituent Assembly, opponents of this principle advocated the necessity of distinguishing between various specialised judicial units with jurisdiction in relation to different areas of law. The result was a compromise between these two extremes. Article 102, on the one hand, proclaims the principle of judicial unity as a fundamental tenet of the Italian legal system and establishes a strict ban on extraordinary judges, ie judges appointed *ex post* to settle specific disputes, who are presumed to lack independence (Article 102.2). On the other hand, however, the Constitution itself envisages a number of special judges who have jurisdiction regarding a defined group of controversies (Article 103).

Moreover, according to Article 102.2, 'specialised sections for specific matters within the ordinary judicial bodies may be established, and these sections may include the participation of qualified citizens who are not members of the judiciary'. According to the Constitutional Court, these sections are not a *tertium genus* between special and ordinary courts, but rather a *species* of the latter, which require the participation of members with special 'expertise', due to the highly technical character of their controversies:[28] including juvenile courts, immigration sections, corporate sections and the like.

The Italian judicial system is therefore a system in which ordinary courts are supplemented by special courts with significant functions.

Some of these are explicitly provided for by the Constitution:

(a) Administrative judges: mainly, the Council of State (*Consiglio di Stato*) (Article 103), which is also entrusted with the function of advising the Government (see Chapter 5), and the Regional Administrative Courts (*Tribunali Amministrativi Regionali-TAR*) (Article 125).
(b) The Court of Accounts (*Corte dei Conti*) is a composite body, empowered to exercise a combination of functions, including an *ex post* audit of the State budget and of other public funding matters (see Chapter 5). It also has jurisdiction as to the responsibilities of public servants.
(c) According to Article 103.3, Military Courts in times of peace have jurisdiction over military offences committed by members of the armed forces. The decisions of Military Courts of first instance

[28] Judgment no 76/1961.

(*Tribunali militari*) can be appealed to the Military Court of Appeal (*Corte militare di appello*), whose decisions can in turn be appealed to the Court of Cassation (adjudicating in its normal composition).

Article 108.2 requires that 'the law shall ensure the independence of special courts judges and prosecutors, and of any outside persons participating in the administration of justice'. Therefore, bodies similar to the High Council of the Judiciary, whose competence concerns only ordinary judges, have been instituted. The Council of the Presidency of the Administrative Judiciary (*Consiglio di presidenza della magistratura amministrativa*) comprises the President of the Council of State, plus 10 'gowned' members and four 'lay' members, elected by the two Houses of Parliament. The Council of Presidency of the Court of Accounts (*Consiglio di presidenza della magistratura contabile*) is composed of the President and the Prosecutor General of that Court, 10 'gowned' members and four 'lay' members, elected by the two Houses of the Parliament. The independence of military courts is guaranteed by the Council of the Military Judiciary (*Consiglio di presidenza della magistratura militare*), chaired by the First President of the Court of Cassation and comprising the Prosecutor General of the Court of Cassation itself, two 'gowned' members and one 'lay' member, appointed jointly by the Speaker of the two Houses and acting as vice-president. The main competence of these councils relates to the careers of the judges falling within their respective jurisdictions.

Although the Constitution (VI Transitory and Final Provision) explicitly stated that a revision of the existing special courts was to be carried out within five years of the effective date of entry into force of the Constitution, the objective of preserving these courts prevailed over the desire to abolish them. Therefore, today there are still other special jurisdictions in addition to those listed by Article 103. The most important ones, especially with respect to the volume of their case-loads, are the tax courts.

B. Administrative Courts: A Dual System

The Italian judiciary follows the French tradition of separation between '*ordinary courts*' and '*administrative courts*'. The origins of this system date back to 1865 (law no 2248, Annex E, of 20 March 1865), although it was effectively established in 1889 (law no 5992/1889), when the Council of State (a body which has existed since 1831, with a purely advisory role) was granted a judicial power to protect individuals affected by the activity of the public administration.[29] The underlying notion is that individuals are not entitled to '*full subjective rights*' before the public administration, but instead have a diminished position, limited to the '*legitimate interests*', because their individual interests are mitigated by concurrent public interests.[30]

The Constitution confirmed this situation in Article 103: 'The Council of State and the other administrative justice bodies shall have jurisdiction over the protection of legitimate interests before public powers and, in particular matters laid out by law, also of subjective rights'. Over time, the legislation has expanded the range of matters in relation to which the administrative courts have jurisdiction to also encompass subjective rights: the so-called matters of 'exclusive jurisdiction'.[31] Furthermore, law no 205/2000 also added to the traditional power of administrative courts to invalidate illegitimate acts of public bodies the competence to award damages, which was originally a power which was confined to the exclusive competence of ordinary judges. Individuals who have been affected by an illegitimate act of the public administration can therefore claim damages alongside seeking a declaration of the invalidity of the act itself.

Today, the Council of State serves as a second instance judge within the administrative justice system, since the Regional Administrative Courts (*Tribunali Amministrativi Regionali* (TAR)) were instituted by law no 1034/1971, implementing Article 125 of the Constitution: 'Administrative Courts of the first instance shall be established in the Region, in accordance with the rules established by the law of the Republic. Sections may be established in places other than the regional capital'.

The administrative justice system represents an important reality in Italy. The Council of State alone decides around 10,000 cases per year. The crucial role of the administrative judges is often the subject of public debate, as its influence on the economy and on the speed of the activity of public authorities are far from being negligible. Although the average time for defining an administrative judgment is definitely shorter than

[29] P Aimo, *Le origini della giustizia amministrativa. Consigli di prefettura e consiglio di Stato nell'Italia napoleonica* (Milan, Giuffrè, 1990).

[30] See Court of Cassation, Judgment no 500/1999. On the difference between 'full subjective rights' and 'legitimate interests' see GU Rescigno, 'La tutela dei diritti soggettivi e degli interessi legittimi secondo la Costituzione italiana' (2006) 12(1) *Diritto Pubblico* 111.

[31] As outlined in Legislative Decree nos 80/1998 and law no 205/2000, as interpreted and delimited by the Constitutional Court's Judgment no 204/2004.

the one needed for settling a civil case, the risk of a complaint to the Regional Administrative Court, raised by those who have been negatively affected by it, is always just behind the corner for any administrative decision.

C. Judges and Public Prosecutors

Within the ordinary judiciary, two figures can be singled out: judges and public prosecutors. The first are in charge of judicial decision-making functions; the second of investigating tasks, acting as public prosecutors (*pubblici ministeri*), within the public prosecutor's office (called *procure*). They both belong to the same judicial body, although from time to time – even very recently – a debate arises about the opportunity to distinguish between the two careers in order to avoid interferences and influences between judges and prosecutors.

Public prosecutors have the power to conduct criminal investigations, to trigger criminal processes and to participate in the criminal process in a dialectic position, prosecuting the person charged with a criminal offence.

The Constitution confirms that the judicial police is at the direct disposal of the judiciary for the purposes of criminal investigations (Article 109). This constitutional provision was not implemented by creating a specialised body of the criminal police, but rather by entrusting specialised sections of the ordinary police force (*Polizia di Stato, Arma dei Carabinieri, Guardia di Finanza*) with the tasks of the criminal police. This choice is not without some downsides, because, in a sense, the members of the criminal police wear 'two hats': generally speaking, the police force belongs to the executive branch and operates under the supervision of the Government, but those who play the role of criminal police are actually directed by the Judge and the Public Prosecutor.[32]

As to their organisation, the public prosecutors' offices are hierarchically ordered structures, in which the heads of the departments may direct, control and instruct their assistants, whose matters can also be assigned or revoked with justification.

[32] On this delicate balance between the power of direction and coordination of the public prosecutors and the hierarchical superiors of the criminal police agents, see Judgment no 229/2018.

These hierarchical relationships must comply with Article 112, which states that 'The public prosecutor shall have the obligation to institute criminal proceedings'. This statement has a twofold meaning. First, it guarantees the independence of the public prosecutors from other branches of government, namely the Executive, which is not allowed to control or interfere with criminal investigations conducted by the public prosecutors. Second, it ideally prevents public prosecutors from exercising any discretionary powers as to whether or not to conduct criminal investigations, although, obviously, it cannot prevent priorities from being established by the head of the office.[33] Be that as it may, if there is sufficient evidence, a criminal trial is to be commenced; otherwise the lawsuit must be dismissed. The rationale of this principle is to ensure the equality of citizens before the law, and respect for the principle of strict legality in criminal matters (Article 25), as well as the impartiality of the judges.

The power to institute penal proceedings falls within the exclusive domain of the public prosecutors, although any citizen is permitted to submit complaints to the public prosecutor, who will eventually set the criminal process in motion. The criminal code draws a distinction between crimes prosecuted *ex officio* by the judiciary and those prosecuted in response to a complaint, which is sometimes a necessary condition for instituting penal proceedings.

V. JUDICIAL RESPONSIBILITY

The traditional perception of the judiciary as a 'null power' was incompatible with the imposition of any liability on the part of judges for their misconduct and wrongdoings. In recent times, a lively public debate has advocated for the members of the judiciary to bear increased responsibilities, especially after the rendering of some judgments of the CJEU, which have questioned the capability of Italian legislation to provide for such responsibility.

The dramatic change of the role of the judiciary in public life and the expansion of judges' discretion has gone hand in hand with the request for stricter regulation of judges' legal responsibility for any improper exercise of their functions. Yet, any regulation of judicial responsibility must also take into account the overarching principle of the independence

[33] Law no 250/2005 and Legislative Decree no 106/2006.

of the judiciary.[34] Today, it is generally accepted that judges are legally responsible for their actions, but the discussion concerns the forms and limits of their responsibility, to be defined according to the distinctive features of the judicial function.[35]

Judges are subject to three types of responsibility: (a) criminal; (b) disciplinary; and (c) civil.

(a) As to *criminal responsibility*, judges are subject to the same common rules applicable to all individuals in relation to crimes committed in their capacity as private citizens. Similarly, there are no exceptions or special procedures for criminal offences perpetrated by judges in the exercise of their judicial function.

(b) A pivotal role is assigned to the *disciplinary responsibility* of judges, which has been reformed by law no 150/2005 and Legislative Decree no 109/2006. These provisions have specified an enumerated list of misdeeds that trigger the disciplinary responsibility of judges, by contrast with the previous legislation, whose broad and generic definition of the behaviours that amounted to disciplinary breaches gave rise to much speculation.[36]

The sanctions applicable to disciplinary matters include: warning, censure, removal from service, temporary restraint from being appointed to direct or partially direct offices, suspension from judicial function for a period of up to three months, and dismissal from office. Once again, for reasons of legal certainty, the law prescribes which sanction may be imposed for which offence.

Jurisdiction with respect to the disciplinary process is entrusted to a special section of the High Council of the Judiciary, according to Article 105.[37] The power to trigger the process lies with the Minister of Justice (following Article 107) as well as with the Prosecutor General of the Court of Cassation, who now bears the obligation to initiate the process.[38] The disciplinary process is classified as judicial; it is to be assisted by all the safeguard measures applicable to judicial processes; and the decision that is ultimately issued can be appealed to the United Sections of the Court of Cassation.

(c) *Civil liability* of judges and prosecutors was first introduced in Italy in 1988, following an abrogative referendum, with law no 177

[34] F Biondi, *La responsabilità del magistrato* (Milan, Giuffrè, 2006).
[35] Judgments nos 2/1968 and 385/1996.
[36] Article 18 of law no 311/1946.
[37] Judgments no 12/1971 and no 270/2002.
[38] Article 14 Legislative Decree no 109/2006.

(the so-called *legge Vassalli* on civil responsibility of judges).[39] This may be regarded as a very delayed constitutional implementation, when one considers that Article 28 of the Constitution states that 'Officials of the State or public agencies shall be directly responsible under criminal, civil, and administrative law for acts committed in violation of rights. In such cases, civil liability shall extend to the State and to such public agencies'. The Constitutional Court, for its part, had clearly stated since 1968 that this provision is concerned with all categories of civil servants, included the members of the judiciary, even if the civil responsibility of judges requires a special regime to take into account the very peculiar characters of the judicial function.[40] Consequently, for a long time, civil responsibility of judges was limited only to exceptional cases of denial of justice, wilful misconduct, bribery, fraud and corruption.[41]

The evolution of the role of the judiciary summarised above eventually brought to the forefront the demand for stricter regulation of the civil responsibility of judges, which was expressed by the people in the abrogative referendum of 1988.

The 1988 legislation that responded to the dominant public opinion was based on 'indirect responsibility' of the judges. Therefore, individuals were allowed to bring an action against the Italian State as a whole, and the latter might, in turn, request compensation from the judge in question. The cases in which the judge could have been held responsible were narrowly expressed and, in any case, the law provided that no liability arose relating to the interpretation of provisions of law or the assessment of facts and evidence, meaning that the independence of the judge acting in a judicial capacity remained shielded from undue pressure.

The regime of civil liability of the members of the judiciary was later reformed by law no 18/2015, in order to also bring it into line with decisions of the CJEU.[42] The law redefined the grounds for liability in a broader way: as a pre-condition for compensation, the damage in question must have resulted from a behaviour, an act or

[39] The abrogative referendum held in November 1987 asked whether the law excluding any responsibility for judicial errors should be abolished; 80.2% of the Italian voters said 'yes', with a turnout of 65.1%.

[40] Judgment no 2/1968.

[41] Articles 55 and 56 of 1940 code of civil procedure.

[42] Case C-224/01 *Kobler*, 30 September 2003; Case C-173/03 *Traghetti del Mediterraneo*, 13 June 2006; Case C-379/10 *Commission v Italy*, 24 November 2011.

judicial decision which was committed by a judge with 'malice' or 'gross negligence' in the exercise of the judge's functions, or which has resulted in 'a denial of justice'. In particular, law no 18/2015 has broadened the notion of gross negligence, removing the reference to an 'inexcusable error', previously provided for by the law.

While formally maintaining the principle of indirect liability of judges, law no 18/2015 made it mandatory for the State to take action for compensation against the judge found liable in the case of denial of justice, or manifest breach of domestic law or EU law, as well as misrepresentation of facts or evidence, with fraud, malice or inexcusable negligence.

VI. CONCLUSION

An overview of the Italian judicial system could not omit mentioning the endemic problem of the *excessive duration of judicial process*, repeatedly denounced by the ECtHR and that, although slightly improved in recent years, looks still unbearable, especially within the dynamics and the timeframe of contemporary society.

As a tentative response to this problem, law no 89/2001 (*Legge Pinto*, repeatedly amended until law no 208/2015) has introduced the 'responsibility of the State for pecuniary or non-pecuniary damage suffered' by citizens. The violation of the right to a reasonable length of process entitles the individual to equitable compensation. The standards for assessing excessive duration include: the 'complexity of the case'; the 'conduct of the parties'; the 'conduct of proceeding authorities', comprising both systemic defects in the judicial organisation and the personal behaviour of the individual judge managing the process. When the excessive duration has arisen due to the conduct of a single judge, the State can request compensation from the responsible judge via a procedure to be commenced before the Court of Accounts (Article 5 law no 89/2001).

This remedy provides the individual with some right to monetary compensation for the delay suffered. However, a radical solution to this problem must be addressed at a systemic level, with reforms concerning the organisation of the judiciary, changes to the judicial procedures and the regulation of new forms of alternative dispute resolution, so that the existing caseloads can be significantly reduced. Proposals in this direction are on the Parliament's agenda, along with the implementation of the aforementioned 'office for the process', providing the judge with judicial assistants, as seen in many other countries.

FURTHER READING

Benvenuti, S, and Paris, D, 'Judicial Self-Government in Italy: Merits, Limits and the Reality of an Export Model' (2018) 19(7) *German Law Journal* 1641.

Comporti, GD, 'The Administrative Jurisdiction in Italy: The Path Toward a Speciality to Serve Full Protection of Rights Against Public Authority' in D Sorace, L Ferrara, I Piazza (eds), *The Changing Administrative Law of an EU Member State: The Italian Case* (Heidelberg, Springer, 2021) 90–112.

Di Federico, G, 'Judicial Independence in Italy' in A Seibert-Fohr (ed), *Judicial Independence in Transition* (Heidelberg, Springer, 2012).

Ferrari, GF, 'Italian Perspective on the Judiciary' (2019) 10(1) *International Journal for Court Administration* 13.

Guarnieri, C, and Pederzoli, P, *The Judicial System: The Administration and Politics of Justice* (Northampton, Edward Elgar Publishing, 2020).

Silvestri, E, 'Administrative Justice in Italy' (2016) 3(2) *BRICS Law Journal* 67.

9

The Constitutional Court

Constitutional Review of Legislation – US model – Kelsenian model – European model – Composition – Functions – 'Living Law' Doctrine – Fascist legislation – Programmatic Norms – Preceptive Norms – Negative Legislators – Interpretative Judgments – Warning Decisions – Ways of Accession – Incidental Procedure – Dissenting Opinion – Collegiality – Relationality

I. INTRODUCTION

THIS CHAPTER OFFERS an account of the activity of the Constitutional Court as the 'living voice of the Italian Constitution'. At the outset, the chapter deals with the *historical reasons for* setting up a new institution in the form of a Constitutional Court, following the tragic experiences of the Fascist authoritarian regime and the Second World War. Despite this backdrop, which ought to have provided compelling reasons for the establishment of a Constitutional Court, a number of political parties, as well as legal and political theorists campaigned against the *judicial review of legislation*. This resulted in the *delayed creation* of the Court, eight years after the Constitution entered into force (1948–56). Following this discussion, the chapter outlines the principal features of the Court and of the Italian system of judicial review of legislation, born out of an amalgamation between the Kelsenian and US models. Finally, after considering the original, unfavourable context in which the Court was created, the main focus of the chapter is an examination of the 'strategy' that was adopted by the Court to overcome the pervasive resistance to it at the dawn of the Republic and the type of interactions the Court has had with its opponents.

The investigation focuses on the cooperative relationship that the Constitutional Court has built over time with other national judicial and political bodies, shaping *new types of decisions* – namely, interpretative and manipulative decisions – and elaborating *judicial doctrines* which are respectful of the powers of other branches of government – such as '*living law*' and '*margin of political appreciation*'. Likewise, the Constitutional Court has incrementally opened up to the broader European and global context, interacting with its European counterparts. As a result, the Italian style of constitutional adjudication and the distinctive contribution of the Italian Constitutional Court to the European model of constitutional adjudication appears to be a *relational approach*, comprising collaboration rather than conflict; interaction rather than isolation; openness rather than antagonism.

This feature can be traced throughout the different stages of the Court's activity. After *a delayed establishment*, during the first years of its existence, the Constitutional Court was mostly engaged in *disposing of the remains of the fascist regime*, aiming at the modernisation of the legislation inherited from the previous system. The following decades were dedicated to *building its toolkit*, with the Court investing its energy in shaping new remedies and new forms of legal reasoning. In the late 1980s, after the Lockheed trial[1] – which thwarted the activity of the Court for some years – the Court had to come to terms with an *overload of cases*. Reducing the docket, trusting the lower courts, and encouraging the interpretation of the law in accordance with the Constitution were the Court's responses to the excess of cases on its docket. The late 1990s were marked by a rise in *conflicts of attributions among powers*, in particular among political bodies and the judiciary, whereas after the constitutional reform of 2001, the Court tended to be overwhelmed by cases regarding *division of competence* between the State and Regions (mainly raised *principaliter*: see Chapter 7).

II. HISTORICAL BACKGROUND

Historical reasons easily explain why the Italian Constitution of 1948, like the German Basic Law of 1949, introduced into the republican

[1] The Court was required to exercise its criminal competence according to Art 134 of the Constitution in relation to two members of the Government who were charged of bribery regarding the purchase of some kind of planes. At that time, under Arts 96 and 134 of the Constitution, criminal procedures against members of the Government fell within the province of the Constitutional Court. The Lockheed bribery trial in 1978 and 1979 created a backlog in the Court's docket. Following a constitutional amendment approved in 1989, the Court now retains this criminal competence only in cases involving the President of the Republic (see ch 6).

constitutional architecture a new institution empowered with the function of judicially reviewing legislation. During the totalitarian regimes of the 1920s and 1930s, a vast number of shameful and atrocious crimes were committed through the law, not despite the law. Generally speaking, during the Fascist and Nazi regimes, the rule of law was formally respected, at least from a procedural point of view. Alas, from a substantive point of view, the content of the 'laws' passed by the national Parliaments during those years were at odds with the most basic sense of justice. One example is the racial legislation issued by the Italian Parliament in the late 1930s,[2] which openly discriminated against and persecuted Jews and other groups on the ground of race. With this background in mind, unsurprisingly, the national constitutions approved after the end of the Second World War, starting with the Italian and the German constitutions, were enriched with a generous catalogue of fundamental rights and with a new function: judicial review of legislation. For similar reasons, other European countries followed the same course, once they were released from the bondage of dictatorship: this was the case in Spain and Portugal in the 1970s, and also, some years later, in all Central and Eastern European countries after the fall of Communist regimes.[3]

At the time of the Italian Constitution's enactment, judicial review of legislation was a long-standing function of the courts on the other side of the Atlantic, since the seminal decision of the US Supreme Court, *Marbury v Madison* of 1803. Nonetheless, the American model of judicial review could not be wholly imported into continental Europe, due to a number of obstacles entrenched in the legal culture.[4]

First, the supremacy of the constitution was not a firm and established doctrine. Generally speaking, the text of the nineteenth century European constitutions did not include explicit 'supremacy clauses', nor did they provide special procedures for the purpose of amending

[2] The Italian Racial Laws were a set of statutes promulgated from 1938 to 1943, the most important of which is Royal Decree 17 November 1938 no 1728. This restricted the civil rights of Jews, banned their books and excluded them from public office and higher education. See ch 1.

[3] See T Groppi and M Olivetti (eds), *La giustizia costituzionale in Europa* (Milan, Giuffrè, 2003) 5ff; M De Visser, *Constitutional Review in Europe. A Comparative Analysis* (Oxford, Hart, 2013) 53ff; W Sadurski, *Rights Before Courts: A Study of Constitutional Courts in Postcommunist States of Central and Eastern Europe* (Dordrecht, Springer, 2014).

[4] See V Ferreres Comella, *Constitutional Courts and Democratic Values: A European Perspective* (Yale, Yale University Press, 2009) 20ff.

constitutional provisions. Second, and more decisively, the very fundamental pillars of modern European constitutionalism contrasted with the idea of judicial review of legislation: the British ideal of the *sovereignty of Parliament* or the French 'myth' of the 'law' as expression of the general will of the people – *la loi expression de la volonté générale* – were influential all over the continent. Moreover, following the French tradition, in Italy the judicial function was narrowly construed. The judiciary consisted of bureaucratic staff and judges, whose roles were defined as *la bouche de la loi* (see Chapter 9). Essentially, the main obstacle to judicial review of legislation in Europe was rooted in the narrow conception of the role of the judiciary – combined with the great emphasis on 'the law' and 'the parliaments' which was part and parcel of the key legal theories of the time.

When it was proposed at the Constituent Assembly, the idea of constitutional review of legislation was caught in the crossfire: on the one hand, some solid historical reasons called for it; on the other hand, the legal and political mindset was at odds with it. Although the necessity of a guardian against abuses by the legislature was imperative, that guardian could not be found in the ordinary courts (which in some cases were still inhabited by judges trained during the authoritarian regimes). As a result, a new special institution was designed for the purpose of judicial review: the establishment of a special judge, a constitutional court or tribunal, appeared to be the natural option in those countries that wished to safeguard the constitution against the legislature, but which traditionally retained – and still want to retain – a narrow conception of the judiciary.

III. THE EUROPEAN MODEL OF CONSTITUTIONAL ADJUDICATION

Unsurprisingly, attention was drawn to the Kelsenian model of the 'guardian of the constitution', which had been advanced as a theory at the beginning of the century and which had been in place in Austria since the 1920s.[5] This model was based on a special court, whose mission would be to act as a 'negative legislature'.

The Italian Constitution, like many others that were enacted in European countries, draws inspiration from, but does not faithfully

[5] See L Vinx, *The Guardian of the Constitution: Hans Kelsen and Carl Schmitt on the Limits of Constitutional Law* (Cambridge, Cambridge University Press, 2015) 8 and 61ff.

reproduce the Kelsenian model. The Italian (and European) model of constitutional adjudication results from the convergence of two paradigms – the American and the Kelsenian models.[6] These two archetypes of constitutional adjudication have been merged in contemporary European constitutional courts, which feature the main elements of the Kelsenian, centralised model, while granting lower court judges some role in the judicial review of legislation. This development has taken place thanks to the 'incidental procedure' (also called '*incidenter* procedure'): when a constitutional issue arises during an ordinary proceeding, the judge, under certain conditions, must refer it to the Constitutional Court for consideration. Thus, the Italian system of judicial review is centralised, following the Austrian prototype, but the initiative is diffused throughout the judiciary, in accordance with the US style. Moreover, judicial review in the Italian system has general effects, but it also has some 'concreteness', ie it is strictly linked to the real case from which it has been referred.

A similar hybridisation can be noted in the effects of the decisions of European Constitutional courts: their judgments have a general effect, as envisaged in the original Kelsenian model; nevertheless, their effects are retroactive, as typically happens in the US system, according to Marbury's understanding of judicial review of legislation.

IV. THE CONSTITUTIONAL COURT: COMPOSITION AND FUNCTIONS

According to the European model of constitutional adjudication, the Italian Constitutional Court is a special, specialised and centralised body.

A. Special Judge

The Constitutional Court performs its function following judicial procedures, but the appointment of its members is different from that of

[6] See M Cappelletti, *Il controllo giudiziario di costituzionalità delle leggi nel diritto comparato* (Milan, Giuffrè, 1968) 25–48, published in English with the title *Judicial Review in Contemporary World* (Indianapolis, Bobbs-Merrill, 1971) and later developed in M Cappelletti and W Cohen, *Comparative Constitutional Law: Cases and Materials* (Indianapolis, Bobbs-Merrill, 1979) 3ff.

ordinary courts. All Constitutional Court judges are senior legal experts, but not all of them are judges by career, most of them being appointed by political bodies, namely the Parliament or the President of the Republic.

In fact, Article. 135.1 provides that of the 15 judges attached to the Court:

- five are appointed by the President of the Republic;
- five are elected by Parliament in joint session; and
- five are elected by the highest ordinary and administrative courts.

The appointments made by the President of the Republic are chosen directly by the President (and this power is normally counted among the President's fully presidential powers: see Chapter 6). Parliamentary elections of members to the Italian Constitutional Court are made by secret ballot and require a broad consensus: two-thirds majority, which becomes a three-fifths majority after the third unsuccessful ballot. As to the judges to be appointed by the supreme courts, the implementing statutes provide that three of them are appointed by the supreme court for civil and criminal cases (the Court of Cassation (*Corte di Cassazione*)), and one each by the highest court for administrative law cases (the Council of State (*Consiglio di Stato*) and the Court of Accounts (*Corte dei Conti*)).

Despite the political character of their appointment, constitutional judges' independence is assured by the high standard of professional requirements required and the duration of their mandate.

As to the professional qualifications required by Article 135.2, constitutional judges are selected from among judges of the highest courts (even if retired), law professors and attorneys of at least 20 years' experience.

The independence of individual judges is pursued through a non-renewable, nine-year term of office. This tenure is relatively long by comparison with other institutional positions (and originally the Constitution established an even longer term of 12 years). The President of the Republic is elected for seven years; and each judge holds office for a term almost double that of ordinary members of Parliament, who are elected for five years. Moreover, the appointment is not renewable, in order to shield the members of the Court from political pressures and other forms of influence in the final stages of their term.

The composition of the Court reflects the Kelsenian philosophical idea that judging legislation is a special kind of judicial activity, located between jurisdiction and politics. Being a constitutional judge requires a combination of excellence in legal skills with an attitude appropriate to the legal discussion of policy-oriented issues. This dual nature of the judges' role gave rise to a lively debate within the Constituent Assembly as to whether the character of the Constitutional Court is political or jurisdictional. By and large, it can be said that constitutional judges have always fulfilled these expectations and that only on a few occasions have certain appointments been sharply criticised.

B. Specialised Body

The Constitutional Court is not only a special judge, but it is also a *specialised body*. Unlike supreme courts, the Constitutional Court is not part of the body of ordinary judges. The province of the Constitutional Court is purely constitutional adjudication.

According to Article 134, the Constitutional Court's most important function is constitutional review of legislation, which can be activated either through the incidental procedure or through the *principaliter* procedure (see Chapter 7). Its second task is to preserve the correct allocation of powers, solving disputes (also called 'conflicts of attributions'), applying either the rules regarding the separation of powers between the different branches of the government (*conflitti fra i poteri dello Stato*) or the division of competence between State and Regions (*conflitti tra enti*). The third function, which has never been exercised to date, is to determine criminal charges against the President of the Republic for high treason or gross violation of the Constitution. In such cases, the President may be impeached by Parliament in joint session, with an absolute majority of its members and then put on trial before the Constitutional Court (see Chapter 6). A further competence was added by constitutional law no 1/1953, which concerns the admissibility of referendums aimed at repealing parliamentary legislation, which are subject to some limitations, according to Article 75 (see Chapter 3).

All these functions are meant to preserve the integrity of the Constitution and fall within the exclusive province of the Court. No other case or controversy besides these enumerated powers may be brought before the Constitutional Court. This choice is a simple consequence of the notion that judging laws is not of the same nature as judging facts.

C. Centralised Body

The last key feature of the Constitutional Court is that it is a *centralised body*, because it has the exclusive power to decide constitutional questions. Unlike in other legal systems, ordinary courts are not permitted to review the constitutionality of parliamentary legislation in Italy. In fact, one of the major concerns at the Constituent Assembly regarding constitutional review of legislation was that of legal certainty, because in civil law countries, the *stare decisis* principle does not have the same binding force as it has in common law countries. Therefore, had the feature of the diffuse, US system that permits any judge to undertake judicial review of legislation been introduced in Europe, then values such as legal certainty, uniform application of the law, and even equality of citizens would have been threatened. Moreover, in Italy and in the continental tradition as a whole, the idea of a strong and powerful judiciary was not desirable. Among other things, a simple fact is worth mentioning: in 1921 Eduard Lambert published his book, titled *Le gouvernement des juges*,[7] which was based on an account of the power of the judiciary in the United States during the Lochner Era (from 1897 to 1937). Legal scholars and politicians were familiar with this book. The description of such an activist Supreme Court became a veritable spectre for the European statesmen of the time. They feared a new rise of the judiciary. For these reasons, ordinary judges are prevented from scrutinising legislation, and whenever a legislative provision conflicts with the Constitution, only the Constitutional Court may nullify the provision once and forever with general effect, *erga omnes*.

V. THE COURT'S DELAYED ESTABLISHMENT AND FIRST YEARS OF ACTIVITY: REVIEWING FASCIST LEGISLATION

The Constitutional Court was only established in 1956. Its creation took more than eight years (see Chapter 1). This delay reveals some unresolved difficulties that also emerged in the *travaux preparatories* at the Constituent Assembly.

For different reasons, the major political parties were hostile towards the Court. Moreover, the judiciary was suspicious, because a new court was likely to compete with the old ones and to overshadow them, due to its paramount position in the courts' hierarchy. The majority of legal scholars were also wary. All things considered, the new institution was established in an inhospitable environment.

[7] E Lambert, *Le Gouvernement des juges et la lutte contre la législation sociale aux États-Unis. L'expérience américaine du contrôle judiciaire de la constitutionnalité des lois* (Paris, Marcel Giard & Cie, 1921).

Even after its creation, the path to constitutional adjudication was not cleared of all hindrances. A new attack arrived from the Supreme Court of Cassation, which adopted a conservative approach to the new republican Constitution that was likely to tame the role of the new Constitutional Court. First, the Court of Cassation argued that pre-republican legislation was not subject to constitutional review: any legislative conflict with the provisions of the new Constitutions was to be treated as an ordinary form of 'abrogation' or repeal, thus allegedly falling within the jurisdiction of ordinary judges, rather than of the Constitutional Court. Second, as to the interpretation of the Constitution, the Court of Cassation developed the 'programmatic versus preceptive norms' doctrine.[8] The proposition was that the Constitution consisted largely of principles, rather than preceptive rules, and those principles – defined as *programmatic norms* – were not suitable to be directly applied by the courts, as legal rules are, but, rather, required prior implementation by Parliament, as mere political principles. As long as such parliamentary legislation was not adopted, the Constitution remained, therefore, essentially ineffective, especially during its initial stages, with respect to rights and duties. Had this doctrine been followed, then the implementation of the Constitution would had been put by and large in the hands of the political bodies, removing it from those of the judiciary. Certainly, had this doctrine taken root, constitutional review of legislation would have been much less effective.

However, despite this early distrust, the Constitutional Court soon became one of the most influential authorities in the Italian institutional architecture, quickly gaining the utmost respect from all other branches of government.

How did the new Constitutional Court overcome such an unfavourable context? How did the Constitutional Court interact with its opponents? What 'strategy' did the Court adopt to overcome the pervasive resistance to it at the dawn of the Republic?

Since its very origins, the Court has adopted a twofold attitude. On the one hand, it has shown solid self-awareness and high regard for its own mission; while on the other hand, it has maintained a very open and relational approach to other actors, both political and judicial. Later, the Court began to interact with its European counterparts following a similar approach. In the search for its own role in the national and European

[8] E Lamarque, *Corte costituzionale e giudici nell'Italia repubblicana* (Bari, Laterza, 2012) 45ff.

institutional order, the Court has proved to be a resolute guardian of Italy's national constitutional identity, while being open to and cooperative with its counterparts.

The basic features of the Constitutional Court's style of adjudication were illustrated by its very first decision: the landmark Judgment no 1 of 5 June 1956.

This case presented the Court with a constitutional challenge to the 1931 Law on Public Security, a prototype of authoritarian Fascist-era legislation. Article 113 of the law provided that those who wished to use posters or flyers to disseminate their views were required to obtain the prior authorisation of the proper police authority. This provision was challenged as conflicting with Article 21 of the Constitution, which addresses freedom of speech. It was emblematic that the first case brought before the Constitutional Court concerned a Fascist piece of legislation in breach of one of the fundamental freedoms of the new democratic order: free speech. Interestingly enough, the Court of Cassation had already expressed its view on this point,[9] considering the challenged provision to be valid even under the new Constitution. To the contrary, the Constitutional Court did not hesitate to declare it unconstitutional, and therefore invalid: 'By requiring an authorization, Art. 113 makes the right conferred to all by Art. 21 of the Constitution dependent on a concession by the public authorities' unlimited discretion'.

Moreover, the Court took the opportunity in its decision to dismiss the aforementioned legal doctrines upheld by the Court of Cassation that could undermine the authority of the Constitution and of the Constitutional Court itself.

First, the Constitutional Court affirmed its own jurisdiction over legislation in existence prior to the enactment of the Constitution, which was questioned by the Attorney General: according to Article 134, 'it is the exclusive competence of the Constitutional Court to decide controversies regarding the constitutional legitimacy of laws, … without any distinction between laws enacted before or after the Constitution'.

Second, the Constitutional Court dismissed the 'programmatic norms' doctrine: 'The well-known distinction between prescriptive norms and norms that have programmatic characteristics … is not dispositive in

[9] Court of Cassation, United Criminal Sections, 15 April 1950, (1950) *Rivista Penale* 377, and Court of Cassation, United Criminal Sections, 31 March 1951.

constitutional judgments, because, in some cases, the unconstitutionality of a law may derive from programmatic norms'.[10]

Thus, in a few short pages the Constitutional Court broke sharply from the juridical and political hallmarks of the previous Italian legal tradition and, at the same time, laid down a series of basic building blocks for the consolidation of the new constitutional order of the Italian Republic and of its own place within it.

It is significant that the Constitutional Court asserted its authority in the context of a dispute regarding the validity of a Fascist law that restricted basic liberties deemed to be essential in a democratic order. In doing so, the Court immediately established its credentials as part of a new, democratic, constitutional order that is protective of human dignity and freedom, and distanced itself from the authoritarian past, avoiding all conflicts with the Parliament in office. During the first decade of its activity, the Constitutional Court continued in this vein, purging the legal system of a number of remnants of the Fascist authoritarian legislation. Just to mention a few examples, the Court quashed a number of authoritarian provisions issued during the Fascist regime limiting the guarantees of *habeas corpus*, infringing on freedom of religion, treating the right to strike as a criminal offence, punishing a wife for adultery, and offending the equal rights of illegitimate children.[11]

During those years, when it was required to review a piece of legislation approved by the Parliament in office, the Court was more careful: conscious of the formidable force of its determinations of unconstitutionality, the Court tried to use them as a last resort and preferred to commit itself, insofar as possible, to finding the means to collaborate with the other actors of the constitutional order.

VI. A VARIETY OF REMEDIES

The concern for maintaining respectful and collaborative relations with other constitutional actors triggered the creativity of the Court as to the typology of its decisions and remedies. Whereas the relevant constitutional and legislative provisions envisage only an 'either/or' solution to a constitutional controversy – that is, either the challenged legislation is in

[10] Judgment no 1/1956. See also Ch. 1.

[11] See, among many, Judgments nos 11/1956, 59/1958, 29/1960, 126/1968, 79/1959, respectively.

conformity with or it is in breach of the Constitution – the Constitutional Court was able, over time, to develop more nuanced types of decisions and remedies.

Indeed, as a matter of principle, the decisions of the Court can either accept or reject constitutional challenges, and these are known respectively as *sentenze di accoglimento* and *sentenze di rigetto*.

The effects of these decisions are regulated by Articles 136 and 137 of the Constitution and by Article 30 of law no 87/1953. Decisions that reject a constitutional challenge do not certify a law as constitutional; rather, they merely reject the specific challenge presented in the form in which it was raised. These decisions are not universally binding, that is, they are not effective *erga omnes*. Consequently, the same question may be raised again, on the same or different grounds; however, the judge who has certified the question cannot raise it again in the same lawsuit. For this reason, such judgments are said to be effective only as between the parties, that is, *inter partes*.

By contrast, judgments that accept a constitutional challenge are universally binding and enjoy retroactive effect (*ex tunc*), in the sense that the statute declared unconstitutional can no longer be applied from the day after publication of the judgment. Such decisions are final and cannot be appealed. Their retroactivity finds its limits in what are usually called '*rapporti esauriti*', which might be translated as 'concluded relationships' or '*res iudicata*': for reasons of legal certainty, these decisions do not affect situations that were already resolved by final judgments, claims that are barred by statutes of limitation, and the like. Yet, there is an exception to this rule where a final criminal conviction has been entered pursuant to the law now declared unconstitutional: the law provides that such a conviction and any related punishment should cease.

This basic approach of alternatives gives the Court very rigid tools for determining the questions submitted to its scrutiny. For this reason, since the first years of its existence, the Court has developed a rich variety of judgments, that arise from the need, recognised by the Constitutional Court itself, to limit the impact of its decisions on the legal system as a whole and on other branches of government, particularly the Judiciary and the Parliament.

The need to establish a relationship with the ordinary courts, which are charged with the task of interpreting statutory law and preserving as much as possible the existing legislation, led the Constitutional Court to develop *'interpretative' decisions*, in which the Court distinguishes between the text of a legal provision and the underlying norm. By using hermeneutic techniques, it is possible to derive multiple norms from a single text, or a single norm from multiple texts. The distinction between text and norm is particularly important in that it permits the separation of the norm from the literal meaning of the text. Moreover, the distinction allows the system to evolve, facilitating the interpreter's creativity and helping to reduce the 'destructive' and 'negative' impacts of the Court's decisions, with its consequent gaps in the legal system, and giving it the ability to operate in a more subtle way.

In some cases (although very rarely by comparison to some other constitutional courts), the Italian Court may decide to start a sort of dialogue with the legislature, either by deferring the effects of the declaration of unconstitutionality to a later time and giving Parliament time to remove the unconstitutional law (*sentenze di incostituzionalità differita*), or by provisionally assenting to the constitutionality of a law, waiting for its repeal as expressly announced by the legislator itself, and postponing the declaration of unconstitutionality to a later time in the event of the legislator's inaction (*sentenze di costituzionalità provvisoria*).

In the same vein, another type of decision, which is even more deferential to the Parliament, is the 'warning-decisions' (*sentenze monito*), whereby the Court upholds the constitutionality of the law, but invites the legislator to amend that law in view of its questionable or problematic content. However, if the Parliament does not intervene within a reasonable time, the Court resolves the problem on its own, by intervening on the norm under scrutiny in order to ensure its compliance with the constitutional principles. In recent years, given the inactivity of the Parliament, the Court has issued a number of decisions in which it assigned a deadline (around one year) for the Parliament to amend existing legislation, while in the meantime suspending its judgment. If this deadline expires without action being taken, the Court is deemed authorised to intervene in partially re-writing the legislation accordingly to the constitutional principles.[12]

By taking into consideration the various kinds of decisions created by the Court through its own case law, we may better understand why the Italian Constitutional Court is not merely a 'negative legislator' in the Kelsenian sense.

[12] The first occurrence was Order no 207/2018, followed by Judgment no 242/2019 (on the so-called *Cappato* case, regarding assisted suicide). Then, Order no 132/2020, followed by Judgment no 150/2021, and Order no 97/2021.

VII. THE INCIDENTAL PROCEDURE AND THE RELATIONSHIP WITH ORDINARY COURTS

As has been noted, at the beginning of its existence, the Constitutional Court had to stand firm and defend its constitutional role from hostile doctrines developed by the Court of Cassation that would have diminished the role and the authority of the Constitutional Court. It is worth recalling that according to Transitional Clause VII, before the creation of the Constitutional Court, constitutional judicial review of legislation was undertaken by ordinary courts. The result was that when the Constitutional Court commenced its activity, the Court of Cassation, as well as other ordinary courts, felt deprived of a function that had hitherto fallen within its jurisdiction. The two highest Courts were competitors in a sense, and their relationship was tense. However, the Constitutional Court cannot function effectively without having smooth and cooperative relationships with the other components of the judiciary. In the Italian constitutional architecture, other judicial bodies are necessary partners of the Constitutional Court, and cooperative relations with them are crucial for the proper operation of constitutional adjudication.

The main pathway of access to the Constitutional Court is the 'incidental procedure', which was established in constitutional law no 1/1948 and further developed in law no 87/1953 (Article 23). The incidental procedure is structured as follows:[13] when a judge, in the course of a judicial proceeding concerning any kind of case – criminal, property, tort, administrative – is called upon to apply a legal provision the constitutionality of which is questionable or suspect, the judge is required to suspend the proceedings and refer the case to the Constitutional Court, so that the legislation may be reviewed. Once the Court has issued a binding decision on the matter, the ordinary judge resumes the case and decides it in accordance with the Constitutional Court's judgment. Two important requirements must be met for a constitutional issue to find its way to the Constitutional Court: it must be *relevant* – meaning that its resolution must be essential to the determination of the case – and it must be *not manifestly unfounded* – meaning that the issue must have a *prima facie* foundation on the merits. These two requirements reveal the objective connection between the original concrete case and the process before the Constitutional Court.

[13] See G Zagrebelsky and V Marcenò, *Giustizia costituzionale* (Bologna, Il Mulino, 2012) 269ff.

The determination of the constitutional validity of the statute at stake is reserved solely for the Constitutional Court, but the initiative is spread throughout the entire judiciary. Therefore, ordinary judges are entrusted with the role of acting as 'gatekeepers' of the Constitutional Court:[14] it is up to the ordinary judges themselves to decide which cases will be admitted for constitutional review and which will not. This mechanism is premised on the cooperation of ordinary judges. If ordinary judges do not activate the procedure, the Constitutional Court cannot play its part.

As seen above, when discussing the early history of the Constitutional Court, smooth relations with the ordinary judiciary were not to be taken for granted. However, the Constitutional Court was well aware of the necessity of encouraging good relationships with ordinary judges, and since first being established, the Court has favoured expansive access by interpreting the notion of 'judge' and 'judicial procedure' set out in Article 23 of law no 87/1953 in a very broad sense. Things changed in the late 1970s, when the Court started being overwhelmed by the number of cases on its docket. At present, it seems that the Court now requires a double qualification for recognising the standing to refer questions to it: a subjective one, regarding the judicial nature of the referring body; and an objective one, regarding the judicial procedure pending before the judge. This change reveals that the Court is now well-established and its position is acknowledged within the institutional system. The Constitutional Court is no longer a new and unprecedented body in search of authority. Rather, the Court is a cornerstone of the Italian form of government, and therefore can afford to regulate and limit its jurisdiction.

An important contribution to the Court's fostering of respectful and synergistic relations with national ordinary courts was granted by the *living law doctrine* and by the method of *interpretation 'in conformity with the Constitution'*.

According to the 'living law' doctrine, the Constitutional Court will review challenged legislation as it is interpreted by ordinary courts, without imposing its own interpretation. Consequently, the Constitutional Court decides the question referred to it on the assumption that the interpretation adopted by the 'living law' (*diritto vivente*) is the correct one.

On the other hand, since the mid-1990s, the Constitutional Court has invited ordinary courts to read statutory texts in such a way that

[14] P Calamandrei, 'Il procedimento per la dichiarazione di illegittimità costituzionale' in P Calamandrei, *Opere giuridiche*, Vol III (Naples, Morano, 1965) 372.

they accord with the principles enshrined in the Constitution. Ordinary judges, following the case law of the Constitutional Court, have adopted the 'interpretation in accordance with the Constitution' doctrine (*interpretazione conforme a Costituzione*): that is, they themselves construct meanings of statutes that are compatible with the Constitution and that do not violate it. The rationale for this doctrine lies in the notion that statutes are to be quashed only if their incompatibility with the Constitution is clear beyond any reasonable doubt and there is no other way to resolve the inconsistency.

A similar doctrine is not unknown in other traditions, such as, for example, the US Supreme Court's case law: 'Where a statute is susceptible of two constructions, by one of which grave and doubtful constitutional questions arose and by the other such questions can be avoided, [a court's] duty is to adopt the latter.'[15] This doctrine enhances the importance of ordinary courts in interpreting, applying and expounding the Constitution. In the name of 'interpretation according to the Constitution', judges may sometimes even enforce the literal meaning of the text, to 'save' the statute and therefore avoid referring the case to the Constitutional Court.[16]

Why does the Constitutional Court encourage lower judges to assume such a broad and anti-formalistic approach to interpretation, through a mechanism that apparently strips the Court of a portion of its power? The answer to this question is partly cultural and partly pragmatic. The Court favours the penetration of constitutional values into everyday life: the more an interpretation conforming to the Constitution is advanced, the more constitutional values percolate through social life and become part of the public discourse. From a pragmatic perspective, as previously mentioned, a judge's obligation to explore a statutory construction which conforms with the Constitution before referring the question to the Court can be viewed as a means of screening cases and controlling the Court's caseload, which increased over time, especially during the 1980.

Through the development of these doctrines, the Constitutional Court has displayed a great deal of trust in the ordinary judiciary, preserving the primary competence of the latter as the interpreter of legislation. In this way, the Constitutional Court has demonstrated respect for ordinary

[15] *Jones v US*, 526 US 227, 239 (1999), quoting *Attorney General v Delaware & Hudson Co*, 213 US 366, 408 (1909).

[16] Lamarque (n 8) 127ff.

judges, and contributed towards building good relationships with them. Without this inter-judicial relationality, the doors of the Constitutional Court would have remained mostly closed, and its pronouncements largely ineffective.

It is worth noting that it is only at first glance that the European model of constitutional adjudication marginalises ordinary judges, for the benefit of a sole, centralised constitutional judge. In actual fact, their marginalisation should not be overstated. Ordinary judges play a crucial role both before and after the decision of the Constitutional Court: before, because it is up to them to identify the question and to refer it to the Constitutional Court; and after, because it is then up to the ordinary judges who raised the question to determine the concrete dispute in light of the answer provided by the Constitutional Court. It is clear that judicial review of legislation in Europe depends upon dutiful cooperation between ordinary judges and special courts.

Both sets of judges have specific roles, each of which is necessary for the smooth and efficient functioning of the system. If ordinary judges do not introduce questions of constitutionality, constitutional courts cannot make determinations; if judges do not apply the decisions of constitutional courts, their case law is rendered meaningless. So, the secret ingredient of the European recipe is a balanced and trusting collaboration between ordinary judges and constitutional courts, both in Italy and elsewhere on the continent.

VIII. THE CONSTITUTIONAL COURT AND EUROPEAN COURTS

A similarly active and dutiful cooperation is also required for the existence of smooth relations between the Italian Constitutional Court and what shall hereinafter be referred to as the 'European Courts': the Court of Justice of the European Union (CJEU) and the European Court of Human Rights (ECtHR).

As a matter of principle, in a centralised system such as the Italian one, the Constitutional Court is endowed with the exclusive and final power to review legislation. This was one of the reasons why the European model opted in favour of setting up an 'ad hoc' and specialist body for undertaking the difficult task of judging the constitutionality of a law. As a matter of fact, however, the Italian Constitutional Court is closely aligned with other judicial bodies: the ordinary judiciary – as seen above – and the two European Courts, the role of which is growing in significance.

Clearly, the mandates of the national constitutional courts and of the European Courts do not fully overlap, and neither European Court has jurisdiction over the constitutional review of national legislation, which falls within the exclusive domain of the national constitutional courts (when existing). Nevertheless, the three legal orders – EU, European Convention on Human Rights (ECHR) and national legal orders – have developed into a 'composite' constitutional system and a number of interactions occur between their respective judicial bodies, especially when they act as fundamental rights adjudicators.[17] Each Court cannot function without the others.

Within the European context, the Italian Constitutional Court has dramatically changed its attitude over time, transitioning incrementally towards an openness to the European environment. While at the beginning of the European adventure, the Italian Court viewed its supranational and foreign counterparts as aliens, a period of informal reciprocal influence followed, during which the Italian Constitutional Court – while avoiding all formal reference to the case law of the European Courts – was actually well aware of the case law developed in Luxembourg and in Strasbourg (see Chapter 2). Today, the European case law is an ordinary element of the legal authorities on the basis of which Italian constitutional adjudication is conducted and justified.

The current framework for the Constitutional Court's relationship with the CJEU was established in 1984,[18] although direct dialogue by means of preliminary ruling was inaugurated only in 2008.[19] The Constitutional Court accepted the two basic principles of EU law – supremacy and direct effect – as pronounced by the CJEU in *Simmenthal* (1978).[20] However, the supremacy of EU law is not without limits within the Italian legal system. The Italian Constitutional Court, like many other national constitutional courts – starting with the German *Bundesverfassungsgericht* – has accepted the supremacy of EU law 'subject to conditions'. According to this doctrine, EU norms are not permitted to override the core principles of the Italian Constitution,

[17] Cf LFM Besselink, *A Composite European Constitution* (Groningen, Europa Law Publishing, 2007). See also M Cartabia, 'Europe and Rights: Taking Dialogue Seriously' (2009) 5(1) *European Constitutional Law Review* 5.

[18] Judgment no 170/1984.

[19] Orders nos 103/2008, 207/2013, 24/2017, 117/2018, 182/2020. See the rich debate published by the Special Issue of the *German Law Journal* ((2015) 16(6) *German Law Journal*) available at https://germanlawjournal.com/volume-16-no-06/.

[20] Case 106/77 *Amministrazione delle Finanze dello Stato v Simmenthal SpA*.

including particular fundamental rights. The fundamental core principles of the national Constitution are considered to be 'counter-limits' to the limitations of sovereignty. As a result, EU legislation and other EU acts prevail over all national legislation, and can even derogate from the national Constitution, with the exception of these counter-limits.

As for the relationship with the ECtHR, for many decades the Constitutional Court regarded the ECHR as a typical international treaty and did not bestow it with any distinctive status. The turning point is represented by the 'twin' judgments issued in 2007.[21] In those decisions, the Court established on the one hand that the ECHR enjoys a higher status than any piece of ordinary legislation. At the same time, it acknowledged that the Constitutional Court itself exercises jurisdiction over any conflicts between national legislation and the ECHR, as interpreted by the ECtHR. According to the Court, the new text of Article 117.1 of the Constitution, as amended in 2001, has given the ECHR a particular status. It is still an ordinary law, but since the Constitution refers to it, it therefore becomes an 'intermediate standard' (*parametro interposto*) for judicial review of legislation.

However, in both cases, long before opening up to direct dialogue with the European Courts, the Italian Constitutional Court maintained an implicit and silent, although influential, regard for their decisions. A similar consideration is paid by the Constitutional Court to foreign law and comparative sources. Whereas in recent years, the Italian Constitutional Court has occasionally openly referred to the case law of other Constitutional courts, the influence of comparative sources is actually much deeper than may be superficially apparent.

In summary, Italian constitutional law has entered gradually into an active relationship with European, international, and comparative law, and especially with the judge-made law of the two European supranational Courts, in particular in human rights cases. While, in some areas, the impact of these external sources has prompted the Constitutional Court to revise its previous case law and to develop new principles and standards, in other cases the Italian Constitutional Court has deliberately adopted a different position to other European or foreign courts, especially when the core values of constitutional identity are at stake. In short, the Court now engages in open and direct relations with external

[21] Judgments nos 348 and 349/2007. See G Repetto, *The Constitutional Relevance of the ECHR in Domestic and European Law: An Italian Perspective* (Den Haag, Intersentia, 2013).

judicial bodies. However, those relations are not oriented towards an unreasoned importation of external judicial solutions; rather, it is a reciprocal relationship between peers: a dialogue that triggers constructive convergence but also leaves room for difference and distinctiveness.[22]

IX. THE RELATIONAL CHARACTER OF ITALIAN CONSTITUTIONAL ADJUDICATION AND INTERNAL COLLEGIALITY

If we consider the attitudes of the Constitutional Court at the beginning of its activity, we can easily affirm, borrowing an expression from John Merryman,[23] that the 'Italian style' of constitutional adjudication lies in its '*relational character*'.[24]

In fact, Italian constitutional law is intensely relational: it speaks of cooperation, connection, interdependence, interactions, links, networks, and the like. Indeed, no single notion is capable of capturing the essence of an institution as rich in history, complexity, and even contradiction as the Italian Constitutional Court. However, many of the interesting aspects of the Court and its case law that stand out when viewed by comparison with other experiences may be summed up with the term 'relationality'.

This is not to imply that the Italian Court is always consistent or successful in maintaining this distinctive identity, nor that its relational approach is always an unambiguous asset. Some aspects of the process and style of the Court's opinions do not provide outstanding examples of openness and transparency.[25] It suffices to notice that some innovations regarding the openness of the procedure and the intervention of the *amici curiae* were only introduced in 2019.[26]

[22] Judgments nos 264/2012 and 49/2015. See D Tega, 'The Italian way: a blend of cooperation and hubris' (2019) 77(3) *The Heidelberg Journal of International Law/Zeitschrift für ausländisches öffentliches Recht und Völkerrecht* 685.

[23] M Cappelletti, JH Merryman and JM Perillo, *The Italian Legal System* (Stanford, Stanford University Press, 1967).

[24] This idea is developed in V Barsotti and others, *Italian Constitutional Justice in Global Context* (Oxford, Oxford University Press, 2016) 234ff and also V Barsotti and others, 'Introduction. Dialogue as a Method' in V Barsotti and others (eds), *Dialogues on Italian Constitutional Justice: A Comparative Perspective* (London, Routledge, 2021) 1.

[25] T Groppi, 'Giustizia costituzionale 'Italian Style'? Sì, grazie (ma con qualche correttivo)' (2016) 2 *Diritto pubblico comparato ed europeo*.

[26] See the deliberation, dated 8 January 2020, which amended the regulations governing the conduct of proceedings before the Court.

Nor can it be suggested that the Italian Court is absolutely singular in these efforts towards relationality: any successful constitutional tribunal must attend, to some degree, to the political realities of its position within the constitutional order, and the Italian Court undoubtedly still has much to learn from other systems in this regard. Nevertheless, when reviewing the history of the institution, it is helpful to adopt a positive approach: to tease out, from a complex jumble of data, that which is of particular value, and to offer it as a narrative that calls forth the best version of the Court. Viewed from this perspective, the relational qualities of the Italian Court are valuable assets, which are worth articulating and sharing.

Indeed, relationality is imprinted into the very structure of the Court. Let us consider again the composition and fabric of the Court. As outlined earlier, of its 15 judges, some are elected by the Parliament, some are appointed by the President of the Republic and some are elected by the other branches of the judiciary: both ordinary and administrative bodies. Therefore, all the other branches of the State have a say in the appointment of the Constitutional Court's 15 members. The members of the Court are fully independent and do not answer to their 'constituencies' – their appointments derive from different bodies.

Moreover, although all judges are jurists, some of them come from academia, as legal scholars; others from the bar; and yet others from the judiciary. The constitutional judges are diverse due to their different sources of appointment – some selected by the highest courts of the ordinary judiciary, others by Parliament, and others by the President – and due to their different backgrounds, with career judges working alongside university professors and practising lawyers. They are united by a common legal education, but differ in terms of their previous professional trajectories and personal cultural formation.

This pluralistic composition is significant when one considers that the Court's rules of procedure are dominated by a paramount principle: that of *collegiality*. Judges are prompted towards dialogue and agreement because of the principle of collegiality that governs the Court's work. The Court's internal organisation and working procedures are designed to encourage the judges to work closely together; they are obliged to engage in dialogue with one another.[27] This fosters reciprocal cross-fertilisation between the Court's members and their respective

[27] See G Zagrebelsky, *Principi e voti: La Corte costituzionale e la politica* (Turin, Einaudi, 2014) 7ff.

ideas, political and social backgrounds, cultures and mentalities; it also serves as the principal growth factor in the Court's capacity for building relations.

Every single step in the decision-making process requires the participation of all 15 members. Some features of the adjudication process are worth noting in order to fully appreciate the strict collegiality that governs the Italian Constitutional Court.

For example, unlike many other constitutional courts, the Italian Court never splits into chambers: every single case is discussed and decided by a plenary panel, even cases that may be minor or repetitive. No filter is applied to the scrutiny of an application's admissibility, and every controversy enjoys the same procedural dignity.

Another expression of the principle of strict collegiality is that the individual voices of the judges cannot be recognised. The Court always speaks with one voice, and separate opinions are not allowed. Although this issue has been debated from time to time, to date the Court has rejected all proposals aimed at introducing the plurality of opinions. Every decision is the result of the deliberation of all 15 members of the Court; even those who do not agree have a say and can contribute to the drafting of the Court's judgment. Without the possibility of publishing a dissenting opinion, even those judges who were not part of the majority of the Court participate in writing the official judgment.

The President of the Court plays an important role, but does not control the jurisprudence of the Court: the President is elected by the judges of the Court from among their number, for a term of up to three years. Usually, the term served is much shorter than that. The President tends to be elected based only on seniority, and sometimes serves in the role of President for only a few months before his or her nine years' term expires. The President's most important power is to choose the reporting judge for a case (who is ordinarily in charge of writing the final opinion) to be submitted to the plenum.

X. CONCLUSION

All this considered, the architecture of the Court's internal deliberation fosters compromise and encourages the judges to broadly incorporate the particular views of their individual colleagues into the final text of the decision. These methods favour efforts to reconcile and unify divergent views into a composite that cannot be reduced to the perspective of a single judge, politician or scholar.

It is no surprise, then, that the Court's internal structural and procedural pluralism, and the principle of strict collegiality governing its operation, are reflected in its external activities. As is the case for any other constitutional court, interactions with other judicial and political bodies are part of the Italian Court's mandate. These interactions may be adversarial or synergistic. The distinctive trait of the Italian experience, however, is definitely the latter. Occasional conflicts do not contradict the general trend, which comprises a dialogical, open, collaborative and accommodating approach.

FURTHER READING

Barsotti,V, and others, *Italian Constitutional Justice in Global Context* (New York, OUP, 2016).

Barsotti, V, and others, *Dialogues on Italian Constitutional Justice: A Comparative Perspective* (London, Routledge, 2021).

Bifulco, R, and Paris, D, 'The Italian Constitutional Court' in A von Bogdandy, P Huber and C Grabenwarter, *The Max Planck Handbooks in European Public Law. 3. Constitutional Adjudication: Institutions* (Oxford, Oxford University Press, 2020) 447–554.

Cappelletti, M, Merryman, JH, and Perillo, JM, *The Italian Legal System* (Stanford, Stanford University Press, 1967).

De Visser, M, *Constitutional Review in Europe: A Comparative Analysis* (Oxford, Hart, 2013).

Repetto, G (ed), *The Constitutional Relevance of the ECHR in Domestic and European Law: An Italian Perspective* (Den Haag, Intersentia, 2013).

Tega, D, 'The Italian Constitutional Court in its context: A narrative' (2021) 17(3) *European Constitutional Law Review*, 369–93.

Voncansek, ML, *Constitutional Politics in Italy: The Constitutional Court* (Basingstoke, Palgrave, 2000).

10

Protection of Rights

Constitutionalism – The 'Age of Rights' – Fundamental Rights – Inviolable Rights – Personalism – Social Pluralism – Solidarity – Duties – Formal Equality – Substantive Equality – 'New Rights' – Reasonableness – Balancing – Proportionality – Judicial Safeguards – Non-Judicial Safeguards – Reserve of Legislation – Reserve of Jurisdiction – Citizens – Migrants – Non-Discrimination – Freedom of Religion – Social Rights – Right to Education – Healthcare System

I. INTRODUCTION

IN THIS CHAPTER, after having analysed the historical roots of the protection of fundamental rights in close connection with the evolution of constitutionalism, the peculiarities of the Italian approach to fundamental rights are examined. The chapter starts with an in-depth analysis of Articles 2 and 3 of the Constitution, the two props on which the relationship between state and society rests. The analysis of the former is divided into three sections. First, the focus is on the notion of the *inviolability* of fundamental rights, as it results from the text and as it has been expounded by the case law of the Constitutional Court. Second, an account of the Italian constitutional approach to fundamental rights based on *personalism*, *pluralism* and *solidarity* is compared with the individualistic approach, typical of the liberal tradition. Third, the interpretation of Article 2 as an *open clause* is explored, taking into account the relationship between the *codified rights* listed in Articles 13 to 54 and the *new rights* developed over time in the jurisprudence of Italian and European courts.

An understanding of the relationship between liberty and authority in the Italian Constitution is not complete without accounting for the relevance and the originality of Article 3, relating to the principle of equality and non-discrimination. This provision is the outcome of a confrontation between the major political parties in the Constituent Assembly: the first paragraph restates the traditional, formal equality of all citizens before the law, deriving from the liberal tradition and the principle of non-discrimination; by contrast, the second paragraph affirms the principle of substantive equality, which paves the way for positive measures in favour of disadvantaged groups.

The chapter then addresses the fundamental problem of *limitations* of fundamental rights, as well as the kind of scrutiny undertaken by the Constitutional Court in cases concerning limitations of rights, based on principles of reasonableness and balancing, and the proportionality test. The *judicial and non-judicial safeguards* of fundamental rights are examined as they developed over time, from the 'reserve of legislation' to the multi-faceted judicial protection provided across the European continent.

A number of examples are offered throughout the chapter and some selected topics are canvassed in greater detail in its final part, such as rights connected to migration, freedom of religion and social rights (related to education and healthcare).

II. THE EVOLUTION OF CONSTITUTIONALISM AND THE 'AGE OF RIGHTS'

Fundamental rights and freedoms lie at the heart of constitutionalism and are integral to a glorious historical evolution upon which the legacy of the Italian Constitution is built.

Their origins may be traced back to the Middle Ages with the English Magna Carta (1215) representing an early attempt to protect personal freedoms vis-à-vis the power of the Crown by means of the writ of *habeas corpus*. This document was a sort of preview of the golden age of individual rights that subsequently developed in the modern liberal state, heralded once again in England with the Bill of Rights of 1689, under the influence of the modern natural law philosophers like Hobbes and especially Locke. Then, the ideal of individual rights became a hallmark of the American Revolution: first, with the Declaration of Independence of 1776 – famously affirming that 'all men are created equal, that they are endowed by their Creator with certain unalienable rights, that among these are life, liberty, and the pursuit of happiness' – and later with the first 10 amendments attached to the US Constitution in 1791 just two years after its entry into force, intended to protect the freedoms of religion, press, speech, assembly and due process, as well as many others aimed at securing the freedom of individuals from the undue interference of public powers (including those authorised by the legislator).

On the European continent it was not until the French Declaration of the Rights of the Man and of the Citizen of 1789 that a written charter of individual rights was approved. However, unlike its English and American counterparts, the French charter was fundamentally a political plan, aspiring to a social reality which was yet to be established: the proper symbol of the revolution. The model of the French Declaration rapidly circulated throughout Europe during the nineteenth century. In accordance with the principle set out in Article 16 of the French Declaration a number of national constitutions were approved in order to guarantee the protection of rights, asserting that 'Any society in which the guarantee of rights is not assured, nor the separation of powers determined, has no Constitution'.

In Italy, that model was followed by the *Statuto Albertino* of 1848, which became the first Constitution of Italy following the completion of the unification process in 1861 (see Chapter 1). However, the *Statuto* was flexible in nature and deferred to the Parliament the implementation of the fundamental rights proclaimed therein. Therefore, the legal protection of fundamental rights was, at that time, rather weak, and ultimately rested in the hands of the Parliament. After the Second World War, a new phase of constitutionalism began, which has been defined as the 'age of rights'.[1] In the aftermath of the horrors of the war and of totalitarian regimes, concern for the protection of individual human rights became the focus of the new national constitutions and of international action. By way of example, the Universal Declaration of Human Rights, which was approved by the United Nations General Assembly in 1948, was immediately followed in 1950 by the Convention for the Protection of Rights and Fundamental Freedoms, which was drafted in the context of the Council of Europe, and was signed in Rome. This new wave of contemporary constitutionalism focused on individual rights and strengthened the protection, in many respects, of each and every person vis-à-vis a range of public powers.[2] Its main features may be summarised in five points.

First, whereas the political or legal nature of the constitution was debated in the modern liberal state, the new constitutionalism assumes that constitutions and, more specifically, charters of rights are vested with binding legal force, and occupy the highest levels of the legal system.

[1] N Bobbio, *L'età dei diritti* (Turin, 1990), English Translation by A Cameron, *The Age of Rights* (Cambridge, Polity Press, 1996).

[2] See G Pino, *Il costituzionalismo dei diritti* (Bologna, il Mulino, 2017) 20–27.

Second, as a consequence, the judiciary – or at least a special branch of it – assumes a central role in the protection of rights: rather than being a neutral *bouche de la loi*, the judiciary has become the guardian of the constitution, and, upon certain conditions, is also vested with the power of reviewing the Parliament's legislation.

Third, the list of rights has been enriched and extended: alongside the 'first generation' of individual freedoms, a number of social and economic rights have been added in order to reflect the reality of citizens' lives.

Fourth, the second generation (and eventually also third and fourth generation) of rights not only provide a defence for the individual against the State and other public powers, but they also require the State to take a proactive stance. Consequently, some of these rights are classified as negative freedoms, while others are instead considered to be positive rights.

Fifth, the new constitutionalism of rights extends beyond national borders and embraces a supranational, international, transnational and global dimension. Treaties, conventions, declarations and charters proliferate at different levels and are all intertwined with one other and with the national constitutions, so much so that adjudicating rights has become an increasingly complex exercise.

The Italian Republican Constitution of 1948 is part and parcel of this new paradigm of the 'age of rights' and expresses the spirit of its time. Yet, it also presents some distinguishing features consisting in an approach based on the principles of *personalism, pluralism and solidarity*, as well as *equality and non-discrimination*, established in Articles 2 and 3 of the Constitution and in its entire first part. In fact, the principles enunciated in the general clause on fundamental rights and in the general principle of equality are followed and complemented by a very rich charter of fundamental rights entrenched in the first part of the Constitution (Articles 13 to 54). It is worth remarking that fundamental rights are listed at the beginning of the Constitution, after the enumeration of the basic principles and before the allocation of powers. This organisation of the text has rather strong symbolic value: it emphasises that fundamental rights serve both as a limit on, and as the foundation of, the public powers.

III. INVIOLABLE RIGHTS

The history of the Fascist era has demonstrated that the liberal approach to fundamental rights was insufficient to protect individuals from abuses by public powers. The Fascist regime managed to suppress all forms of personal and social liberty and offended the basic notion of human dignity, despite the constitutional provisions of the *Statuto Albertino* on the protection of rights remaining in force and never having formally been repealed.

As a reaction to the former totalitarian regime, the Italian Constitution contains a strong commitment to the protection of inviolable rights at its outset. Although there is no Preamble, the Constitution opens with a list of *Fundamental principles*, among which Article 2 is the keystone for the protection of fundamental rights. It reads:

> The Republic recognises and guarantees the inviolable rights of the man, both as an individual and in the social groups where human personality is developed. The Republic requires that the non-derogable duties of political, economic and social solidarity be fulfilled.

This provision was carefully discussed in the Constituent Assembly and is the result of a conciliation between two divergent positions presented by Giorgio La Pira (Catholic) and Lelio Basso (Socialist). This provision conveys the cultural understanding of the protection of fundamental rights in the Italian Constitution, which resulted from a convergence of all the different political visions represented in the Constituent Assembly. There are some keywords in this provision that reveal the Italian approach to the protection of fundamental rights and that deserve attention.

The first keyword is the verb *recognise*. This verb covers a broad semantic spectrum. On the one hand, it relates to knowledge; on the other hand, it is concerned with giving value.

'To recognise' means to come to know something that already exists. In fact, this verb was chosen to stress the priority or antecedence of human rights in respect of the power of the State and of the legal order. In other words, first comes the person and her fundamental rights, and then the State.[3] This statement marked a very relevant theoretical shift, rejecting the *Reflexrechte* theory – which had been pretty popular in Italy, under the influence of the nineteenth century German legal scholarship of Gerber, Jellinek and Laband – defending individual rights as the result of a self-limitation of the all-encompassing power of the State, which remains free to take back its power at any time and to therefore arbitrarily infringe the personal liberty of its citizens. Recognising rights means that the Constitution does not create fundamental rights, but ascertains

[3] A Baldassarre, 'Diritti inviolabili' in *Enciclopedia Giuridica* (Rome, Istituto dell'Enciclopedia italiana, 1989) 10ff.

the rights that already exist. Therefore, it is implicit in the use of the verb *recognise* that the public powers come second, and are instrumental to the human individual and are intended to serve her needs: the State is made for man, rather than man for the State, one could say, paraphrasing the Gospel of Mark 2:28.

Moreover, the verb *recognise* suggests that the Republic attaches a legal value to fundamental rights, indeed a value of utmost importance; it certifies their value and their authority. Rights are characterised as *inviolable*, meaning that they are given the highest position in the legal order, one that is beyond the reach of any constituted authority. The proclamation that fundamental rights are inviolable is not merely a means of lending moral weight to the rights subsequently listed in the Constitution, but it has a precise legal and cultural significance. Affirming that fundamental rights are inviolable means that they must be respected by all public authorities: not only do they restrain executive power – as in the nineteenth-century liberal state – but they also constitute a limit on acts of Parliament, even those issued in its capacity of amending the Constitution. Inviolability therefore means that the State has no power to annul or to withdraw fundamental rights. This is the legal sense of the inviolability proclaimed by Article 2: fundamental rights are definitive and untouchable, at least at their core, in their essential content.

The Constitutional Court shares this opinion, which was openly stated in Judgment no 1146/1988 (see also Chapter 1): 'The Italian Constitution contains some supreme principles that cannot be subverted or modified in their essential content, either by laws amending the Constitution, or by other constitutional laws'. Thus, despite the lack of an explicit 'eternity clause' – as is the case, for instance, in Articles 19.2 and 79.3 of the German Basic Law or Article 53.1 of the Spanish Constitution – the Italian Constitutional Court has clearly developed a similar doctrine and declared that some basic constitutional principles and rights are unamendable.[4]

IV. THE ITALIAN APPROACH TO FUNDAMENTAL RIGHTS: PERSONALISM, PLURALISM AND SOLIDARITY

A typical trait of the Italian protection of fundamental rights is an approach based on the intertwined principles of personalism, pluralism

[4] P Faraguna, 'Unamendability and Constitutional Identity in the Italian Constitutional Experience' (2019) 21(3) *European Journal of Law Reform* 329.

and solidarity, which are the three pillars of the constitutional protection of fundamental rights in Italy. In fact, the Constitution considers the rights-holder as each person viewed not only as an individual, but also having regard to that person's relational dimensions. In fact, Article 2 speaks of 'the inviolable rights of the man, both as an individual and in the social groups where human personality is developed'. Rights and duties are inseparable: the two sides of the same coin. Article 2 concludes that the Republic requires the fulfilment of the 'non-derogable duties of political, economic and social solidarity'.

The rights-holder in the Italian Constitution is indeed the individual. However, unlike some versions of the libertarian conception of fundamental rights,[5] the rights-holder is not an abstract individual, unencumbered, comprising only her autonomy, but is a person qualified by her constitutive attachments, history, circumstances and relationships.[6] That is why individual rights, protection of social groups and duties of solidarity are entangled in the Italian approach with the protection of rights, starting with Article 2 and continuing in the first part of the Constitution, entitled, significantly, 'Rights and Duties'.

Although, in many respects, the members of the Constituent Assembly belonged to divergent cultural universes, they all agreed on a concrete and social understanding of the human person, one that viewed the individual in her context – *l'homme situé*[7] – living in specific social conditions, facing tangible social problems and taking part in a number of social groups, starting with the family, the school, the workplace, the religious community and the like. The human person is portrayed in her social, living dimension, not as an isolated, abstract subject.

This approach can also be seen in Article 3 of the Constitution, relating to the principle of equality. Its first paragraph – 'All citizens have equal social dignity and are equal before the law' – is anything but new. It is an idea with ancient roots, which has been widely constitutionalised since the French Revolution, and which was adopted during the liberal era by all states governed by the rule of law. Since the Second World War,

[5] MA Glendon, *Rights Talk: The Impoverishment of Political Discourse* (New York, The Free Press, 1991).

[6] A similar point is made by MJ Sandel, *Liberalism and the Limits of Justice* (2nd edn, Cambridge, Cambridge University Press, 1998) 178. This different vision of the rights-holder has been developed in M Cartabia, 'The Age of "New Rights"' (2010) 3 *Straus Working Paper*, available at https://www.law.nyu.edu/institutelawjustice/2009-2010fellows.

[7] G Burdeau, *Traité de science politique. T. 7. La démocratie gouvernante, son assise sociale et sa philosophie politique* (Paris, LGDJ, 1980) 27ff.

however, the principle of equality has gradually assumed new meanings and broader scope. In addition to these 'formal' requirements of equality, Article 3.2 also inserts into the Constitution the principle of 'substantive' equality when it states:

> It is the task of the Republic to remove those obstacles of an economic or social nature which, by limiting in fact the freedom and equality of citizens, prevent the full development of the human person and the effective participation of all workers in the political, economic and social organization of the country.

Not only does the principle of formal equality prevent all forms of direct and indirect discrimination,[8] but it also requires public bodies to take into consideration the factual conditions of life of a given category of people in order to level the playing field via affirmative, positive or privileged measures for the purpose of giving the disadvantaged groups effectively equal opportunities and effectively equal social dignity.[9]

The same tangible, social, factual approach explains why the Italian Constitution provides for a broad range of social rights, and why the protection of fundamental rights in the Italian Constitution is strictly related to the protection of social pluralism and, moreover, why it requires the discharge of duties and obligations. In fact, the reference in Article 2 to the social groups, in which the relevant person lives and flourishes, is further developed in the first part of the Constitution, which includes a long list of rights divided into different sections that take into consideration a variety of relational contexts, such as 'civil relations', 'ethical and social relations', 'economic relations' and 'political relations'.

Many of the rights set out in the first part of the Constitution, and especially in Title I on *Civil Relations*, are generally recognisable as the classic formulations of the modern liberal era. These include guarantees of personal liberty, freedom of movement and residence, freedom of expression, freedom of religion, the principle of *nulla poena sine lege* (no punishment without law), and the right to judicial protection (including a right to be heard by the 'natural judge' of a dispute).

Title II on *Ethical and Social Relations* primarily addresses the family, health and education. It has no less than three articles regarding the family, marriage, the rights and duties of parents, and the obligation of the State to support family life. It also recognises the State's obligation

[8] See for example Judgment no 163/1993.
[9] See for example Judgment no 109/1993.

to protect health both as a fundamental right of the individual and as a collective interest, and to provide free care to the destitute. Various provisions not only guarantee the freedom to educate and to run private educational institutions, but also that primary education be free, as well as requiring the State to provide support to individuals and families who do not have the means to pay for higher education.

Economic Relations, covered in Title III, address many aspects of the right to work: the State's responsibility to promote the training and advancement of workers and even the protection of Italian workers abroad; the right to a limitation on maximum working hours and to periods of rest; the right to compensation that is both proportionate to the quantity and quality of one's labour and adequate 'to ensure them and their families a free and dignified existence'; special care for the conditions of working women, especially mothers; and the right to social security and other protection in the case of unemployment or disability. Unions and the right to strike receive special attention as well. At the same time, Title III also recognises the freedom of private economic initiative and the right to private property, although both are subject to limits in order to ensure their social function and compatibility with human dignity. This section also explicitly provides for both the nationalisation of certain industries and essential public services, as well as land redistribution programmes. As can be seen, economic and social rights are granted a very high level of protection.

The fourth and last Title, on *Political Relations*, includes the right to vote, to form political parties, and to petition Parliament. It guarantees equal opportunities to accede to public office. It also enumerates several duties of citizens, including to participate in the defence of the Nation, to pay taxes which are to be established on a progressive scale, and to abide by the Constitution and the laws of the Republic.

Even this very brief overview of Part I identifies certain distinctive qualities of the Italian Constitution's approach to fundamental constitutional rights. First, and most importantly, it is immediately clear that the text pervasively reflects the confluence of several different and competing ideological currents, namely Liberal, Christian Democrat and Socialist-Communist (see Chapter 1). At the same time, however, it categorises those rights in interesting ways, clearly reflecting a strong emphasis on community, on social relations, and on civil society, and a comparatively weaker emphasis merely on the autonomous individual, by comparison with other constitutional bills of rights or international human rights instruments. The names of each of the four Titles attest to this: they refer to their subject matter not as rights, values or principles, but as *relations*.

Similarly, the sprinkling throughout the document of the language of duties – both the duties of the State and the duties of solidarity among citizens – speaks of a tradition of rights discourse, grounded in Mazzini's thinking, which is more similar to that of the French, epitomised by Rousseau and Latin America,[10] than the more libertarian dialect of rights typical of the Anglo-American world.

V. CODIFIED RIGHTS AND NEW RIGHTS

The list of enumerated rights in Part I of the Italian Constitution is rich and well-articulated; indeed it was one of the largest and the most generous for the epoch when it was approved. Nevertheless, social life evolves and new needs emerge requiring protection, which are often brought before the courts, both at the national and at the European level.[11] New technologies give rise both to new opportunities and also to new threats to personal and social life, for example in the fields of data protection, privacy and personal reputation. The massive migration flows necessitate the consideration anew of the implications of well-established constitutional principles, such as equality and non-discrimination, and, furthermore, suggest that a new balance ought to be struck between the right to security and the right to migrate. New understandings of issues related to human dignity have also given rise to requests for new rights concerning marriage, family, reproduction and end of life. Additionally, increased awareness of the risks caused by climate change calls for new individual and collective rights related to the protection of the environment. The examples of 'migration of constitutional ideas' could go on.[12]

Having regard to these developments, many scholars speak of different generations of rights, where the first refers to the liberal negative freedoms of the nineteenth century, the second generation includes social and economic rights recognised by many constitutions after the Second World War, and the third and fourth generations encompass the most recent developments of individual rights in the fields of biotechnologies, the internet, the environment and security.

[10] See, for instance, the 1948 American Declaration of the Rights and Duties of Man.

[11] MR Ferrarese, *Il diritto al presente. Globalizzazione e tempo delle istituzioni* (Bologna, Il Mulino, 2002) 187ff.

[12] See S Choudhry, 'Migration as a New Metaphor in Comparative Constitutional Law' in S Choudhry (ed), *The Migration of Constitutional Ideas* (Cambridge, Cambridge University Press, 2010) 1–36.

Some recently enacted constitutions and charters of rights protect these 'new rights' via explicit provisions.[13] Older documents, like the Italian Constitution, obviously do not contain specific provisions regarding these issues. Consequently, a question arises: is it necessary to amend the Constitution in order to recognise these new rights? Is the list of rights enumerated in the Constitution closed, or does it provide for some flexibility to cope with the new requests for protection emerging in social life? Can the general clause of Article 2 be interpreted as a source for recognising new unwritten rights without requiring a constitutional amendment?

Until the last decade of the last century, the prevailing opinion in the Italian scholarship assumed that the Constitution does not leave any room for integrating new rights. With some remarkable exceptions,[14] the common shared position was that the introduction of new fundamental rights had the potential to alter the overall picture of the constitutional values and to jeopardise the protection of codified rights by weakening or undermining some of them. Article 2 tended to be interpreted as a 'closed' provision by the majoritarian scholarship, as well as by the Constitutional Court.[15]

Moreover, the same scholarship was very reluctant to promote constitutional revision with respect to the first part of the Constitution, for fear that the level of protection offered by this part might be diminished by means of constitutional amendment, thereby contradicting the principle of the inviolability of fundamental rights. As a matter of fact, the first part of the Constitution concerning *Rights and Duties* has been altered only three times via very specific amendments: Articles 48, 51 and 27.[16] These amendments, although relevant and significant, do not even begin to cover the broad scope of topics affected by the 'new rights' of the third and fourth generations.

Although the Constitution 'on the books' has remained almost untouched, the Constitutional Court has offered a very dynamic interpretation of the text,[17] so much so that the Constitution 'in action' covers

[13] Or, if not recent, at least easily amendable as it is, for instance, the Swiss Constitution.

[14] A Barbera, 'Commento all'Art. 2' in G Branca (ed), *Commentario della Costituzione. Principi fondamentali* (Bologna, Zanichelli, 1975) 50–122.

[15] For example, Judgments nos 29/1962 and 102/1975.

[16] See constitutional laws nos 1/2000, 1/2003, and 1/2007, respectively. See ch 1.

[17] Recently, see F Viganò, 'Il diritto giurisprudenziale nella prospettiva della Corte costituzionale' (2021) *Sistema penale* 7ff.

a number of new, unwritten rights. Moreover, even 'old' rights have been given an evolutive interpretation,[18] and their scope is open to new implications and applications.

The Constitutional Court has followed two methods to expound the rights protected by the national system.

First, it considers the Constitution to be a living instrument, which is open to incorporating the evolving requests for protection identified in the social life of Italy's citizens. Although the Court is reluctant to interpret Article 2 as an open clause as such, it admits the existence of 'fundamental inviolable rights ... which necessarily derive from those enjoying explicit constitutional protection',[19] ie unwritten rights that are both assumed and implied by the text of the Constitution.

One of the most remarkable examples concerns the *right to life*, the first and most important of all the inviolable rights, which is solemnly pronounced by the Universal Declaration of Human Rights (Article 3), by the European Convention on Human Rights (Article 2) and by the Charter of Fundamental Rights of the European Union (Article 2). By contrast, this right is *not* expressly provided for by the Italian Constitution.

Significantly, the fact that the Constitution does not explicitly mention the right to life cannot be understood as constituting a denial of the protection of such a fundamental value. Rather, the opposite is true: the right to life was considered by the Constitution's drafters to be so relevant and self-evident that its existence was assumed and taken for granted by the Constitution.

The Constitutional Court recognised the right to life on the basis of a combined reading of Articles 2 and 27, which prohibits the death penalty in Italy.[20] This case was about an Italian citizen who was convicted of first-degree murder on trial in Florida, and detained in Italy. The question was whether extradition to the United States in such circumstances violated Articles 2 and 27, because that crime was punishable by the death penalty in Florida. The Constitutional Court struck down the challenged norms, underlining the inviolability of the right to life, and stating that the mere fact that a legal system provides for capital punishment contrasts with the prohibition of it enshrined in the Italian Constitution.

Adopting the same broad interpretation of various written provisions along with the general clause in Article 2, the Court has recognised, in

[18] As had been suggested by A Pace, *Problematica delle libertà costituzionali. Parte generale* (Padoua, Cedam, 2003) 20ff.

[19] Judgment no 98/1979.

[20] Judgment no 223/1996. See also Judgments nos 27/1975 and 223/1996.

addition to the right to life: the right to sexual identity and to sexual freedom;[21] the rights to privacy and data protection;[22] the right to housing;[23] and the right to keep one's own name as an essential distinguishing mark of personal identity,[24] to offer just a few examples.

Second, a dynamic interpretation of constitutional rights reflects the influence of the European Court of Human Rights and the Court of Justice of the European Union (see Chapters 2 and 9). Although each system has its own field of competence, the jurisdictions of the three courts overlap. Due to a number of interconnections between the three systems, many cases begin in one court and end up another. Therefore, the courts cannot ignore one another.[25]

The interpretation of the rights involved is affected by the reciprocal influence of the case law of the relevant judge. In recent times, the areas in which the influence of the European courts has been clearest within the Italian legal system have been criminal law;[26] control orders and non-conviction based confiscation orders;[27] administrative sanctions of a punitive nature;[28] criminal procedural law;[29] excessive length of proceedings;[30] women's rights;[31] migrants' rights;[32] workers' rights;[33] military trade unions;[34] and indeed the '*Taricco* saga', on the principle of legality in criminal matters in relation to the statute of limitation.[35]

VI. LIMITING RIGHTS

> The notion of limits is inherent in the notion of rights … within the legal system the various legal positions are inevitably bound to limit each other in order to coexist in a well-ordered civil community.[36]

[21] See, respectively, Judgments nos 98/1979 and 161/1985 and Judgment no 561/1987.
[22] Judgments nos 366/1991 and 20/2019.
[23] Judgments nos 404/1988 and 44/2020.
[24] Judgment no 13/1994.
[25] P Ridola, *Diritto comparato e diritto costituzionale europeo* (Turin, Giappichelli, 2010) 273ff.
[26] Judgment nos 25/2019 and 32/2020.
[27] Judgment no 24/2019.
[28] Judgments nos 223/2018, 63, 112 and 117/2019, 84/2021.
[29] Judgments nos 317/2009, 210/2010, 113/2011, 200/2016.
[30] Judgments nos 88/2018, 34/2019, 169/2019.
[31] Judgment no 286/2016.
[32] Judgment no 187/2010.
[33] Judgment no 187/2016.
[34] Judgment no 120/2018.
[35] Starting with Order no 24/2017 and ending with Judgment no 115/2018 (see also ch 2).
[36] Judgment no 1/1956.

Ever since its very first decision, the Italian Constitutional Court has vigorously affirmed that all fundamental rights are limited, even the most basic ones, such as freedom of speech. This statement is all the more relevant if one considers that it was in fact pronounced in a decision in which the Court was upholding and strongly reaffirming the freedom of speech protected by Article 21 of the Constitution, in the face of blatant violations perpetrated by Fascist legislation (see Chapter 9).

Indeed, paradoxical as it may sound, fundamental rights and inviolable rights are always susceptible to limitation. Their inviolable character does not imply unconditional, absolute protection. There is no contradiction between their inviolability and their limitability.

From a comparative and transnational perspective, it is of note that limitations on rights may be enounced either in a *general clause* or in *specific provisions*. An example of the former technique is Article 52 of the Charter of Fundamental Rights of the European Union: 'Any limitation on the exercise of the rights and freedoms recognised by this Charter must be provided for by law and respect the essence of those rights and freedoms. Subject to the principle of proportionality, limitations may be made only if they are necessary and genuinely meet objectives of general interest recognised by the Union or the need to protect the rights and freedoms of others'.

The Italian Constitution, instead, follows the latter approach and provides specific limitations right by right, in each *specific provision* declaring them. For example, Article 16 reads: 'Every citizen has the right to reside and travel freely in any part of the country, except for such general limitations as may be established by law for reasons of health or security. No restriction may be imposed for political reasons'.

Yet, limitations to each and every constitutional right are required by the very protection of other rights. This idea has underpinned all declarations of rights since their origins. For example, Article 4 of the Declaration of the Rights of Man and of the Citizen of 1789 expresses this notion as follows: 'the exercise of the natural rights of each man has only those borders which assure other members of the society the fruition of these same rights'. This is all the more relevant in a time of inflation and expansion of rights.[37] As has been stated, the Constitution protects a wide range of fundamental rights, and the scope of rights' protection is always enlarging. Indeed, over time new implicit rights

[37] K Moeller, *The Global Model of Constitutional Rights* (Oxford, Oxford University Press, 2012) ch 1.

have been added to the codified rights, by means of interpretation of the broad textual provisions, read in light of the general clause of Article 2 and of the case law of the European Courts. Moreover, in addition to fundamental rights, other public interests are also to be protected, such as public order, public security and many others. As a result, different constitutional rights and principles overlap. They also tend to clash with one another, and must be reciprocally limited in order to coexist.

To offer just a few, basic examples taken from real cases. The obligation to vaccinate is instrumental to the protection of personal and public health, but at the same time mandatory vaccination contradicts the freedom of self-determination with respect to personal health issues.[38] An even clearer example is a law requiring the publication of the financial assets of some categories of civil servants, which is intended to pursue the goal of transparency in public offices in order to prevent corruption, but which concurrently imposes significant limits on the right to privacy of the people involved.[39] These are but a few of many examples, to give the flavour of the kind of legal issues involved in rights adjudication.

In order to handle these conflicts between rights, the Constitution does not provide a hierarchy of rights. Indeed, the Constitutional Court rejects the notion of hierarchies between rights. Therefore, in abstract terms, it is impossible to establish which of two or more rights in question prevails over the others. Rights, even when fundamental and inviolable, are all of the same legal ranking. They must therefore be balanced against one another, especially in hard cases.[40]

The Italian Constitutional Court has clearly explained its doctrine with respect to balancing rights, in particular deciding a complex case concerning a company, ILVA, which is one of the largest steel producers in Europe.[41] The case was brought before the Constitutional Court because ILVA's method of production was, and still is, very problematic vis-à-vis the protection of the environment, and even in relation to workers' and citizens' health and lives. The Court's consideration of this hard, if not tragic, case required it to strike a sensitive balance between a number of rights and constitutional principles: the rights to health and to a clean environment, but also the right to work and to conduct economic activity, all of which are protected by the Constitution. In doing so, the Constitutional Court adopted the following principle: 'All fundamental

[38] Judgment no 5/2018.
[39] Judgment no 20/2019.
[40] R Dworkin, *Taking Rights Seriously* (Cambridge, Harvard University Press, 1978).
[41] Judgment no 85/2013.

rights protected by the Constitution are mutually related to one another and it is thus not possible to identify any one of them in isolation as prevailing absolutely over the others'.

As affirmed also in other cases, their protection must at all times be 'systematic and not fragmented'.[42] Otherwise, 'the result would be an unlimited expansion of one of the rights, which would 'tyrannise' other legal interests recognised and protected under constitutional law'.

With reference to the ILVA's controversy, this means that no fundamental right 'may claim absolute status'. Even values classified as 'primary', such as environment and health, are not 'placed at the pinnacle of a hierarchically absolute order'. The point of equilibrium between rights is dynamic and 'must be assessed – by Parliament when enacting legislation and by the Constitutional Court upon review – according to the criteria of proportionality and reasonableness in such a manner as to ensure that their essential core is not sacrificed'.[43]

Here, the Court identified the doctrinal tools that serve to resolve cases involving competing rights. There are three key words to be highlighted: *reasonableness*, *balancing* and *proportionality*. Although these doctrines have different origins and set different standards of review, they are generally referred to as equivalents in the Italian case law.[44] To be more precise, the traditional doctrine, which characterises the Italian jurisprudence, is the principle of reasonableness:[45] the Court's job is to review whether the balance set by the legislator is reasonable.

In recent times, conventionally starting from its case law on electoral legislation, the Court has occasionally adopted the more structured test of proportionality,[46] which originated in the German jurisprudence,[47] and which is now widespread at a global level, as a sort of common currency in rights adjudication.[48] In a sense, the standard of review

[42] Judgment no 264/2012.

[43] Again, Judgment no 85/2013.

[44] M Cartabia, 'Ragionevolezza e proporzionalità nella giurisprudenza costituzionale italiana' in A Giorgis, E Grosso and J Luther (eds), *Il costituzionalista riluttante. Scritti per Gustavo Zagrebelsky* (Turin, Einaudi, 2016) 463–75.

[45] See, among many, G Scaccia, *Gli 'strumenti' della ragionevolezza nel giudizio costituzionale* (Milan, Giuffrè, 2000) and A Morrone, *Il custode della ragionevolezza* (Milan, Giuffrè, 2001).

[46] See Judgments nos 1/2014 and 35/2015 (see ch 3), but also Judgment no 20/2019.

[47] An historical overview is offered by A Barak, *Proportionality: Constitutional Rights and Their Limitations* (New York, Cambridge University Press, 2012) 175ff.

[48] K Moeller, 'Constructing the proportionality test: An emerging global conversation' in L Lazarus, C Mc Crudden and N Bowels (eds), *Reasoning Rights* (Oxford, Bloomsbury, 2016) 31ff.

based on reasonableness and balancing is a shortcut. It skips the first stages of the proportionality test and goes straight to the final and more contentious step.

The proportionality test, after ascertaining whether a constitutional right has been limited, requires assessment of: (a) whether the limitation serves a legitimate goal (legitimate goal stage); (b) whether the measure taken is suitable for the purposes of furthering that goal (rational connection stage); (c) whether there is a less restrictive means of pursuing the same objective (necessity stage); and (d) whether the measure has a disproportionate impact on the rightsholder (balancing stage). The reasonable balance test applied by the Italian Constitutional Court boils the proportionality test down to its final stage.

In its case law, the Constitutional Court stressed that some elements of the balancing test are essential: first, balancing rights requires a *concrete* analysis in light of the specific situation in question, an analysis that cannot be conducted in the abstract and which can never be determined in advance; second, it implies some burden and sacrifice with respect to all the rights and principles at stake, but the sacrifice and burden are only partial, as both proportionality and reasonableness require that the *essential core* of each right and principle is always preserved.

VII. JUDICIAL AND NON-JUDICIAL SAFEGUARDS

Not only have the content and the number of rights protected expanded throughout the history of human rights' preservation, but so too have the safeguards provided for the protection of those rights increased and become more sophisticated.

From a historical perspective, the first step was *writing* down the rights: the first *charters* of rights were considered to be a safeguard *per se*. Committing the rights of citizens to writing imposed a limitation on the Crown's power and on her government: writing down rights implied that the Crown was bound to respect the principles agreed in the Charter. The first era of constitutionalism was, indeed, the time of writing.

During the modern liberal constitutionalism of the nineteenth century, Parliaments gained a central position within the institutional system. Accordingly, one of the central guarantees for the protection of fundamental rights was the *reserve of (parliamentary) legislation*. The aforementioned Article 4 of the Declaration of the Rights of Man and of the Citizen of 1789, for example, established that the limits to each right 'can be determined only *by the law*' (emphasis added). 'The law' is not the equivalent of any particular rule. Rather, 'the law' is a typical act issued by Parliament, which is, in turn, made up of the people's representatives.

The liberal constitutions required that only the Parliament should be vested with the power of regulating the rights of citizens. At the time, individual rights were to be protected mainly from the capricious and arbitrary interference of the Sovereign and the Government. Therefore, it was appropriate that the power to establish the scope of each right be taken out of the hands of the Crown and the Government, and instead given to Parliament, acting by means of general legislation, in respect of the equality principle.

The Italian Constitution, like many other constitutions, has inherited this guarantee from the liberal period, which still requires respect for the *reserve of legislation*. This means that any limitation to constitutional rights falls within the exclusive domain of the Parliament (absolute reserve of legislation) or should at least be based on an act of the Parliament (relative reserve of legislation).

For example, Article 15 on the freedom of personal communication states: 'Freedom and confidentiality of correspondence and of every other form of communication is inviolable. Limitations may only be imposed by judicial decision stating the reasons and *in accordance with the guarantees provided by the law*' (emphasis added). The same structure is followed by other provisions, like Article 13 on personal freedom, in accordance with the traditional meaning of *habeas corpus*, reading that 'Personal liberty is inviolable. No one may be detained, inspected, or searched nor otherwise subjected to any restriction of personal liberty except by judicial order stating a reason and only *in such cases and in such manner as provided by the law*' (emphasis added).

An interesting judgment was issued by the Constitutional Court, when requested to review Article 224.2, of the Code of Criminal Procedure, which empowers the investigating judge to require an indicted person, as well as certain third parties, to undergo a compulsory blood test. The Court found that this provision violated the right to personal liberty and personal integrity because it failed to precisely define the circumstances and the manner in which the blood test could be ordered, and thus granted the investigating authority an overly broad and unlimited discretionary power.[49]

[49] Judgment no 238/1996.

As can be seen, the reserve of legislation is always accompanied by a *reserve of jurisdiction*, meaning that the power to implement the limitation on each of the rights set out by the Parliament can only be implemented by an independent judge. Many of the above-mentioned constitutional provisions concerning individual freedoms require that 'limitations may only be imposed by judicial decision' or 'by order of the judiciary'. In particular, arrest and detention (Article 13), search and seizures (Article 14), and interference in personal correspondence and wiretapping (Article 15) cannot be enforced by the police in the absence of a judicial warrant explaining the reasons and the justification for the intrusion. In cases of urgency, the police can act on their own initiative. However, the subsequent immediate approval of a judge is required, within a strict time limit of 24 to 48 hours. As already remarked, the independence of the judiciary, as established by Article 101, and effective access to justice, as established by Article 24, as well as the principle of the 'natural judge' (Article 25) and all the other constitutional safeguards for the impartiality of the judiciary are necessary prerequisites for the respect of the rule of law and are essential pillars for the effective protection of individual rights (see Chapter 8).

These traditional safeguards deriving from the liberal state were complemented in the Republican Constitution by the institution of the Constitutional Court, vested with the power of judicial review of legislation (see Chapter 9). In the face of violations of individual constitutional rights resulting from bad legislation, only the Constitutional Court is entitled to declare the relevant legal provisions invalid and to restore proper respect for the infringed rights.

The Italian system does not prescribe a specific constitutional remedy for the violation of fundamental rights, such as the *Verfassungsbeschwerde* or the *Recurso de amparo*. There is no such instrument in the Italian system as a direct complaint. In the event of the violation of fundamental rights, the wronged individuals address ordinary judges, who in turn address the Constitutional Court *via* the incidental procedure when the violation derives from a legislative provision.

As a result, the protection of fundamental rights in Italy depends upon the strict cooperation of all the judicial bodies: ordinary, administrative and constitutional. Yet, while all the judicial bodies are involved in the protection of fundamental rights, the Constitutional Court plays a special role, as the privileged interpreter of the Constitution. As the content and the scope of fundamental rights have been expounded in its case law over time, their limits have been specified and the balancing between different constitutional rights has been outlined.

Therefore, in order to properly understand the implications of the constitutional provisions concerning individual rights, it is important to take into account the jurisprudence of the Constitutional Court.

As already observed, an overview of the safeguards of fundamental rights offered by the Italian legal system would be incomplete without consideration of the role of the European Courts. Fundamental rights have become heavily protected throughout Europe, not only via the national constitutions, but also as a result of the European Convention on Human Rights (ECHR), established in 1950 in the context of the Council of Europe, and more recently due to the Charter of Fundamental Rights of the European Union, which was given legal binding force by the Treaty of Lisbon in 2009. Indeed, the rights enunciated in the Constitution, in the Convention and in the Charter are very similar, although the most recent instrument – the Charter – encompasses a number of third and fourth generation rights that are were not included in the earlier documents. What is more relevant, however, is that the interpretation of similar rights may diverge.

Over the last few decades, the Court of Justice of the European Union, based in Luxembourg, and the European Court of Human Rights (ECtHR), based in Strasbourg, have gained a growing importance as human rights adjudicators, and their jurisprudence has a substantial impact on the national legal system. Although the mission of the national courts and that of the two European Courts are different and encompass distinct domains, their jurisdictions nevertheless overlap in an increasing number of areas. In Europe, in the field of human rights, a 'composite' constitutional system has clearly developed, whereby a number of interactions occur between the national and the supranational systems and their respective judicial bodies[50] (see Chapter 2).

As a result, the safeguards of individual rights are the outcome of the reciprocal influences of, and the cross-fertilisation between, the national Constitution, the European Convention on Human Rights and the EU Charter of Fundamental Rights,[51] as interpreted by the courts. The provisions of the national constitution concerning fundamental rights are often read and applied in light of the interpretation developed at the

[50] M Cartabia (ed), *I diritti in azione. Universalità e pluralismo dei diritti fondamentali nelle Corti europee* (Bologna, il Mulino, 2007).

[51] AM Slaughter, 'A Typology of Transjudicial Communication' (1994) 29(1) *University of Richmond Law Review* 100ff. See also S Cassese, *I tribunali di Babele. I giudici alla ricerca di un nuovo ordine globale* (Rome, Donzelli, 2009).

European level (for its part, often influenced by some national Courts' case law).

It is possible to consider as an example some case law of the Italian Constitutional Court.

The Court was requested to review some Italian legislative provisions regarding custodial sentences for the offence of defamation committed by the press. The provisions were challenged not only for allegedly violating Article 21 of the Constitution, but also for a violation of Article 10 of the ECHR, as interpreted by the settled case law of the Strasbourg Court. In a rather recent case, following an in-depth analysis of the case law of the Strasbourg Court and many other Council of Europe documents, the Constitutional Court affirmed the urgency to rethink the balance 'between freedom of expression and protection of individual reputation, in particular with regard to journalism'.[52] On the one hand, the Court recognised that 'freedom of expression constitutes – even more than a right proclaimed by the ECHR – a fundamental right recognised as "co-essential to the freedom guaranteed by the Constitution", a "keystone of the democratic order" and a "cornerstone of democracy in the whole legal system". On the other hand, the legitimate exercise by the press and other media of this freedom 'requires a balance to be struck with other interests and rights, of equal constitutional standing, which mark its possible limits from both a constitutional and ECHR perspective', among which is a person's reputation, which constitutes an inviolable right within the meaning of Article 2 of the Constitution[53] and an essential component of the right to privacy outlined in Article 8 ECHR.[54]

It appears from this reasoning that national and supernational protection are closely intertwined: the Constitutional Court refers equally to national sources and case law, as well as to European and international sources and case law. Therefore, not only does the Strasbourg Court offer a further recourse to an individual complaining about a violation of a fundamental right that has not been remedied at the national level, but the principles developed in its case law also impact on the case law of the national courts, including the Constitutional Court, and contribute to the development of the protection of fundamental rights. Indeed,

[52] See Order no 132/2020, addressed to the legislature, from which the excerpts are taken (then followed by Judgment no 150/2021).

[53] Judgments nos 37/2019, 379/1996, 86/1974 and 38/1973.

[54] See, *inter alia*, ECtHR Judgment of 6 November 2018, *Vicent del Campo v Spain*.

the case law of the European Courts endorses a very dynamic attitude toward fundamental rights and has consequently impressed upon the Italian legal system not only the importance of adaptability, but also some tensions.

VIII. KEY RIGHTS

In order to better appreciate the Italian approach to the protection of fundamental rights, it might be useful to turn to some specific cases in which the distinctive features of the Italian Constitution more clearly emerge.

A. Citizens and Migrants

The Italian constitutional text reflects the traditional understanding of Italy as a country of emigration rather than of immigration. The only relevant wording on this subject is found in Article 35, which recognises the freedom to *emigrate* and which grants protection to Italian workers abroad. Italians fled to other countries in massive numbers after the unification of the country in the late nineteenth century, as well as after each of the two World Wars of the twentieth century. In Europe many Italians, taking advantage of international agreements specifically made for this purpose, went to work in Belgium, France, Germany and Switzerland. Outside the continent, a large number of Italians live in Argentina, Brazil and Canada, as well as the United States and Australia. It is no surprise, then, that Article 35 also states that the Republic 'shall promote and encourage international agreements and organizations which have the aim of establishing and regulating labour rights'.

The law on citizenship (no 91/1992) has consistently reflected an approach based on the principle of *ius sanguinis*, and the prevailing path for achieving citizenship has therefore been through family lineage. This was also intended to provide those Italians who emigrated and their descendants the possibility of retaining Italian citizenship, even if they were born and lived abroad. This traditional approach has never been abandoned, although it has been called into question several times especially in consideration of the fact that Italy has become, in the meanwhile, a country of immigration, being one of the main first countries of entry for people coming from the Mediterranean (for some discussion on this point see Chapter 3). Yet, at present, the ordinary means through which foreign nationals can acquire Italian citizenship is only after residing in the Italian territory for at least 10 years, with some shortcut for European citizens and for those who are born in Italy.

It was in the late 1970s and early 1980s that Italy began to experience significant waves of immigration, both documented and undocumented. Its geography has made the Italian peninsula a destination, as well as a European hub, for masses of immigrants coming from practically everywhere in the Mediterranean area. While the 1990s saw the arrival of thousands of Albanians after the fall of the communist regime, during the last two decades immigrants and refugees from North Africa and the Middle East have arrived in huge numbers, seeking shelter and economic opportunity in Italy and in Europe.

As to the legal status of non-nationals, Article 10.2 provides that the 'legal status of foreign nationals shall be determined by [Italian] law in accordance with international treaties'. Consequently, the Italian legislation on this issue is to be understood as taking into account the international and EU law.

Moreover, the Constitution deals with the right to political asylum. Pursuant to Article 10.3, 'foreign nationals who cannot actually enjoy the democratic liberties protected by the Italian Constitution in their own countries shall be entitled to the right to asylum within the territory of the republic, subject to the conditions established by law'. In order to enjoy this right, it is not necessary that non-nationals be persecuted in their own country (in this case, the rights of refugees would apply, as per international law). Rather, in order for political asylum-seeker status to be granted, it is sufficient that a country does not guarantee the main fundamental freedoms protected by the Italian Constitution, even if those freedoms are formally recognised in a bill of rights.

On the basis of these principles and of the general constitutional principles concerning the protection of fundamental rights, equality and the duty of solidarity, the Constitutional Court has developed a body of case law on immigration that revolves around three basic ideas: security, equality and solidarity.

As to *security*, the Constitutional Court has affirmed that 'the power to regulate immigration is one of the essential features of State sovereignty as an expression of territorial control'. The State 'cannot relinquish the ineluctable task of guarding its own borders'.[55] The legislation governing the entry into and stay in Italy by foreign nationals is

[55] Judgment no 250/2010, also quoting Judgment no 353/1997.

'associated with the consideration of various public interests such as, for example, security and public health, public order, restrictions of an international nature and the national policy on immigration', with restrictions and policies that 'are the result of assessments relating to the socio-economic "sustainability" of the phenomenon'.[56]

This means that that, in order to regulate immigration, Parliament is free to decide whether criminal sanctions are appropriate, or if it is sufficient to impose administrative penalties in this context. The interests protected by laws prohibiting illegal immigration not only encompass public order and security, but also the fundamental rights of people unlawfully transported within the country, who are often exposed to the risk of death and or suffering torture, or inhuman and degrading treatment in the promotion of economic interests.[57]

The second concern for the Constitutional Court is *equality and non-discrimination.*

Article 3 of the Constitution textually requires the equal protection only of the rights of citizens. The Constitutional Court has, however, basically overcome the formal distinction between citizens and non-citizens by developing strong protection of immigrants' human rights. For many years,[58] the Court has affirmed the idea that, even though many articles of the Constitution relating to human rights, and the very principle of equality, refer specifically to 'citizens', they must however also apply to foreign nationals where it is necessary to respect fundamental human rights.

A relevant decision on the equal treatment enjoyed by citizens and non-nationals was the one in which the Court invalidated an 'aggravated circumstance' that permitted punishment of a person convicted of a criminal offence more severely if that indicted person was an illegal migrant.[59] The Court found that this provision was discriminatory against migrants because the substantive rationale underlying the contested provision was a general and absolute assumption that illegal immigrants are more dangerous than other people. Therefore, this provision contrasts with Article 25, which 'stipulates that criminal responsibility must be based on a person's actions and thus imposes the rigorous requirement that a

[56] Judgment no 250/2010, quoting Judgments nos 148/2008, 206/2006 and 62/1994.

[57] Again, Judgment no 250/2010. On the use of criminal penalties see also Judgment no 142/2017.

[58] Judgment no 120/1967.

[59] Judgment no 249/2010.

person may only be punished for his or her own conduct and not for his or her personal characteristics'.[60]

In similar fashion, the Court removed a number of provisions which were discriminatory against non-nationals. A recent example of unconstitutional discrimination against non-nationals was identified in a provision according to which the residence permit for asylum seekers 'shall not constitute grounds for registration in the residents' register' (which is the basis for enjoying social benefits and for exercising other rights). The Court insisted on the fact that Parliament cannot place foreign nationals in a position of social 'subordination' and that a person's status as a foreign national cannot in itself be viewed 'as an admissible reason for different and less favourable treatment'.[61]

Yet the Court went beyond combating discriminatory legislation. In the name of the principle of *solidarity*, the Court expounded a number of rights, namely social rights, for the benefit of non-nationals, concerning the basic needs of each human person. This package of rights does not pertain solely to refugees, but also to asylum seekers and immigrants moving to Italy for reasons of employment, and even to undocumented immigrants. In sum, the Constitutional Court has committed itself to an affirmative interpretive effort to expand the social rights of immigrants, whatever their legal status might be.

This approach has had a strong impact on national, regional and local welfare policies. According to the Court, however, benefits and services cannot be conferred only on citizens if there is no reasonable justification for excluding non-citizen immigrants from such treatment. The Court has therefore expanded many social rights – in the fields of health care, rights of disabled people, housing and educational services[62] – to extend to non-citizen immigrants. It has imposed on the State a special duty to justify all differentiated treatment: policies that discriminate between citizens and non-citizens must be appropriately justified.

Moreover, the Constitutional Court has recently introduced a new aspect to the notion of solidarity, by asserting that social integration is achieved not solely through the recognition of further rights, which turn the immigrant into a passive subject of the legal order benefiting from social security, but also through the conferral of duties, which enable the foreign national to become an active participant in solidarity. To refuse

[60] Judgment no 249/2010.
[61] Judgment no 186/2020.
[62] See, among many, Judgments nos 306/2008, 11/2009, 187/2010, 329/2011, 40/2013, 22/2015, 230/2015, 170/2018 and 140/2018.

foreign nationals the ability to participate in an activity of social solidarity therefore constitutes an unjustified limitation on the full development of their personality, and for this reason a provision restricting the ability to perform voluntary civil service to Italian nationals has been ruled unconstitutional.[63]

It is not surprising that this trend of the Court has taken place in the field of social rights and the welfare system, since these are conceived as ways of redressing social inequalities and meeting the necessities of people in need. Here the principles of equality and solidarity converge to expand the protection of fundamental rights. By contrast, non-citizens do not enjoy political rights and do not have the right to vote in Italy. Article 48 of the Constitution, which states that '[a]ll citizens, male and female, who have attained their majority, are voters', has usually been interpreted as endowing *only* citizens with the right to vote. Non-citizens can therefore participate in elections only once they have become Italian citizens. This interpretation of Article 48 is disputed, however, especially with reference to regional and local elections, which, according to some critics, are not covered by the article and therefore should not be constitutionally limited to citizens. Indeed, citizens of the European Union already enjoy the same rights as national citizens, except for the right to vote and to be elected for the national Parliament.

B. Freedom of Religion

The Constitution takes religion into consideration in many of its provisions, namely in Articles 3, 7, 8, 19 and 20.

In order to understand the overall constitutional framework with respect to religious matters, it might be relevant to recall that Italy has for centuries been a country in which the vast majority of the population were followers of the Catholic Church. Moreover, since the origins of the Catholic Church, its headquarters have been located in the Vatican State, in the heart of Rome, both before and after Rome became the capital of Italy, in 1871 (see Chapter 1). It comes as no surprise, then, that the Catholic Church enjoys a peculiar status within the Italian State and the Italian Constitution, specifically in Article 7:

> The State and the Catholic Church are independent and sovereign, each within its own sphere.

[63] Judgment no 119/2015.

> Their relations are regulated by the Lateran pacts. Amendments to such Pacts which are accepted by both parties shall not require the procedure of constitutional amendments.

In the past, the Catholic Church was granted a privileged position. The Albertine Statute and then the Lateran pacts (*Patti Lateranensi*) of 1929 established Roman Catholicism as the official religion of the Italian State. All other religious denominations were disadvantaged, since they were only allowed to operate after the Government had certified that their basic principles were not in conflict with the national public order (law no 1159/1929).

Things have changed as a result of the Republican Constitution, which ensures that equal treatment is afforded to all religious beliefs. Despite the Roman Catholic Church still enjoying a distinguished position Article 8 states that 'all religious denominations are equally free before the law' and that 'their relations with the State are regulated by law, based on agreements with their respective representatives'. Therefore, each religious denomination maintains specific relations with the Italian State which are regulated by individual agreement, and the Constitutional Court considers that the Constitution does not require that all religious denominations should enjoy the same legal treatment, and that a range of different regulations might be compatible with the Constitution.[64]

In recent years, however, considering the secularisation of the Italian society and its pluralistic composition, the orientation of the Constitutional Court in such matters has tended to shift towards a more secular interpretation of the State's role as an impartial legal guarantor of all religious denominations. This has especially been the case since the new Concordat with the Church was agreed in 1984, which established that the Catholic religion was no longer the official religion of the Italian State.

Indeed, the Constitutional Court has consistently reaffirmed that the principle of the secular state, on the basis of Articles 2, 3, 7, 8, 19 and 20, does not mean that it is indifferent to the existence and operation of religious denominations, but rather that it is committed to guaranteeing freedom of religion, within a context of cultural and confessional pluralism.[65]

[64] Judgment nos 125/1957, 79/1958, 39/1965 and 86/1985.
[65] See Judgment no 203/1989.

A fundamental tension can be identified in the constitutional provisions concerning religious issues. On the one hand, Italy is a secular state, which embraces the principle of distinction between State and religious denominations: *laicità* is a supreme and inviolable principle characterising the Italian form of state as a pluralistic one, in which diverse faiths, culture, and traditions coexist with equal liberty. Consequently, it requires equal freedom to be afforded to all religious denominations and to religious and non-religious people alike (Article 19, on the right to freely profess religious beliefs and to celebrate rites). According to the fundamental principles of equality and the prohibition of all discrimination on the basis of religion (Article 3), the State's position must be one of equidistance and impartiality with respect to religious denomination.

On the other hand, the Constitution envisaged the possibility for the State to regulate in a bilateral way, and therefore in a specific and differentiated way, its relations with the Catholic Church through the Concordat (Article 7) and relations with other religious denominations via 'agreements' (Article 8).

Judging on the facilities for religious services, the Constitutional Court explained the balance between equal treatment and the special status of religious denomination in the Italian Constitution, highlighting that 'the principle of separation of church and State (*principio di laicità*)' has been defined in constitutional case law, 'not as indifference to religious experience, but as the guardian of religious freedom in a system grounded on religious and cultural pluralism'.[66]

At the same time, the Court affirmed that 'the free exercise of religion is an essential aspect of the freedom of religion' (Article 19) and is, moreover, 'recognized equally for all people and every religious denomination' (Article 8), 'with or without any formal relationship with the State'.[67]

Therefore, the principle of *laicità* has to be understood not as the indifference of the State to religious experience generally, but rather as the equi-*distance* – or equi-*proximity* – and impartiality of the law with respect to all religious confessions. Although *laicità* is sometimes translated into English as 'secularity,' 'secularism' or 'laicity,' or with the French word *laicité*, none of these terms perfectly captures the somewhat distinctive meaning of the term in Italian constitutional jurisprudence.

[66] Judgment no 63/2016, quoting Judgments nos 508/2000, 329/1997, 440/1995 and 203/1989.

[67] Judgment no 63/2016.

In recent years, similarly to what has occurred in other countries, many disputes have arisen regarding the display of religious symbols in public areas. In the Italian case law, such problems have originated almost exclusively in relation to the presence of crucifixes in polling stations, courtrooms and classrooms. In particular, the presence of the crucifix in the classroom of a public primary school has been the subject of a very complex and controversial dispute that originated in the Veneto Administrative Court (TAR Veneto) and involved the Council of State, the Constitutional Court and even the European Court of Human Rights. The crucifix case provides a good example of the relationship between the State and religion in Italy.

The case began in 2002, when the parents of two students enrolled in a public primary school asked the local school board to remove the crucifix from their children's classrooms. Following the decision of the board not to remove the crucifix, the parents challenged the board's decision as infringing the supreme and inviolable principle of *laicità*, the principle of non-discrimination and the freedom of religion – which includes the right not to profess any religion – protected by Article 19 of the Constitution and Article 9 of the ECHR.

The Veneto Administrative Court referred the question to the Constitutional Court in 2004, but the latter dismissed the case for procedural reasons. As a follow up, the Administrative Court resumed the case and held that the crucifix could remain in the classrooms because it was a symbol of Italian history, culture, and identity: a symbol of equality, freedom, and tolerance for all, that did not offend freedom of religion.

This decision was appealed to the Council of State, the court of last resort for administrative matters (see Chapter 8), which dismissed the appeal in 2006. The Council of State held that, in Italy, the crucifix symbolised the values of Italian civilization (tolerance, mutual respect, dignity of the person, affirmation of one's rights, consideration of one's freedom, the autonomy of one's moral conscience vis-à-vis authority, human solidarity, and the refusal of any form of discrimination), and their Christian origins. In that sense, when displayed in classrooms, the crucifix could serve a highly educational symbolic function, even from a 'secular' perspective, irrespective of the religion professed by the pupils.

The litigation did not end in the Italian courts, and ultimately reached the European Court of Human Rights in Strasbourg. In November 2009, the Second Chamber of the Strasbourg Court unanimously held that the Italian State, by allowing the display of the crucifix in the classroom of a public school, had violated the principles of religious freedom. The decision was severely criticised in Italy and led to a very bitter public debate.

At one end of the spectrum were those who viewed the public display of the symbol of a religion followed by the majority of the population, such as the crucifix, as a violation of the freedom of religion of those persons who do not recognise this symbol, either because they follow other religious beliefs or because they subscribe to none. At the opposite end of the spectrum were those who considered the crucifix to represent a legitimate expression of the national identity, the mere display of which did not in any way violate basic guarantees of religious freedom or education; together with those, whether believers or not, who did not feel offended by the presence of a religious symbol in public buildings.

The Italian Government asked for the case to be referred to the Grand Chamber, which granted the request. Testifying to the importance of the case, the Grand Chamber gave leave to intervene in the case to 33 members of the European Parliament acting collectively, many nongovernmental organisations, and 10 Member States of the Council of Europe. They provided written (and in the case of the other States, oral) arguments. In March 2011, the Grand Chamber issued a judgment reversing that of the Second Chamber[68] and holding by 15 votes to 2 that there had been no violation of the Convention.

The Grand Chamber remarked that a 'crucifix on a wall is an essentially passive symbol' and 'cannot be deemed to have influence on pupils comparable to that of didactic speech or participation to religious activities'. It also considered that 'the presence of crucifixes is not associated with compulsory teaching about Christianity' and that 'Italy opens up the school environment in parallel to other religions'.

For these reasons, taking into consideration the overall diverse cultural context, open to diversity, the Grand Chamber found the question to fall within the scope of the 'margin of appreciation' to be accorded to the State, essentially remanding the controversy to the Italian legislature and courts, according to the pluralistic nature of the protection of fundamental rights in Europe.

More recently, the Court of Cassation opted for a constitutional oriented interpretation of the old provision which includes the crucifix among the school furnishings (Article 118 of the royal decree no 965/1924), arguing that it is neither an obligation nor a prohibition. Thus, the school community has full power to choose whether to display the crucifix in the classroom through a vote that represents the precipitate of

[68] *Lautsi and Others v Italy*, Application no 30814/06, ECtHR, 9 November 2009.

all the convictions of the same community. In the event that discordant positions emerge, it is necessary to seek a point of connection through a 'reasonable accommodation', following the Canadian example.[69]

C. Social Rights

The Italian constitutional framework reserves a special place for social rights, laying the foundations for the construction of the welfare state. Philosophical personalism, Catholic social teaching and socialist theories – all well represented within the Constituent Assembly – favoured the idea of a proactive State for the protection and the promotion of human dignity. Moreover, in the Constituent Assembly, the socialists, the communists, and the Catholics were all entirely convinced that a rapid recovery from the destruction of the war required a significant State presence in the market and in the provision of health care, education and housing. The efforts of the State were understood as an indispensable part of democratic life and the development of the country. Thus, in enshrining the right to receive an education, to have a family, to bear children, to have a job, or to receive healthcare, the Constitution not only grants the State certain powers, but also imposes a positive obligation to actively intervene in these fields by promoting housing, establishing schools and hospitals, encouraging higher rates of savings, and so on.

Social rights were considered to be the most effective instrument to foster substantive equality.

This social side of the Italian bill of rights is documented in a series of Constitutional Court decisions that expanded the protection accorded to people in need. Some examples can offer assistance in understanding the Italian approach to social rights.

With regard to the *right to education*, the Court viewed the State as being responsible for the duty to remove obstacles to the enjoyment of this right. The Court remarked that the provisions of Article 34 of the Constitution 'focus on economic obstacles, since the founders were well aware that such obstacles are the main component of unequal starting points in life, and that it was, therefore, essential to provide express prescriptions in order to guarantee the effectiveness' of the right to education.

[69] See Judgment no 24414/2021 of the Court of Cassation, United Sections. See M Cartabia, 'The Many and The Few: Clash of Values or Reasonable Accommodation?' (2018) 33(4) *American University International Law Review* 667.

However, the suppression of other limits and obstacles of other kinds – as for students with disabilities – is 'a general duty of the Republic', deriving from Articles 2 and 3.2, as 'school attendance and the acquisition of a complete education are fundamental tools for the "full development of the human person"'.[70]

Another meaningful example can be found a decision by which the Constitutional Court struck down the law that limited the number of relatives who had the right to take a leave of absence from their jobs in order to assist persons with disabilities. The Court, stressing the essential role of the family in the provision of assistance to and socialisation of the disabled, stated that the constitutional system requires the most effective protection of persons in need, and that such protection includes their right to enjoy human relationships. Consequently, people with disabilities had the right to be assisted by their family members, and the limitation imposed on the category of relatives permitted to take leave to assist was unconstitutional.[71]

The examples of cases concerning the protection of social rights are countless. The Italian Constitution offers a wide spectrum of social rights so that citizens are entitled to be assisted and to receive social services from the State, the regions or the municipalities in the fields of work, social security, education, health and many others. Yet, the *health-care system* is indeed one of the more relevant sectors in which the Italian approach to the care and welfare system can be appreciated.

Article 32 provides that 'the Republic safeguards health as a fundamental right of the individual and as a collective interest', and provides that the Republic 'guarantees free medical care to the poor'. Notwithstanding the limits set by this provision, Parliament established the National Health Service, committing public authorities to ensuring the physical and mental health of the entire population, regardless of social and individual backgrounds.[72] In this respect, the right to health obviously gives rise to a positive burden for public administration and, as such, is subject to budgetary limits. Consequently, the offer of free health care may vary, depending on the economic situation of the country. The National Health Service may require the citizen to contribute a 'fee' to

[70] Judgment no 215/1987. See Judgment no 275/2016 (on the right for students with disabilities to receive free public transportation to school).

[71] Judgment no 203/2013. See Judgment no 152/2020 (on pensions for disabled people, in which the Court doubled the amount envisaged by the legislator).

[72] See law no 883/1978 and legislative decrees nos 502/1992 and 513/1993.

cover some of the costs, depending on the income of citizens and on the economic cycle and the financial condition of the public funds.

Indeed, social rights have a cost and their full and free implementation for everyone's benefit depends on the availability of economic funds. The Court acknowledges that the right to medical care 'is conditioned by the way the legislature chooses to implement it, balancing the interest it protects against other constitutionally protected interests and also considering the objective limits it encounters in doing so (eg the organisational and financial resources available at the time)'.[73]

This approach of the Constitutional Court has superseded the previous position, well-established in the 1980s, which tended to favour a more expansive approach toward social rights, regardless of their financial implications.

The huge public debt and the inefficiencies generated in this system have become apparent over the decades, and have progressively led to a reconsideration of the sustainability of social rights and of the welfare system itself. As to the former, starting in the early 1990s, public institutions have tried to put a cap on increasing public debt, in part due to pressure from the European Union, which wanted to secure the performance of the euro through fiscally sound State budgets. This led to the 2012 constitutional reform, which required balanced budgets (see Chapters 2 and 5) and which also contributed to a new perspective in the Constitutional Court. The Court became particularly concerned about the financial sustainability of social rights, and it began to temper its expansive attitude – anticipating and taking into consideration the financial implications that its decisions might entail.

Yet, the level of health care can never fall below a minimum standard, which guarantees the essential content of the right to health. In this regard, following the 2001 reform of Title V of the Constitution (see Chapter 7), which attributed the subject matter of 'health' to the concurrent legislative powers of the State and the Regions (Article 117.3), the central State still retains the exclusive legislative power in relation to the 'determination of the essential levels of benefits relating to civil and social entitlements to be guaranteed throughout the national territory' (Article 117.2, letter m).[74]

The need to protect health as a collective interest may also require people to submit to certain medical treatments such as, for instance,

[73] Judgment no 445/1990.
[74] Judgment no 187/2012.

mandatory vaccinations.[75] In this regard, however, the Constitution provides that health care can only be imposed by Parliament pursuant to an express piece of legislation and that any such law cannot violate 'the limits imposed by the respect for the human person' (Article 32.2).

The Constitutional Court stated that a law imposing mandatory health-related treatment is not incompatible with Article 32 if: (a) the treatment is intended not only to improve or maintain the health of the individual receiving the treatment, but also to preserve the health of others; and (b) it provides that the treatment may not have a permanent negative impact on the health of the recipient, and, in the case of further injury, the payment of equitable compensation to the injured party is provided for, separate from any damages to which they may otherwise be entitled.[76]

The co-existence of these multiple principles within Article 32 leaves room for legislative discretion so that, depending on the context, at any given time, Parliament might select the technique of recommendation and, at others, that of obligation. In the latter case it may calibrate the measures (including those imposing sanctions) that are intended to guarantee the effectiveness of the requirement. This legislative discretion must be exercised in light of the various health and epidemiological conditions in question, as ascertained by the scientific and medical authorities[77] and having regard to the constantly evolving discoveries of medical research, to which the legislator must turn for guidance in the exercise of its choices in this area.[78] In any event, the Court stressed that even in cases of mandatory medical treatment and vaccination, some space must necessarily be preserved for a relationship between the medical authorities and the citizenry based on information, dialogue and persuasion. Indeed, mandatory medical treatments impose a limitation of individual self-determination in the sensitive field of health. For this reason, the Court favoured an approach encouraging the individual responsibility, even if in a context of a regulatory scheme. This allows for lifting the obligation when conditions change and the medical and

[75] See Decree Law no 73/2017, converted with amendments into law no 119/2017, which has added 10 mandatory vaccinations for school-aged children.

[76] Judgments nos 307/1990, 258/1994 and 169/2017.

[77] Judgment no 268/2017.

[78] Judgment no 282/2002.

scientific knowledge evolve or when the same results may be achieved by less intrusive means.[79]

IX. CONCLUSION

The principles affirmed by the case law of the Constitutional Court on vaccinations have obviously represented the guidelines for the activity of the legislator to promote the campaign for vaccination against COVID-19. An obligation to be vaccinated has so far been imposed only to people working in the health care system. Access to many services, events and workplaces, however, requires a 'green pass': an official certificate proving that the person has been vaccinated or has recently tested negative for COVID-19. At the same time, more generally, the measures adopted in order to face the pandemic and to prioritise the protection of people's lives, health and physical integrity, have determined a temporary but severe abridgement of many fundamental rights protected by the Constitution.

As the Italian Constitution does not contain clauses suspending fundamental rights, which can be triggered by exceptional circumstances, nor provisions that allow for changes to the power structures in times of crisis, similar to Article 48 of the Weimar Constitution, or Article 116 of the Spanish Constitution or Article 16 of the French Constitution,[80] the mechanisms of rights protection illustrated in this chapter have been challenged further. The non-judicial mechanisms such as the reserve of legislation (formally respected by the adoption of decrees of the President of the Council, as foreseen by a decree-law, being quickly and almost unanimously converted by the Parliament) as well as judicial tools – such as requirements for measures to be temporary, necessary, proportionate and balancing – have been placed under stress, in Italy as well as in other democracies, by the pandemic.[81]

[79] Judgment no 5/2018.

[80] See M Cartabia, 'Summary of the Report on the work of the Constitutional Court in 2019' (28 April 2020) 18ff, available at www.cortecostituzionale.it/documenti/relazione_cartabia/2_sintesi_eng.pdf.

[81] On this issue, see Judgments nos 37/2021 (recognising the measures aimed at combating COVID-19 as included in the exclusive State competence on 'international prophylaxis') and 198/2021 (rejecting the objections on the respect of the principle of legality raised on the decrees of the President of the Council limiting personal freedoms because of the pandemic).

FURTHER READING

Cartabia, M, '"Taking Dialogue Seriously". The Renewed Need for a Judicial Dialogue at the Time of Constitutional Activism in the European Union' (2007) 12 *Jean Monnet Working Paper*, 1–43.

Fabbrini, F, and Pollicino, O, 'Constitutional Identity in Italy: European Integration as the Fulfilment of the Constitution' (2017) 6 *EUI Working Papers*, 1–15.

Federico, V, and Maggini, N, 'Italy' in V Federico and N Maggini, N (ed), *Solidarity as a Public Virtue? Law and Public Policies in the European Union* (Baden Baden, Nomos, 2018) 109–28.

Pin, A, 'Public Schools, the Italian Crucifix, and the European Court of Human Rights: The Italian Separation of Church and State' (2011) 25(1) *Emory International Law Review* 97–149.

Index

Introductory Note

References such as '178–79' indicate (not necessarily continuous) discussion of a topic across a range of pages. Wherever possible in the case of topics with many references, these have either been divided into sub-topics or only the most significant discussions of the topic are listed. Because the entire work is about the 'Italian Constitution', the use of this term (and certain others which occur constantly throughout the book) as entry points has been restricted. Information will be found under the corresponding detailed topics.

www.ingramcontent.com/pod-product-compliance
Lightning Source LLC
Chambersburg PA
CBHW071251180926
51613CB00001B/3
9781509905720